URBAN RESEARCH METHODS

PERSPECTIVES IN URBAN GEOGRAPHY

VOLUME FIVE

Concept's International Series in Geography

No. 1 Perspectives in Agricultural Geography (In Five Volumes) Edited by **Noor Mohammad**

No. 2 Perspectives in Geomorphology (In Four Volumes) Edited by **H.S. Sharma**

No. 3 Perspectives in Urban Geography Edited by **C.S. Yadav**

1. New Directions in Urban Geography
2. Comparative Urban Research
3. Comparative Urbanization : City Growth and Change

4.A Models in Urban Geography (Theoretical)

4.B Models in Urban Geography (Mathematical)

5. Urban Research Methods : Central Place, Hierarchical and City Size Models
6. Contemporary City Ecology
7. Slums, Urban Decline and Revitalization
8. Contemporary Urban (Issues)
9. Rural-Urban Fringe
10. Morphology of Towns
11. Cities and Housing
12. Perceptual and Cognative Image of the City
13. Urban Economics
14. City Planning : Problems and Prospects
15. City Planning : Administration and Participation

16.A Urban Planning and Policies

16.B Urban Planning and Policies

Concept's International Series in Geography No. 3

PERSPECTIVES IN URBAN GEOGRAPHY

VOLUME FIVE

Urban Research Methods

Central Place, Hierarchical and City Size Models

Edited by

C. S. YADAV

CONCEPT PUBLISHING COMPANY, NEW DELHI

First Published 1986

Published by

Naurang Rai
Concept Publishing Company
H-13, Bali Nagar
NEW DELHI-110015 (India)

Printed in India by

Printway India
at S. Narayan and Sons
7117/18, Pahari Dhiraj,
DELHI-110006

PREFACE

NATURE OF URBAN GEOGRAPHY

THERE are several studies on urban geography which reveal that, as a major sub-discipline, it has a long tail but a short body. However, the spectrum is so vast and broad that researchers are able to make general statements in defence of its conception, philosophy, nature and orientation. Urban geography today encompasses and interfaces with various disciplines which are interested in urban studies. As an introduction to this series, our task here is to make an attempt to briefly review the development of geographical interest in various aspects of cities.

There are several reviews of the early development of urban geography which have been dealt with by Berry and Harton (1970)[1] and Carter (1974).[2] Berry and Harton in their book, *Geographical Perspective on Urban System*, have made an attempt to introduce readers to its present-day status. They have clearly resolved that "the formative years of the social science in the late nineteenth century and early twentieth century were also the years in which urban studies first developed,"[3] thus providing the context for the geography's emerging interest in cities. However, the emergence of urban studies dates back to the writing of Greek scholars, but as a sub-discipline, it has reached its present-day status only in the past 30 years.

In their historical perspective the works on urban geography show that the pre-20th century studies primarily concerned themselves with themes of location, size and shape of the cities. The initial findings were strongly subjective, descriptive and dependent more on observation such as the works of Hassert (1907)[4] and Blanchard (1911).[5] In the succeeding years the conceptual framework of site and situation was criticized by Aurousseau (1924)[6] and Crowe (1938)[7], their conception being that cities were not inanimate objects in landscape, but also organic elements which involved people and their movements. The morphologist, later in 1960, truly brought the indigenous line of evolution in the sphere of urban geography and studies on the build-up fabric of cities (Conzone, 1960).[8] Smails (1955)[9] constituted the prime base of urban geography, which remained articulated without any major conceptual change till early 1960s. The studies on the morphological aspects of the urban system were influenced by external forces, consequently the methodological frameworks got impetus within the discipline. At this juncture the evolution of concepts was not based on environment but took shelter under the umbrella of economics of location, and incorporated analysis of land values and rents, and the concept of nodality and accessibility. These concepts were derived from the economic theories of Cooley (1894)[10], Weber (1899),[11] and Hurd (1903).[12]

The Chicago School of Urban Ecology hastened the evolution of urban geography. In his monumental work Park (1925)[13] developed the idea of order and analysis of towns. Further, a powerful thrust and much of the rationale was provided to the studies of urban geography by the Central Place Theory of Christallar (1933).[14]

The impact of the statistical method was powerful and it brought rapid and enormous changes in the field of urban geography. It also brought new insights into the development and application of urban geography towards increased quantification. Brian J. Berry, a pioneer in the field, analysed the spatial order, size and location of towns and cities. There was widespread use of innovative techniques to explore the nature of urban problems, hypotheses were tested, new theories propounded and old theories remodelled. The statistical methods were put to a variety of uses. Smith (1965)[15] evaluated the classification of settlements ; Berry and Garrison (1956)[16] examined the utility of the rank-size rule for urban populations. The models of Park and Burgess (1925),[17] Harris and Ullman (1945)[18] and Homar Hoyt (1939)[19] were tested and re-examined by various geographers.

A new impetus to urban geography came from social area analysis which was initially propounded by Shevky and Bell (1955)[20] and later on this provided a basis for factorial ecology. The collaboration of this stream in urban geography was offered by Berry (1971),[21] Herbert (1972)[22] and Johnston (1971).[23] As a consequence of these thrusts in geography after 1960, the techniques of investigation were sharpened and this has provided the basis for a scientific explanation of cities. Attempts were made to introduce new theories and frame laws to make the explanation of events more rational and logical. Sophisticated models were propounded as urban geography entered a new era of rationalizing the subject matter of urban studies on the basis of new philosophies, new concepts, new theories, new methodologies and applications.

However, the status of contemporary urban geography has been elevated only recently by the behavioural approach. The studies of perception and cognition which have a long tradition in physiology were first introduced into the field of geography by Lynch (1960),[24] Dowson and Stea (1973)[25] Gould and White (1974).[26] At present there is a sudden spurt in the studies on the subject with a new paradigm. But the full impact of behavioural approaches upon urban geography has yet to be realized.

The aim of this series is to seek reorientation of the discipline strengthened by new philosophies, methodologies, subject matter or application. The series has been arranged in such a way that all contemporary view points are covered comprehensively. Hopefully, this series will inspire researchers to appreciate the work already done by geographers in studying cities. Geography by nature seems to be a synthesizing field of inquiry. As such we have made an endeavour to combine some of the otherwise disparate facts garnered by other disciplines in such a manner that we can gain a better understanding of the urban system. The study of urban geography is essential if we are to analyse the human consequences of the settlements in which we live. It is useful to planners, decision makers in government and corporations and also to each one of us as citizens. Finally, it gives us a perspective on what may be happening to our cities and to the nature.

To achieve the above goal only those contributions with originality and contrasting viewpoints were selected for inclusion in this series. In doing so the editor does not wish to compete with the journals in the field in which innovative research and methodological aspects are presented. But he does wish to convey, and convey with conviction, that significant researches are being undertaken in the different branches of urban geography and in other allied disciplines. The present series is an attempt to provide a selective reappraisal and rigorous examination of the assumptions and the urge to disseminate new knowledge created by the mutual interaction. Emphasis is also placed on the conceptualization and theorization of the subject matter so that general laws may emerge. A conscious effort has been to organize the series in such a way that it reflects the philosophical approach parallel to that of the behavioural school. Finally, a vigorous attempt has been made to demonstrate throughout the series now geographers are basically involved in solving the urban problems.

REFERENCES

1. Berry and Harton, *Geographic Perspectives on Urban Systems : With Integrated Readings*, New Jersey, Prentice Hell, INC, Englewood Cliffs, 1970.
2. Carter, *The Study of Urban Geography*, Edward Arnold, London, 1974.
3. Berry and Harton, 1970.
4. Hassert, K., *Die Stadte Geographisch Betrachect*, Leipzig, 1907.
5. Blanchard, R., *Grenoble : Etude De Geographic Urbanine*, Paris, 1911.
6. Aurousseau, M., "Recent Contributions to Geography : A Review," *Geographical Review*, 1924, 14, p. 444.
7. Crowe, P. R., "On Progress in Geography", *Scottish Geographical Magazine*, 1938, 54-1-19.
8. Conzone, M.R.G., "The Plan Analysis of an English City Centre", Ink. Norkorg (Ed.), *Proceedings of I.G.U. Symposium on Urban Geography*, C.W.K. Gleerup, Lund, 1962.
9. Smails, A.E., "The Urban Mes of England and Wales", *Transactions and Papers*, Institute of British Geographers, 1946, 11, 85, p. 101.
10. Cooley, C.H., "The Theory of Transportation", *Publications of the American Economic Association*, 1894, 9, p. 5-7.
11. Weber, A.F., *The Growth of Cities in the Nineteenh Century : A Study of Statistics*, New York, 1899.
12. Hurd, R., *Principles of City Land Values : New York Record and Guide*, 1903, p. 19-21.
13. Park, R.E., "Suggestions for the Investigation of Human Behaviour in an Urban Environment", in R.E. Park, E.W. Burgess, R.D. Mackenize (eds.), *The City*, University of Chicago Press, 1925.
14. Christallar, W., *Central Place in Southern Germany*, Gustar Fischer, Teno, 1933.
15. Smith, R.M.T., "Method and Purpose in Functional Town Classi-

fication", *Annals of Association of American Geographers*, 1965, 55, pp. 539-548.
16. Garrison, W.L., "Applicability of Statistical Inference to Geographical Research", *Geographical Review*, 1956, 46, 427, 429.
17. Burgess, E.W., "The Growth of City", in R.E. Park, E.W. Burgess and R.D. Mackenzie (eds.), *The City*, University of Chicago Press, 1925.
18. Ullman, E.L., "The Nature of Cities", *Annals*, American Academy of Political and Social Science, 1945, 242, 7-17.
19. Hoyt, H., *The Structure and Growth of Residential Neighbourhoods in American Cities*, Washington, Federal Housing Administration 1939.
20. Shevky, E. and Bell, W., *Social Area Analysis*, Stamford University Press, Stamford, 1955.
21. Berry, B.J.L., (ed.), "Comparative Factorial Ecology", *Economic Geographic (Supplement)*, 1971, 47.
22. Herbert, D.T., *Urban Geography : A Social Perspective*, David and Charles, Newton Abbot, 1972.
23. Johnston, *Urban Residential Pattern*, Bell, London, 1971.
24. Lynch, *Image of the City*, Massachusetts, Cambridge, 1960.
25. Dowson and Stea, "Image and Environment", Chicago and London, 1973.
26. Gould and White, R., *Mental Maps*, London, 1974.

ACKNOWLEDGEMENTS

We thank Editors Gerd-Michael Hellstern, Frithjof Spreer Hellmut Wollmann *Heft 2, Vol. II* for their permission to use material from "Applied Urban Research." Proceedings of the European Meeting on Applied Research, Essen Oct. 1981.

CONTENTS

LIST OF CONTRIBUTORS

M.M. Chandna : Department of Geography
Government College, Nahan (India)

Oded Izraeli : Associate Professor of Economics
Oakland University
Rochester, Michigan, USA

Jawahar Lal Jain : Lecturer, Department of General and Applied Geography
University of Saugar, Sagar (India)

K. B. Kankure : Lecturer, R. K. Talreja College
Ulhasnagar (District Thane)
Maharashtra (India)

Jin Hwan Lee : Department of Geography
Michigan State University
East Lansing, MI 48 824, USA

Barry Lentnek : Associate Professor of Geography
Suny at Buffalo, USA

P. T. Malshe : Reader, Department of Geography
University of Poona
Pune-411 007 (India)

Thomas R. McCarthy : Assistant Professor of Economics
Oakland University
(Currently on leave at the Federal Trade Commission, Washington D. C.)

N. Damson M'tizwa-Mangiza : Lecturer, Regional and Urban Planning Centre
University of Zimbabwe, Zimbabwe

D. C. Pandey : Lecturer, Department of Geography
Kumaun University
Nainital-263 001 (India)

Richard E. Preston : Department of Geography
University of Waterloo
Waterloo, Ontario. N2L 3G1

J. S. Rawat : Lecturer, Department of Geography
Almora Campus (Kumaun University)
Almora-263 601 (India)

Prabha Shastri : Lecturer and Head, Department of Geography
Vanijya Mahavidyalaya
Yavatmal, Maharashtra (India)

Mohan Singh : Lecturer, Department of Geography
Garhwal University Campus
Pauri-246 001, U.P. (India)

M. L. Soni : D. N. College
Fatehgarh-209 601 (India)

P. C. Tiwari : Research Fellow, Department of Geography
Kumaun University
Nainital-263001 (India)

Joe U. Umo : Department of Economics
University of Lagos, Lagos, Nigeria

R. K. Wilkinson : Division of Economic Studies
University of Sheffield
Sheffield, S10 2TN, England

C.S. Yadav : Reader, Department of Geography,
Bhagat Singh College, Delhi University, New Delhi.

ONE

C.S. YADAV

INTRODUCTION

GEOGRAPHERS have long been fascinated by the galactic patterns of human settlements. They have sought answers to questions like what form they take and have identified whether it is random or chaotic. They have also laboured hard to discern regularities in their patterns and processes. The 19th century investigators have made vigorous attempts to seek city-size relations, and the first to actually fiind a significant one was German geographer Felise Auerbach (1913)[1] who arranged settlements in order of size (first, second, third, fourth and so on).

Auerbach has stated that there is a simplest relationship between population and city size. Accordingly, the fourth-ranking city was found to have approximately one-fourth population of the largest. This inverse relationship between the population of a city and its rank within a general fabric of settlement is termed as the rank-size rule Peter Haggat (1972).[2] Accordingly it can be postulated that the size of any one city is linked to the size of all other settlements in a region which implies that the whole set of cities form an interlinked chain system distinguished from the largest to the smallest city. These are termed as rank-size chains. Urban geographers found these chains more meaningful when they subdivide the distribution of settlements into distinct segments. There is enough evidence available to prove that regular rank-size chains are recognizable for settlements in different parts of the world during different time periods.

THE LOGIC OF RANK-SIZE CHAINS

Geographers are not the only ones to solve the puzzle demonstrated by the rank-size distribution of cities. Similar attempts have been made by botanists to study the number of plant species. Nevertheless the pervasiveness of the type of distribution has led organization theorist Simon (1955)[3] to postulate rank-size rule as the equilibrium slope of a general growth process. According to this process a city initially has a random size and thereafter grows in an exponential manner that is proportional to size.

The problems in rank-size distribution are posed due to comparisons of city populations and ranks. In any national system, cities are ranked from the largest to the smallest, according to population. The largest city would rank number one, the second largest number two and so on. If these ranks are plotted against city population sizes, the rank-size relationship emerges. There is an apparent empirically regular relationship between the rank of a city and its population Berry and Garrison (1958).[4]

City-size relations have been noted by a number of scholars. The distribution of city sizes was first attempted by Auerbach[5] in 1913 and Onski (1972)[6] who developed the idea of city-size distribution. However, the best known elaboration of rank-size regularities was developed by G.K. Ziffp (1949).[7] He presented the rank frequency distribution of the 100 largest metropolitan districts in the United States in 1940. He stated the rank-size rule by the best fitting equation as follows :

$$R=(P^{-1})\ 1{,}00{,}00{,}000$$

where P is the city size and R is the city rank. He indicated that K=1,00,00,000 and was equal to the population of the largest metropolitan district. He drew the line calculated by least squares. This was simple regression line with a negative slope.

Rank Size vs Primacy

Berry (1961)[8] argued that when Ziffp advocated the concept of rank-size regularity to analyse the distribution of city size his contemporary Mark Jefferson (1939)[9] introduced the concept of "Primate" City. According to him, Primacy does exist when the population of the largest city is several times larger than that of the city which is second in rank. And those who followed Jefferson have applied the term to the whole system of cities of different sizes. According to them primacy also exits when a stratum of small towns and cities is dominated by one or more very large cities.

Berry (1961) synthesizes the conceptual issues related to both these procedures. He has commented that rank-size regularities had been associated with the existence of integrated systems of cities in economically advanced countries whereas primate cities had been associated with colonial economies in underdeveloped countries. He attempted to divide the 37 countries into three distinct categories using the lognormal distribution of cities with over 20,000 people : rank-size, intermediate size, and primate distribution. He concludes that rank size distribution was found when many forces affected the urban pattern in various ways due to complex economic, political and historical organizations. Intermediate city size distribution comprised the countries of a variety of sizes at various levels of development. Primacy, he advocates, is the simplest city size distribution. According to him, the Primate Cities are either orthogenetic, political and administrative capitals, "heterogenetic" capitals of the emerging nations or empire capitals Redfield and Singer (1954).[10]

The other pioneers who attempted the rank-size distribution of cities over time are Cesar A. Vapnarky (1969)[11] who examined cities of Argentine, Gary, L. Fowler (1972)[12] who tested Berry's model of the lognormal distribution and Harry W. Richardson (1973)[13] who described the similarities and differences among lognormal, Pareto and rank-size distributions.

Central Place Model

The terminology of Walter Christaller's model is straightforward. In an urban system analysis it seems normal to use the following terms : hierarchy, nodality and circulation patterns. However, the term central place denotes "urban centre". It consists of a series of hierarchical rankings of urban centres according to size and the function they render. They are evaluated as hamlets, villages, towns and cities and associated market areas and transportation networks. Contemporary urban analyists have shown the usefulness of the theory by evaluating the spatial structure of retail and service business. After its initial formulation over a period of time the contents of the theory have increased. Consequently these changes have increased generality of the application of the theory. Today the theory is more widely used in different cross cultural regions. Berry (1970)[14] remarked that it is a powerful theory and its assertions are plausible, its logical consequences more explicit.

THE CHRISTALLER CENTRAL PLACE MODEL

There are various models which explain the urban growth and their systematic arrangement. However, Christaller (1933)[15] has constructed a general, purely deductive theory to explain "size, number and distribution of towns" with the assumption that there is some ordering principle governing the distribution. His ideas were based on those of locational theorists like Von Thunen Peter Hall (1966)[16] and Weber (1929).[17] Christaller's works had little impact on contemporary Germany, and it was not until their introduction into the United States in the 1940s and 1950s that their value was established. Since then Christaller's model has been varified and extended and widely used to analyse the pattern of central places domain and structure of the Central Place Theory.

The domain of Walter Christaller's theory is usually described as embracing the location of urban trades and institutions, interpreted as narrowly as tertiary and consumer-oriented activities. He intended a broader interpretation of central goods and services. The theory was initially propounded to analyse the territorial arrangements at the intercity scale of not only retail and service trades but of transportation and communication activities, wholesaling, public and cultural institutions, some financial activities and certain types of market oriented industries Christaller (1966)[18] ; Berry and Harris (1968)[19] and thereby concentrate on a solution of general problems of explaining the size, number and distribution of urban places.

EXTENSION OF THE CHRISTALLER MODEL

Since its publication the Central Place Model has evoked two main reactions from fellow urban geographers. First, there are those who have confirmed in the absolute sense the general arguments presented by Christaller, with one condition that it be adopted with some refinement. Second, there are those who have taken extreme steps and found Christaller's model too rigid and static. They have reacted by providing an alternative procedure with a stronger time dimension and closer correspondence to actual settlement history. Loseh represents a logical extension of the Christaller model. It is based on the same hexagonal unit and hence suffer from the same rigidity. However, it explains a relationship between the size and function of central places and, therefore, is more closer to the observed distributions. The domain and structure of the theory are quite different from the substantive interpretations offered in key reference works Ullman (1941)[20], Dickinson (1958)[21], Wherwein (1942)[22], Brush (1953)[23], Berry and Garrison (1958, *a*, *b*, *c*)[24], Berry and Pred (1961)[25], Berry (1967, *b*, *c*)[26], Beavon (1977)[27].

This in the general fabric of settlement which extends from hamlet to metropolis, only the central places constitute the hierarchic class system which is the prime postulate of the central place model. As it has been identified a national spatial system consists of hierarchy of central places, hierarchies of tributary areas and transport routes. When a socio-economic system changes due to technological innovations and advancement, the hierarchic pattern also changes correspondingly.

ABOUT THIS VOLUME

In this volume those articles are included which postulate the principle of Christaller and Losch. The volume provides a glimpse of rank, size rule and the hierarchical system of settlement in different cross cultural regions. A glance at the list of the numerous articles in the volume on central place, rank-size relationship, effect of city size, hierarchical structure of the central places would show both the current extreme concern with the system of cities and the empirical foundation of the models propounded.

The first article by Richard E. Preston, "A Reassessment of the Structure of Classical Central Place Theory", demonstrates that there is a marked differentiation between the published description of Christaller's Central Theory and its original presentation as a consequence of which existing analyses fail to convey how the theory provides a basis for describing and explaining both real world and idealized central place patterns in both space and time. The objective in this paper is threefold : (i) to establish the domain and structure of the classical central place theory, (ii) to present some of Christaller's views regarding his theory and (iii) to consider implication of this assessment for several aspects of research on the urban system. The author with his comments draws the attention of the readers towards an apparent confusion and oppotunity in the central place research which are enlisted as under : (i) the pertinence of empirical evidence to the domains classical centre places theory, (ii) confusion of fundamental meanings centrality vs nodality, (iii) economic base theory, potential theory and a dynamic system perspective, (iv) exogenous forces and changing central places system, (v) central place theory and industrial location and (vi) mixed hierarchies.

The question of what determines the size of an urban population has practical as well as theoretical interest. Urban geographers have explored the question of whether towns and cities are "too small or too big" and consequent determinants of city size. Thus the existence of a pattern to the growth of individual areas and the apparent stability of a hierarchy of city sizes demand explanations. To resolve these questions urban geographers, first, concentrate on the individual city and try to seek to explain why economic and technical factors together determine its size. This type of analysis follows the concepts and approach of the neoclassical theory of a firm. The second approach is macro in concept and seeks to explain the hierarchy of urban sizes on the assumption that there is a system of urban areas. The explanation of "rank size rule" is the central theme of the works on urban system. It is identified that there is a lot of controversy on the question of optimum size. R.K. Wilkinson in his article, "Theories of Urban Area Size", first concentrates on the question of optimum size. In this paper he has rightly chosen the subject matter to demonstrate that government, business and commercial organizations have all different kinds of hierarchies. He has tried to explore the possibility, just as there would appear to be optimum units for administration and production, it wouid seem feasible to expect them to be similar optimum size units for urban areas. The author clearly reveals that there must be sufficient theory to rationalize the observed structure of the urban system, and the size of the individual urban areas has a concomitant relationship to economic forces. He finds it suitable to define the optimum size and expiain the observed hierarchy. He reveals that related theory has a rather negative than a positive operational use and he finds that such a theory serves to define what may be possible in trying to influence the size of urban areas rather than what are likely to be desirable lines of policy to pursue.

Journey to work behaviour represents an important dimension of location theory. The location models postulate that commuters travel to worksites in central business districts of a monocentric city built on a featureless plain. Households choose their optimal location based upon the traditional utility maximization subject. Oded Izraeli and Thomas R. McCarthy in their article, "The Effect of City Size in Journey to Work Behaviour," adopt the basic framework of the location theory to investigate not only the important travel distance parameter of journey to work behaviour but also travel time. The authors in this paper demonstrate how journey to work place behaviour, as measured by travel time and travel distance, is affected by a change in city size. The authors have made an attempt to prove that under the assumption of a monocentric city, the effect of an increase in the population of the city on average travel distance would depend upon the elasticity of the supply of urban land. The authors find that as a city grows in size, business is able to realize sufficient agglomeration economics at sites other than CBD and consequently the development of new centres or sub-centres would become attractive. Besides the effect of city size on travel time and travel distance two other aspects of J.T.W. behaviour are of concern to the present study. One is the examination of the effect of city size on the means of transportation used. In this paper the authors have made an attempt to examine the choice of means and transportation, especially mass travel. The authors have finally tried to explore the effect of city size on travel speed. In the paper they have, in Section II, discussed the theoretical framework of the monocentric model of urban locations as the basis for the empirical analysis which follows in Section III.

Since the inception of the concept of rank size rule in 1920 various academicians have made an attempt to analyse how groups of cities in regions, countries or the world have a consistent regularity in size. The organizing principle which explains this regularity was derived from "Ziffps Rule" of "Rank Size Concept" which states that the distribution of all cities by rank and size in many countries is such that the population of any city multiplied by its rank is a constant. The distribution of city size based on population has been studied in Korea. Nevertheless there are very few studies which have surveyed the recent rank-size distribution of Korean cities. Therefore, it is significant to survey the recent distributions by rank-size of Korean cities. The present paper by Jin Hwan Lee on "Korean City Size Distribution Based on the Rank Size Relationship" is an attempt in this direction.

The object ve of the author in this paper is two fold. First, he attempts to survey the changes in the distribution of city size in Korea over time. Secondly, he feels it appropriate to reveal the relationship between the distribution of city system in Korea and that of the rank size rule. The author briefly examines the methodology in order to investigate the rank-size rule for Korea. In doing so he provides a brief review of literature. He provides an analysis of distribution of rank size of cities in Korea and concludes his investigation as follows : (i) More than 60 per cent of the urban population in Korea is concentrated in four largest cities : Seoul, Pusan, Daegu and Indean, (ii) the author finds it interesting that distribution of Korean city size is developing towards the lognormal distribution over time, (iii) the author postulates that the distribution of city size is inconsistent with the distribution of the rank-size rule, (iv) the medium sized cities provided the most consistent relationship between rank-size rule and size of the city.

Until recently, the administration and planning of Harare, the capital if Zimbabwe has been characterized by fragmentation and discriminatory practies. Consequently past research work on suburban shopping centres has concentrated on centres located in the low density residential areas which are high-income areas. However, since Zimbabwe's independence in 1980, urban planning policy has shifted substantially, with the desired attempt to improve. The long neglected high density residential areas accommodate 70 per cent of the total population of the city.

In view of this, there is an urgent need for a critical appraisal of the structure of urban activity in Harare. N. Damson

M'tizwa-Mangiza through his article, "The Hierarchical Structure and Spatial Distribution of Suburban shopping Centres in Harare", makes an attempt to draw attention to the neglected region of Harare. He conducts a critical appraisal of the structure of urban activity in Harare. The aims of his present study are : (i) to investigate the hierarchical structure and spatial distribution of suburban shopping centres in Harare, (ii) to analyse the functional composition of the centres and (iii) to provide a comprehensive picture of the whole city with respect to suburban shopping centres with the ultimate view of furnishing much needed data for planners. The study matter is sequentially divided into conceptual framework of analysis, area of study, data collection, analysis and discussion of results and conclusions. The present study has limited itself to four theoretical approaches (i) location theory formulations originating from Christaller's Central Place Theory, (ii) spatial behaviour concepts derived from gravity model, (iii) the gravity behaviour approach and in structural approach. However, the Central Place Theory has been chosen as a conceptual framework for the present study.

The studies of both intracity and interregional income inequality as they relate to city size in developed countries can hardly be generalizable to contemporary 'LDCS' for at least two reasons : (i) the single instrument used as a measure of inequality, i.e., income, fails to capture the key concerns of poverty eradication in LDCS and (ii) the impact of primate city phenomenon which can make a difference to accessibility to basic needs. Joe U. Umo in his article, "Basic Needs Gradients in a Primate City State : The case of Lagos", seeks to develop an intraregional/intraurban distributional hypothesis based on the basic needs concept. In this paper the author points out that a negative basic needs gradients with radial distance from the core characterise of a primate city region. Using Lagos City State as a case study, it has been verified that all basic needs indicators used—education, employment, revenue, housing and health—have distance decay trends from the core. The gradients suggest in particular that basic needs distribution in the city region is highly regressive. Explanation for this phenomenon includes distance friction, political neglect and excessive concern for city growth at the expense of welfare distribution. The need for a threshold analysis for identifying its real growth potentials and encouragement of local participation in community development concerns have identified. The paper seeks to develop an intraregional/intraurban distributional hypothesis based on the basic needs concept. This the author has tested against the background of city-primacy in an LDC Nigeria. The paper has attempted to advance a basic needs gradient hypothesis and used primate City State, Lagos, for empirical verification. The first section of the paper reviews a theoretical background and develops a basic needs gradient hypothesis (BMGH.) The second section examines the empirical materials relating to BMGH. The third concluded with a possible explanation of BMGH and an analysis of policy implications.

The focus of the paper of Barry Lentnek on "Primacy's Peak 20th Century Mexican Urbanization", is on the manner in which the evolution of city distributions may statistically be characterised. In this paper an application is made to the 20th century experience of urbanization in Mexico. The author finds that the rank-size rule is one method of characterizing city-size distribution. Gini's coefficient of concentration is another. This article presents the mathematical relationship between the two and applies these statistics to population date from 57 cities in the 20th century Mexico. Empirical analyses show that primacy increased during 1900-1950 and has been decreasing since then. Also, the scope of the rank-size equations for all cities except Mexico City have approached "1" since the close of the Mexican Revolution and probably will approximate a perfect rank-size rule around 2000. The relationship of these findings to the theory of urban development is discussed. However the paper is organized as follows : (i) A Re-examination of the rank-size rule as one of a number of alternative ways to stylize facts concerning national urban systems. (ii) A presentation of alternative Maxican data bases. (iii) A critique of the methodology and suggestions for improvement in time series and cross national studies of urban population size distribution are offered.

Jawahar Lal Jain in his paper, "Urban System of Malwa" (India) seeks to provide a method for an analysis of spatial organization within the conceptual framework of central place system. It thus attempts grouping or ranking of towns as central places and demarcating their hinterlands or areas of their command, i.e., defining the central place hierarchy—its structure, organization and functioning as a spatial system. Besides, it investigates the structural organization and functional efficacy of the region under study as a coherent system and interprets it in the context of the geographical disposition of the region and recent historical developments. However, in order to avoid the tantalizing problem of defining the lower limit of central places, only all the towns of the region, as per the 1971 Census, have been reckoned with.

The Region covers the portion of Malwa Plateau falling under Madhya Pradesh only, for which the simplified name of "Malwa" is adopted in this paper. It is an extensive plateau surface covering north-western M.P. extending from Narmada river in the south to State border with Rajasthan in the north, and from Sagar district in the east to the western border of the State with Gujarat and Rajasthan, though a little of actual Malwa extends over the adjacent parts of these States also. It covers an area of little under 105,000 sq. km. The total population of the region, as per the 1971 Census, is 11,045,000, living in 19,304 villages and 84 towns, the latter ranging in size from under half a myriad to well over a half million and containing approximately 24 per cent of the total regional population. The distribution of rural population as well as the spacing of towns is notably even. The region is essentially a somewhat undulated plateau surface (general altitude a litle over 500 metres above sea level) covered with thick piles of extrusion lava, upon which have developed the typical rich, black soils, dotted here and there.

The central place interactions are referred to as the principal element leading to the organization of space around the focal point. Various urban geographers in their attempt to analyse the interaction areas have adopted different terms. They have observed that the centripetal and centrifugal forces provide the actual parameters to demarcate the zone of central place interactions and spatial organizations. The main objective of authors D.C. Pandey, P.C. Tiwari and J.C. Rawat in their article, "Central Place Interactions", is to identify the central place interactions in a three-tier functional hierarchy with the help of the quantitative as well as qualitative technique. The authors in the paper have analysed the factors affecting spatial interaction pattern in hills and plains. The authors find that there were marked differentiations in delineation and nature of the areas of interaction of central places of hills and plains. They reveal that the interaction areas of the central places taken as basic planning units are helpful to analyse spatio-functional gaps as well as integrated spatial organization in the region.

Every inhabited part of the world is characterized by a variety of settlements of human occupance. These settlements may be grouped into two categories from the viewpoint of spatial organization. The first category comprises those settlements that primarily serve other settlements and the second category includes others which are served. Dr. M.M. Chandana in his article, "Locational Patterns of Service Centres in the Outer Himalayas", intends to identify all the service centres in the Sirmaur district of Himachal Pradesh and to render a detailed analysis of their locational pattern. The author gives a brief des ription of the district methodology. He analyses the distribution of service centres in relation to the physiography of the region.

The concept of hierarchy has attracted the interest of a number of geographers in recent years who have made an attempt to conduct empirical studies in specific areas Neverthe-less M.L. Soni in his article, "Hierarchy of Service Centres in the Umland of Lucknow", attempts to work out the hierarchy of service centres by Godlund's centrality method. The central functions taken into consideration in the present paper are, however, different from those taken by Godlund and K.N. Singh. The latter has considered only the persons engaged in trade and commerce whereas in this paper non agricultural population has been taken into account for centrality calculations. Centrality values have been tabulated and mapped. A close examination of the map reveals that the service centres in the umland of Lucknow vary greatly in importance. The population and centrality of all the service centres have been plotted on a single graph to observe its centrality index and to observe natural break points which could be used as reference points for classifying the various service centres into certain central categories.

A central place connotes a place of manifold activities for surrounding countryside. A central place can be defined as a pemanent human establishment where an exchange of central goods and services for population, other than the local one, exists and which, therefore, commands a tributary region surrounding it. All central places perform certain non-primary functions for the region. The central places vary in size according to their service capacities. The small market centres, large market centres, small regional centres and large regional centres are all central places but they vary in functional characteristics and importance. K.B. Kulkarni and P.T. Malshe in their article "Growth Hierarchy and Functional Classification of Urban Settlements in Marathwada", have made an attempt to present a picture of urbanization, centrality, hierarchy and functional classification of towns in Marathwada. The analysis is based upon the cause-and-effect model with a process approach. The functional classification has been attempted according to the method. The authors have analysed the changing processes and patterns of urban growth. They identify five hierachies of settlement in Marathwada : (i) Large Regional Centre, (ii) Regional Centre, (iii) Sub-Regional Centre, (iv) Large Market Town, and (v) Small Market Town. According to the functions they render they are classified as : (i) Agricultural Towns, (ii) Mining Towns, (iii) Household Industry Towns, (iv) Manufacturing Towns, (v) Construction Towns, (vi) Trading Towns, (vii) Transport Towns and (viii) Other service towns.

During the decade 1971-81 the number of "Million Plus" cities of India increased from 9 to 12 with the addition of Nagpur, Lucknow and Jaipur. Located in the heart of the country, Nagpur is the major city in the eastern part of Maharashtra State. Though Nagpur ranks 10th in population size among the "Million Plus" Cities, it ranks 7th when the cities are arranged in descending order of growth rate. Dr. Prabha Shastri in her article, "The Emergence of Nagpur as a Million Plus City and Changes in the Urban Size Hierarchy of Vidarbha", attempts to study the growth of population in Nagpur city, which emerged as a "Million Plus" city for the first time in the 1981 Census. The paper also analyses how far the urban size hierarchy and primacy indices in Vidarbha have changed during the decade 1971-81 as a consequence of the emergence of a "Million Plus" city. The extent to which the urban size hierarchy deviates from "Rank Size Rule" in both these years is also measured.

Mohan Singh in his article, "Sub-System of Towns Within the Urban System of Uttarakhand", feels that most of the central place models are quantitative which are basically propounded by Western scholars. In this paper the author does not take shelter under quantitative approach and tries to present his matter fully as a qualified device. He has made a bold attempt to select a subject matter of a neglected area where the process of urbanization as envisaged by models has not been experienced—hill areas. The authors' main objective of making such a study is : (i) to justify the towns in Uttarakhand as a system, (ii) trace out the sub-system with the urban system and (ii) explore the relevance of applying systems approach in the spatial organization of towns.

FOOTNOTES

1. Auerbach, F., Das Gestz der Bevolkar ugskonzent railion, Peterman's, *Mitteriluragen*, 1913, 59, 74-6.
2. Haggatt, Peter, *Geography : A Modern Synthesis*, Harper International Edition, Harper and Row, 1972.
3. Simon, H.A., "On a class of Skew Distribution Functions", *Brionmetrika*, 42, 1955, 425-40.
4. Berry, B.J.L. and W.L. Garrison, "Alternate Explanations of Urban Size Relationship", *Annals of the Associations of American Geographers*, Vol. 48, March 1958, 83-87.
5. Auerbach, F., *op. cit.*
6. Onski, K. Dziew, "General Theory of Bank Size Distribution in Regional Settlement Systems" ; "Reappraisal and Reformulation of the Rank Size Rule", *Papers of the Regional Science Association*, Vol. 29, 1972, p. 73.
7. Ziffp, G.K., *Human Behaviour and the Principle of Least Effort*, Addison Wessler, New York, 1949.
8. Berry, B.J.L., "City Size Distributions", *Economic Development and Cultural Changes*, Vol. 9, 1967, p. 575.
9. Jefferson, Mark, The Law of Primate City : *The Geographical Review*, xxix, 1939 (2), 1226-32.
10. Redfield, Robert and Singer, Milon, "The Cultural Role of Cities", *Economic Development and Cultural Change*, 1954, III, 53-73.
11. Cesar, A. Vapnarky, "On Rank Size Distribution of Cities : An Ecological Approach", *Economic Development and Cultural Change*, 1969, 17, 584-585.
12. Fowler, G.L., "Development of City Size Distribution for the Egyptian Urban System", *The Professional Geographer*, 1972, Vol. 24, pp. 317-319.
13. Richardson, H.W., "Theory of the Distribution of City Size : Review and Prospects", in *Systems of Cities* (ed.), L.S. Bourne and J.W. Simmons, Oxford University Press, New York, 1973.

14. Berry and Hartson, *Geographic Perspectives on Urban System*, Prentice Hall, 1970.
15. Christaller, Walter, *Central Place in Southern Germany* Translated by Carlisle W. Barkin, Prentice Hall Inc., Englewood Chiffs, N.J., 1966.
16. Hall, Peter, (ed.), *Von Thunen's Isolated State*, London Pergamon Press, 1966.
17. Weber, Alfred, *Theory of Location of Industries*, University Press, Chicago, 1929.
18. Christaller, *op. cit*,
19. Berry and Harris, C.D., "Central Place" in D.L. Sills (ed.), *International Encyclopedia of the Social Science*, 1968.
20. Ullman, "A Theory of Location for Cities", *American Journal of Sociology*, 46, 1941, 453-69.
21. Dickinson, The Economic Regions of Germany", *Geographical Review*, 28, 1938, 609-626.
22. Wherwein, "The Rural Urban Fringe", *Economic Geography*, 18, 1942, 217-228.
23. Brush, "The Hierarchy of Central Places in South Western Wisconsin", *Geographical Review*, 43, 1953, 380-402.
24. Berry and Garrison, "Functional Basis of the Central Place Hierarchy", *Economic Geography*, 34, 1958a, 145-154.
25. Berry and Pred, *Central Place Studies : A Bibliography of Theory and Applications*, Regional Science Institute, Philadelphia, 1961.
26. Berry, *Geography and Market Centers and Retail Distribution*, Prentice Hall, Englewood Cliffs, N.J., 1967b.
27. Beavon, K.S.O., *Central Place Theory : A Reinterpretation*, New York, Longman, 1977.

TWO

RICHARD E. PRESTON

A REASSESSMENT OF THE STRUCTURE OF CLASSICAL CENTRAL PLACE THEORY

IN this essay it is suggested that published descriptions of the structure of Christaller's central place theory omit numerous critical aspects included in its original presentation. As a result, existing descriptions and evaluations fail to convey how the theory provides a basis for describing and explaining both real-world and idealized central place patterns in both space and time. Accordingly, the intent here is threefold ; to establish the domain and structure of classical central place theory,[1] to present some of Christaller's views regarding his theory, and to consider implications of this assessment for several aspects of research on urban systems.

The arguments presented are based on an interpretation of central place theory that is different from those usually offered in the published literature. Four differences are as follows. First, it is argued that almost all published central place studies interpret the theory's domain too narrowly. It was intended to embrace far more than the retail and service trades and a limited number of governmental and cultural institutions. Second, it is argued that central place theory as presented in Christaller's basic work, *The Central Places in Southern Germany : An Economic-geographical Investigation of the Regularity of the Distribution and Development of Settlements with Urban Functions* (1933, 1966), consisted of five steps or components rather than of the two steps implied in later publications. Third, it is argued that *Central Places in Southern Germany* includes both an explicit appreciation of the role of change in the formation of central place systems and a systematic framework that incorporates within Christaller's theory the main factors shaping such systems (Preston 1983). And fourth, it is argued that some of the operational definitions utilized in the central place literature and urban geography text-books differ substantially from those in Christaller's original presentation.

This interpretation relates to the status of central place research in numerous ways. For example, it is possible that the complete structure of central place theory has not been considered formally during the more than twenty years that this subject has been at the forefront of research and teaching in urban-economic geography. It is also possible that failure to recognize and develop the overall theory, and particularly its dynamic component, has slowed the pace of research on urban systems. Such is the case because the original theoretical domain embraced a wider range of central goods and services than are usually included under the "trades and institutions" view, and because the dynamic component together with the widely accepted static component provide an as yet unmatched "unified theoretical perspective" embracing both the territorial organization and development of central place systems, a prespective that has been sought by geographers for some time. Finally, because of lack of comparability between research procedures employed in the empirical literature and the original structure of the theory, it is possible that at least some of the findings and conclusions about classical theory offered in applied central place studies are open to question.

THE DOMAIN AND STRUCTURE OF CENTRAL PLACE THEORY

Because the context for this study is the original statement of Christaller's theory, it is necessary to emphasize that the theory's domain and structure are quite different from the substantive interpretations offered in key reference works (Ullman 1941 ; Dickinson 1938, 1947 ; Wherwein 1942 ; Brush 1953 ; Berry and Garrison 1958, a,b,c ; Berry and Pred 1961 ; Berry 1967b ; Beavon 1977) and in standard urban geography textbooks (Dickinson 1964 ; Murphy 1966 ; Yeates and Garner 1980 ; Carter 1975 ; Berry and Horton 1970 ; Northam 1979 ; Beaujeu

Garnier and Chabot 1967 ; King and Gollege 1978 : Palm 1981 ; Hartshorn 1980 ; Christian and Harper 1982).

As noted earlier, the theory's domain is usually described as embracing the location of urban trades and institutions, interpreted narrowly as tertiary and consumer-oriented activities. Moreover, empirical studies have been directed overwhelmingly at the retail and service trades, with an occasional examination of institutional and administrative activities thrown in. This view is incomplete. Christaller intended a broader interpretation of central goods and services. The theory was created to describe and explain the territorial arrangement, at the intercity scale, of not only retail and service trades, but of transportation and communication activities, wholesaling, public and cultural institutions, some financial activities, and certain types of market oriented industries (Christaller 1966 : 7, 20-21, 140-141 ; Berry and Harris 1968 : 365), and thereby to contribute to a solution for the general problem of explaining the size, number, and distribution of urban places. The theory is also virtually always described as static in nature, when, in reality, it was Christaller's intent to describe and explain central place patterns in a dynamic systems context. In application, his perspective called for a conceptualization, quantification, and interpretation of both stable and changing relations between system components in terms of magnitudes of surplus energy, or centrality, the generation, distribution, and changing nature of which relate directly to the satisfaction of societal needs. Christaller also stated that central place theory was a partial theory of the space economy and that it was intended to supplement the location theories for agriculture and industry developed by Weber and Thunen, respectively. He was, moreover, aware of the need for a common framework for these partial theories, and for this he relied on the work of Englander (Christaller 1966 : 7).

Regarding structure, classical central place theory included both clearly defined static and dynamic components in the context of *five distinct and interrelated* steps.[2] In this sequence each successive step resulted in an increasingly comprehensive view of the structure and development of central place systems. The entire theory was presented in Part 1, "The Theoretical Part" of Christaller's (1933, 1966) basic work. Reasons for the persistent ignoral of two-thirds of Christaller's theory by urban-economic geographers for a period of fifty years are unclear (Preston 1983 ; Harris 1978), particularly, since : its structure was laid out in detail in the original presentation (Christaller 1933, 1966 : 14-135) ; Berry (1967a) and Rydell (1967) noted the presence of the dynamic component in their reviews of Baskin's translation ; and attention has been drawn to the dynamic component in several recent publications (e.g., Borchert 1967 : 327 ; Carter 1975 : 89 ; Preston 1979 : 202).

Before discussing the theory's five steps, it is important to point out that Christaller (1933) made it clear in the full title and introductory materials of his basic work that the intent of his theory was to describe and explain the territorial organization of central places in both space and time (Table 2.1). This was done by inclusion of the words "Distribution and Development" in

TABLE 2.1 : **Table of contents**[1]

CENTRAL PLACES IN SOUTHERN GERMANY : An Economic-geographical Investigation of the Regularity of the Distribution and Development of Settlements with Urban Functions

Introduction

I. THE THEORETICAL PART : Economic-Theoretical Foundations of Town Geography

A. Fundamental Meanings

1. Centralization as a principal of order
2. Central Places
3. Importance and Centrality
4. Central goods and services
5. The complementary region
6. The economic distance and the range of a good

B. Static Relations

1. *The consumption of central goods and the development of central places*
2. *The distribution of population and the central places*
   (a) no central place, (b) a small central place, (c) a large central place, (d) several central places, (e) excentric central places, (f) results, (g) dispersed places.
3. *The density and the structure of the population*
   (a) population density, (b) social and professional structure of the population, (c) amount and spatial distribution of income.
4. *The Central Goods*
   (a) main kinds of goods, (b) goods of a given quantity with a fixed price, (c) goods of a given quantity with a market price.

(d) goods, the production of which can be increased as desired with a fixed price, (e) goods, the production of which can be increased as desired with a market price, (f) results, (g) generalizations about the price of goods, (h) several types of goods, (i) production costs

5. *The Region*
   (a) size of the region, (b) communication potential of a region, (c) natural endowment of the region, (d) special cases
6. *The Traffic*
   (a) general importance of traffic, (b) lesser and better possibilities in passenger transportation, (c) lesser and better possibilities in goods transportation
7. *The Range oj the Central Goods*
   (a) influence of the distribution of population, (b) influence of the structure of the population, (c) influence of economic distance, (d) influence of the main types of goods and of the price of goods, (e) upper and lower limits of the range, (f) central goods of higher and lower order, (g) competing central places
8. *The System of Central Places*
   (a) problem situation, (b) development of the systems of central places, (c) continuation, (d) imperfections, (e) the transportation principle and the pattern of central places, (f) the separation principle and the pattern of central places

C. Dynamic Processes

1. *The dynamic point of view*
2. *The population*
   (a) uniform increase, (b) non-uniform increase, (c) results, (d) changes in the structure of the population, (e) decline
3. *The Central Goods*
   (a) increase in demand, (b) increase in supply, (c) decline in supply or demand, (d) price changes, (e) several types of goods
4. *Production costs and technical progress*
   (a) importance of the production costs, (b) capital costs, (c) labour costs, (d) land rent, (e) other cost features, (f) technical progress
5. *The Region*
   (a) change in the size of the region, (b) change in transportation possibilities, (c) change in the natural endowment
6. *The Traffic*
   (a) general importance of transportation in dynamic processes, (b) special problems of rail-road transportation, (c) special problems of automobile transportation
7. *The Range of Central Goods*
   (a) suppression of change, (b) change in the size and importance of central places, (c) change in the price-willingness of

TABLE 2.1 : (*Contd.*)

purchaser, (d) change in subjective economic distance, (e) change in the price and amount of central goods, (f) change in the lower limit of the range

8. *The Dynamic Aspects of a System of Central Places*
(a) introduction, (b) change in the situation : the competition among the three principles, (c) change in the number of central places, (d) change in the spacing, (e) change in the size-types, (f) historical development, (g) territorial development, (h) economic policy and planning

9. *Business Cycle Problems*

D. Results

I. *General and Special Economic Theory*

II. THE CONNECTING PART : Application of the Theory of Location of the Actual Geography of Settlements

III. REGIONAL PART : The Number, Sizes, and Distribution of the Central Places in Southern Germany

IV. CONCLUSION

APPENDIX

BIBLIOGRAPHY

1. To emphasize the more detailed table of contents in the original publication, those parts appearing in the 1966 translation are underlined in the title and in the sections dealing with Static Relations and Dynamic Processes.

Source : Abstracted from the Table of Contents of Christaller (1933).

the subtitle, by inclusion of separate and sequential chapters on "Static Relations" and "Dynamic Processes" in a clear-cut four-part division of the first of his book's four major sections, "The Theoretical Part : Economic-Theoretical Foundations of Town Geography", and by stating in the Introduction that the theory begins with a theoretical statement that is divided into static and dynamic parts. Moreover, in a paper published thirty-five years later, Christaller reaffirmed that it was his intent in *Central Places in Southern Germany* to produce a unified perspective embracing both spatial and dynamic aspects of central places :

> In the theoretical portion of my investigation, I thus did not satisfy myself with setting up a model for an invariable and constant economic landscape (thus, for a static condition)—but I also tried to show how the number, size, and distribu-

> tion of the central places change, when the economic factors change : the number, the distribution and the structure of the population, the demands for central goods and services, the production costs, the technical progress, the traffic services, etc. (1968 : 97 ; 1972 : 608).

The five steps comprising classical central place theory are outlined in Figure 1.1 and are considered according to the format used by Christaller (Table 2.1).

Step 1. Fundamental meanings

After the problem statement, the theory begins with a consideration of "Centralization as a Principle of Order". This is followed by a presentation of operational definitions (Christaller 1966 : 14-26) that underly the four following steps and spell-out a logical framework serviceable as a basis for the definition and explanation of the territorial organization of the central place function in any environment and at any point in time (A1-6 in Table 2.1, Figure 2.1) ; namely :[3]

1. *Central Places* are urban settlements that provide central goods and services not only for their own residents but for consumers living in their complementary regions and for the travelling public, i.e., a centre for a region.
2. *Importance and Centrality* are related concepts that identify respectively the aggregate and relative importance of settlements as central places. The term *Nodality* represents the aggregate importance of a place as a provider of central goods and services both for its own residents and for other consumers, while the term *Centrality* represents the importance of a place as a provider of central goods and services in excess of the needs of its own residents.
3. *Central goods and services* are those "produced and offered at a few necessarily central points in order to be consumed at many scattered points" (Christaller 1966 : 19). They are thus provided by functions that are bound by necessity to a central place because of both objective and subjective economic and social advantages, and that serve both local and extra local consumers.

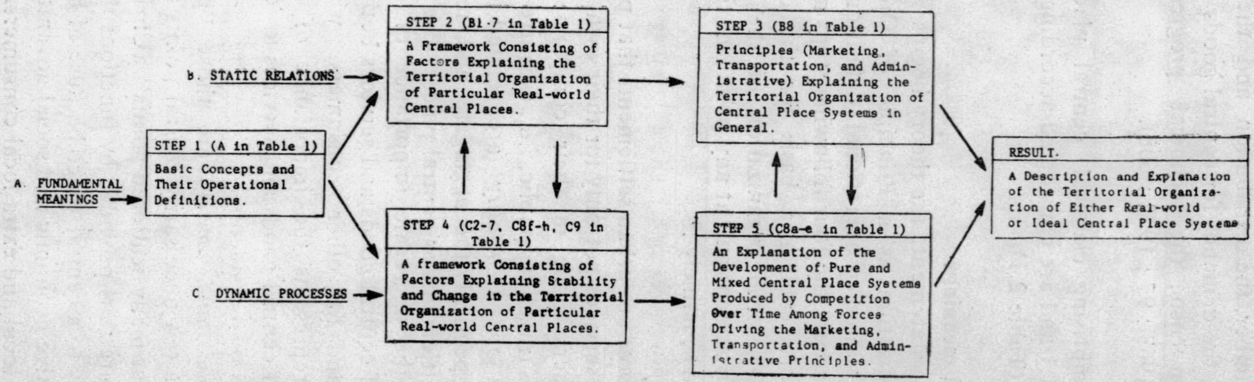

FIG. 2.1 : *Steps comprising classical central place theory*

4. A *Complementary Region* is an area for which a central place is the diffusion point for central goods and services.
5. *Economic Distance and Range of a Good* :

   (a) *Economic Distance* represents not just linear distance but embraces (Christaller 1966 : 22) "costs of freight, insurance, and storage ; time and loss of weight or space in transit ; and as regards passenger travel, the cost of transportation, the time required, and the discomfort of travel." Christaller (1966 : 51-52) developed this idea into concepts of "time-cost-distance" and "subjective economic distance".
   (b) *The Outer-Range of a Good* is the distance beyond which the total cost of acquiring a good by a potential customer becomes greater than the value of the good or service to that customer. The range thus delimits the spatial extent of sales (complementary area) of a particular good or service.
   (c) *The Inner-range of a Good* or *Threshold* embraces the area containing the minimum purchasing power needed to support a particular function.

6. A *Central Place Hierarchy* is an idealized stair-step like distribution of central places in which each level, *or order*, is distinguished from other orders by a distinctive group, *or order*, of central goods and services not offered by lower order places (Christaller 1966 : 19-21, 49-72).

That these concepts and definitions were intended to assist attempts to describe and explain both stability and change in the structure of central place systems was stated clearly by Christaller (1966 : 111) :

> The system of central places is developed only on the assumption that there are many types of central goods, from the lowest to the highest order, each having a special range. The specific ranges differ with regard to time and location, and, . . . , are themselves subject to steady changes soon

after a change in any one of the factors determining the range. Every birth and every death, every change of profession by an individual, every change in fashion, every change in individual wants for certain goods, every invention, every price fluctuation, every new tax, etc., influences the size of the range of the central goods, even if only to a small degree. Every change in the range of any central good at any place causes simultaneous deviations within the systems of central places.

Step 2. An abstract framework for the analysis of individual central places

In step two of his theory Christaller (1966 : 27-58) developed an abstract but flexible framework suitable for "discovering relationships with which we can explain the size, number, and distribution of central places in individual concrete cases" (1966 : 58). This approach was intended to facilitate examination of the limited number of general factors listed in B1-7 in Table 2.1, both individually and in combination with regard to their influence on the territorial organization of particular real-world central places. Broadly speaking, the factors highlighted were : the distribution, density, and structure of population ; the type, quantity and price of central goods and services ; the size and nature of a region ; the state of transportation ; and the range of a good. Range of a good was accorded particular importance in that it was taken to represent the combined spatial effects of all factors considered previously.

Discussion of each factor was based on the question, "What is the relationship between that factor (e.g., distribution of population) and the consumption of central goods ?" The significance of each factor was often demonstrated by a concentric zone model of one or more central places systems, by verbal, numerical, and graphical examples of a hypothetical nature, and by occasional references to actual situations. In most cases, generalizations summarizing the relations examined were offered.

Step 3. Abstract frameworks for analyzing central places in general

After considering relations between the factors listed in B1-7 of

Table 2.1 and central place importance, Christaller expressed dissatisfaction with having discovered only an abstract framework for exploring and explaining the territorial structure of individual central places. He wanted to discover "...laws that bring order to the apparently arbitrary distribution, to the apparently accidental number, and to the apparently individually conditioned sizes of the places" (1966 : 58). This is attempted in the third step in his theory and appears in a section of the book appropriately called "The System of Central Places" (1966 : 58-80). The result (B8 in Table 2.1) was an abstract, normative, framework for interpreting and planning central place systems in general that was based on three comprehensive principles (marketing, transportation, and administration), each representing an ideal territorial expression of groups of pervasive forces shaping central place patterns.

Christaller concluded his discussion of step three with explicit recognition of both a fourth comprehensive principle of central place organization (the mixed hierarchy) and of the need to incorporate change in his scheme. Both positions are related to his view that in reality there is ongoing competition for dominance in a region among the forces driving the three principles and that a dynamic component was necessary in this theory to understand such competition (Christaller 1966 : 76, 80).

This section also provides periodic evaluations of his evolving theory and represents a bridge between its static and dynamic components (Christaller 1966 : 69, 70, 72), for example :

> Hence it should be borne in mind and emphasized again and again in order to avoid misunderstanding that we have only a scheme, a rational scheme of general economic theory, or, in more picturesque but less explicit everyday speech, we have the most favourable state, not in the sense of valuation but in the sense of the highest rationality with the least loss of value. Yet the real values which are most rational change constantly as a consequence of change in population, custom of life, technology, etc. (1966 : 70).

Step 4. An abstract framework for analyzing the evolution of individual central place systems

The chapter on Dynamic Processes is introduced with a crystal-clear declaration of Christaller's (1966 : 84-85) "Dynamic Point of View". Thereafter, the fourth and fifth steps in the theory are presented. Step four offers an abstract flexible framework consisting of general factors intended to facilitate the explanation of evolving real-world central places (C2-7, 8f-h, 9 in Table 2.1). Step four is organizationally parallel to, and builds upon, step two, while at the same time expands the range of explanatory factors included. Therein, Christaller discussed how change in each of the factors treated under step two (plus the factors of production costs and technical progress) could individually and in combination alter the structure of individual central place systems (1966 : 84-111). The concept of range of a good retains the synthesizing quality identified under Static Relations, and it is shown how the range can be altered by change in (1) the importance of central places, (2) the price-willingness of consumers, (3) consumer perceptions of subjective economic distance, and (4) the price of central place goods (Christaller 1966 : 107-111).

Some of the examples used in step four also build on those introduced under step two, and once again, they are verbal, numerical, graphical, and usually hypothetical. In most cases, the likely impacts of various kinds of change on the territorial organization of central place systems are summarized in generalizations suitable for further study (e.g., Christaller 1966 : 87-91, 95-96, 101-104, 109).

Therefore, by abstracting from reality what he considered to be key factors shaping individual central place systems, by isolating each factor and thinking through what the influence of change in it should be, Christaller provided both a basic, but flexible, framework for explaining both the evolving and contemporary territorial organization of any central place system and generalizations describing the likely territorial expression of numerous kinds of change.

Step 5. Analysis of "The dynamic aspects of a system of central places"

The fifth step in the theory deals with dynamic aspects of a system of central places (C8a-e in Table 2.1). It consists of an abstract framework demonstrating how a theoretical central place system generated by one of the principles introduced in step three changes when forces producing one of the other two theoretical landscapes become significant in the evolution of a settlement system. This discussion not only complements step three (B8 in Table 2.1), but both develops further the principle of the "Mixed Hierarchy" introduced there and embraces additional shaping factors.

At this point, however, Christaller became overly ambitious regarding the comprehensiveness of his theory. He accurately summarized the position developed up to that point (1966 : 112).

> Up to this point, we have formulated our theory on the bases of the simple, more or less isolated facts, population, number of types of central goods, etc. In the static theory we explained the mutual relationships; and in the dynamic theory we explained the effects of changes in the simple facts, on central places.

He (1966 : 112) then proposed "...to consider complex phenomena as found in concrete reality, and seek to discover all the factors and processes which serve to explain those phenomena." He fell short of that goal. What he did provide was an analytical framework for explaining why actual central place systems are structured differently from the models generated by his three principles (1966 : 113-122).

In this framework the marketing model was *assumed* to be the norm. Situations considered were :

(1) the impact of the transportation principle on a marketing landscape,

(2) the decline of a transportation system in a formerly predominantly marketing landscape,

(3) the impact of the administrative principle on a marketing landscape, and

(4) the reorganization of an administrative landscape (Christaller 1966 : 112-116).

Then, a more detailed consideration of circumstances that cause deviations from or prevent establishment of, central place systems corresponding to the assumed marketing scheme was presented. The approach was to confront four problems; namely, under what conditions will the (1) location, (2) number, (3) distance between, and (4) importance of central places differ from the assumed norm (Christaller 1966 : 116-122). Each problem was explained by showing how temporal competition between the forces driving the marketing, transportation, and administrative principles could reshape the territorial organization of central places. Probable outcomes (central place patterns) were offered for each of the four problems, and, as in earlier analyses, discussions were supported by verbal, numerical, and graphical examples of a hypothetical nature, and by occasional references to historical situations. He emphasized that in actual situations one of the principles will rarely triumph completely. Thus, studies of evolving central place systems employing his theoretical framework may not produce clear-cut results, that is, the central place systems revealed can represent every kind of transitional situation, or mixed hierarchy (Christaller 1966 : 116).

Additional key factors useful in analyzing the evolution of central place systems

The materials presented in the last part of the chapter on Dynamic Processes integrate the fourth and fifth steps in the theory by recognizing several additional factors that consistently influence the formation of central place systems (1966 : 122-130 ; C8f-h and C9 in Table 2.1). Factors considered first were the length of time a central place network had been in place and how the influence of an existing network influences the structure of subsequent settlement systems. The next factor recognized that central places evolving under different political or cultural systems can have different territorial characteristics. Another factor related to the uses of planning to produce more efficient central place systems. The last factor emphasized that forces associated with various business cycles can greatly influence the formation of central place systems. This section, along with earlier discussions of the influence of long distance trade (1966 : 72-76, 113-114, 191), demonstrates conclusively that Christaller did not ignore the role of exogenous forces in the formation of central place systems.

SOME OF CHRISTALLER'S VIEWS ON THE NATURE OF HIS THEORY

Considerable discussion has appeared in the geographical literature on the interpretation of central place theory. The intent in this section is to clarify some of the issues raised by presenting Christaller's views on some controversial dimensions of his theory.

Factors not included in the theory

Although Christaller was comfortable with his theoretical approach (1966 : 4-5, 27, 71, 84-85), he was well aware that there were important factors that influence the development and organization of central places in addition to those encompassed by either his flexible analytical framework for analyzing particular central places or by his principles. Moreover, he felt (1966 : 72, 199-200) that most aspects of central place patterns not accounted for by his approach could and should be explained (1966 : 5),

> The unexplained facts must then be clarified by historical and geographical methods, because they involve personal, historical, and naturally conditioned resistances – factors which cause deviations from the theory.

In the "Regional Part" of his basic work (Christaller 1966 : 122, 166, 170-188 ; 1933 ; 165-251 ; Barnum 1966 : 140-168) attempted to take at least some of these other factors into account.

Laws

Basic to the application and interpretation of his theory is what Christaller meant by law. He stated that the geography of settlements was part of the social sciences and that its study could be approached by the application of *special economic-geographical* laws. "These laws, to be sure, are of a different type from natural laws, but no less 'valid' on that account. They should, perhaps, be designated not as *laws*, but, more conveniently, as *tendencies*, because they are not so inexorable as natural laws" (Christaller 1966 : 3).

The necessity of formal mathematical expression

In the interest of maintaining the flexibility embodied in his theoretical framework and in his view of social science laws as tendencies, Christaller saw little need for a formal expression of his theory. After establishing that the range of central goods can vary over time and that central places emerge and decline in his theoretical landscape (1966 : 60-63), it appears that he had shown to his satisfaction how change could be introduced into his abstractions, that is (Christaller 1966 : 70) :

> It seems unnecessary to express in mathematical formulas the results discussed in the previous paragraph [dealing with central place dynamics]. The possibility of mathematical expression is self-evident and is easily realized. But in economics, in anthropogeography, and in all the disciplines combined, only a few factors can be given precise values ; and since most of these factors are unmeasurable intensities of desire, action, valuation, and comparison, which can be put into mathematical terms only quite roughly by estimation and comparison, the mathematical expression of a relationship *a priori* cannot be exact. The formula could be highly symbolic but then the reader would be inclined, as a rule, to take it as absolute and as allowing no exception, and finally the author himself might mistake the numerical symbol which ought to serve as an expression of the valid laws, as a genuine mathematical formula. (Information in brackets inserted by the author.)

The nature of the original test

In *Central Places in Southern Germany*, Christaller presented the results of his partial test of his theory. The static component received nearly all his attention, while the dynamic component was largely ignored. After developing an operational model for application of his theory, he presented some general findings in the section on "Preliminary Results" and still broader generalizations in the section on "Verification of the Theory". Detailed findings were presented in Baskin's translation only for the Munich central place system. A translation of the detailed findings for the Stuttgart system is provided by Barnum (1966 : 140-168). Details for the Strassburg, Frankfurt, and Nurnberg systems are available in the original.

In Christaller's mind, the theory and the test were quite separate (1966 : 4, 137, 152, 165-166 ; 1969 : 209). That is, he developed his theory largely independent of conditions in any particular area, and he tested only certain aspects of it in Southern Germany. Thus, findings presented in his basic work regarding the validity of the theory represent the products of a partial test conducted in a limited area. It is suggested that, fuller testing of Christaller's theoretical ideas could produce findings and conclusions that could both modify and enlarge those presented in *Central Places in Southern Germany.*

CONCLUSIONS AND IMPLICATIONS FOR RESEARCH

This essay called for a reassessment of the present understanding, as presented in the literature, of the domain and logical structure of classical central place theory. Based on the materials reviewed, it is concluded, first, that the original presentation of Christaller's theory offered a far more comprehensive and fully qualified theory of the territorial organization and development of central places than that described by the two-step representation offered by the English language geographical literature, and second, that recognition of this situation, and particularly of the theory's dynamic nature, offers substantial scope for research directed toward further development of the classical theory. This essay concludes with comments on a few areas of apparent confusion and opportunity in central place research.

The pertinence of empirical evidence to the domain of classical central place theory

A problem with virtually all applied central place studies is a failure to report whether individual studies fall under the domain of Christaller's original statement or under some broader version of the theory. Since the middle 1960's this problem has been magnified by the need for researchers to explain whether and how their contribution relates to the classical version or to the newly defined modern central place theory, or to both. Whereas classical central place theory includes only Christaller's contribution, modern central place theory represents an attempt to generalize and broaden the original theory, on the one hand, from a partial to a wholistic theory of the spatial structure of urban systems, and, on the other hand, to include the arrangement of retail and service functions at the intra-city scale (Berry and Garrison 1958c; Berry 1965; 1967b; Beavon 1977). This is a noble and valuable effort in its own right, but one that is much broader in scope than Christaller's endeavour.

A confusion of fundamental meanings : centrality vs. nodality

An example of the general situation just described is afforded by a widespread practice in research which fails to take into account a basic logical and operational fact of classical central place theory. This is the uncritical substitution of the concept of nodality for Christaller's key concept of centrality in the determination of central place importance. This has resulted in considerable confusion regarding the meaning of much of the evidence produced over the last three decades (Preston 1970, 1971, 1975). Such substitution is done formally and for good reasons in the case of modern central place theory where the stated domain is much broader than that of the classical version. The result is the replacement of centrality by more general but less clear characterizations like "the essence of the point of focus" (Berry 1967b : 3) and "the information content of central places" (Berry and Barnum and Tennant 1962a : 104 ; Berry and Barnum 1962b : 38). However, such substitution has taken place both consistently and informally in the empirical literature, and given that the concepts are logically incompatible, the implications of the evidence offered by nodality based studies for the status of research on Christaller's original theory are potentially far reaching and must at least be questioned. What it means, in essence, is the replacement of centrality defined unambiguously as surplus product by various measures reflecting the concept of aggregate functional importance. It must be noted, moreover, that in both the empirical literature generally and in studies tied explicitly to the modern theory, the critical distinction offered by classical theory between the contribution of local and extra local consumers to the importance of a settlement as a central place is lost.

The nature of this logical conflict is more than semantic. For example, in the empirical literature all places studied are granted central place status automatically. By contrast, under Christaller's scheme settlements can be deficit places (non-central places providing insufficient central goods and services to meet the needs of their residents), auxiliary places (neither clearly deficit nor central in terms of their provision of central goods and services), or central places. Only those settlements and markets exhibiting centrality qualify for central place status. This fact cannot be determined conclusively on the basis of indices of nodality. As a result, in the empirical literature the distribution of the central place function may well remain unrevealed. Neither the situation just described nor its consequences for the status of central place research have been reported consistently or evaluated fully.

Economic base theory, potential theory, and a dynamic systems perspective

It has been established that the specific aspect of urban activity upon which classical central place theory focusses is the region serving function of towns, or their centrality. This emphasis on surplus product places the theory under the broader approach to the study of space economies represented by economic base theory. In this context, that part of a town's total production of central goods and services accounted for by centrality can be considered basic or export, while that part accounted for by local consumption can be considered as service, or non-basic. Given the dynamic nature of classical central place theory, and its identification of both centrality and local consumption, a union with economic base theory enhances the theory's ability to explain overall town and urban system growth, stability, and decline. Dziewonski (1978 : 43) has also noted advantages of an integration of the economic base and central place theories. He stated (1978 : 46) with regard to attempts to blend various partial theories :

> The integration of the economic base and central place theories is at present the most advanced. Here the concept of economic base, originally dealing only with individual settlements, has been widened and connected with the analysis of the whole settlement network or system. At the same time through the use of the additional concept of specialized functions within the economic base central place theory has been extended beyond the limits of its original assumptions.

A similar argument might possibly be made for a union with the "Potential" concept as used in studies of spatial interaction. Self-potential could be regarded as a measure of local consumption or non-basic activity, while the potential estimate for the same place could be regarded as an overall measure of centrality or basic activity. Continued work on the fusion of these three theories should prove rewarding.

The approach represented by classical central place theory rests firmly in a systems format (Russwurm 1972). Christaller (1966 : 164) took a central place system to be a number of central places grouped around a system-forming central place according to given rules. He identified the elements of such a system as : the system-forming central places ; the central places grouped around them ; the distances between the central places ; the positions in which the central places lie with regard to the system-forming central places as well as other central places of the system ; and, the area occupied by such a system, or the region of the system-forming central place (Christaller 1966 : 164). In summary, he saw the territorial organization of central places in a systems perspective, one in which nested hierarchies of central places, auxiliary central places, and deficit places were linked together in complex dependency relations by flows of surplus product (or centrality), the magnitudes of which represent the response by central places to the biological and social needs of all dependent consumers.

Exogenous forces and changing central place systems

Vance (1970 : 2-10, 140-148 ; 1977 : 89-93) suggests that a basic deficiency in Christaller's theory is that it fails to deal with exogenous forces and change, especially long distance trade, or wholesaling (Vance, 1970 : 6). In fact, in addition to other key factors (Table 2.1) Christaller (1966 : 84) identified specifically the place of exogenous forces in his perspective at the start of his chapter on Dynamic Processes. "The individual factor either creates the change out of itself according to its own nature—then the change is endogenous—or the change is forced by other elements—then the change is exogenous." Moreover, change in central place systems caused by exogenous factors is given explicit recognition in discussions of (1) long distance trade (Christaller 1966 : 72-76, 113-114, 191) ; (2) government economic and planning policies (1966 : 123-126) ; (3) reorganization of political boundaries (1966 : 124) ; (4) cultural and political differences (1966 : 123) ; and (5) of the manifold influences of business cycles of different duration and originating at different scales (1966 : 126-130).

Not only did Christaller identify exogenous forces generally and consider those just noted, he attempted to accommodate long distance trade in his scheme in at least four specific ways : (1) by an explicit consideration of the impact of the introduction of long distance transportation into a central place system organized according to the marketing principle (1966 : 113-114) ; (2) by the incorporation into his theoretical hierarchy of two levels above that to which Munich, Stuttgart, Nurnberg, Frankfurt, and Strasbourg were assigned in his basic work (1966 : 157-159). These Reichsteilstädte and Reichshauptstdäte serve to integrate entire regional and national urban systems into mixed central place hierarchies focussing on one centre, and play critical roles in Christaller's theoretical interpretation of a post-World War II central place system for western Europe (Christaller 1950). Such within and between national central place system links cover hundreds of miles and facilitate high order flows of complex and varied aspects of commerce and governance in addition to the journey to shop ; (3) in a list of establishments exemplifying the exchange of central goods and services, he associates explicitly the following activities with higher order central places : wholesalers, brokers (non-agricultural), foreign trade agents and agencies from other German lands, stock exchanges, branches of national banks, state agencies and chambers of commerce of trade (Christaller 1966 : 140-141) ; and (4) Christaller's key concept of centrality embraces, along with that of other central place functions, the contribution of wholesale trade to central place importance.

Central place theory and industrial location

As noted earlier, central place theory is a partial theory of the space economy. By embracing retail trades and services, wholesaling, transportation and communications, public and cultural institutions, some financial activities, and certain types of market oriented industries, Christaller (1966 : 7, 20-21, 140-141) intended to supplement Weber's theory of industrial location. Nevertheless, an examination of the numerous attempts in the literature to apply central place theory could easily leave the impression that Christaller's theory treats only the tertiary sector and therein focusses on retail and service or consumer-oriented activities. This impression is inaccurate on both counts. While the pertinence of central place theory to activities in addition to urban trades and services should now be clear, it is not usually revealed that Christaller took pains to explain how the locational behaviour of some types of industry fall under his theory and that he attempted to discuss the pertinence of his theory to industrial location in general.

First, Christaller (1966 : 20) stated :

> Above all, those manufacturers which, according to Alfred Weber's terminology, are *Consumer-oriented* (excluding those which can be found in almost any village), belong in central places ; . . . Centre-oriented production occurs when the collection and further manufacture of dispersedly produced unfinished goods or raw materials occur at the centre. Typical illustrations of centre-oriented production are the many handicraft industries, frequently the food industries, breweries, dairies, sugar refineries, and container industries. Breweries are consumer-oriented and dairies, sugar refineries, and container industries are raw material-oriented.

Classes of industry reliant on ubiquitous materials fall directly under the marketing principle, while those reliant on non-ubiquitous materials fall under and enrich Christaller's mixed hierarchy perspective. Parr (1973 : 186) has reminded us of how Christaller's theory accommodates certain market-oriented industries and both suggests and considers how the theory might be modified to embrace more fully industries that "tend to locate themselves in order to gain ready access to material inputs which are only available in a dispersed pattern." Parr's examples include industries that process agricultural and forestry products and emphasize the importance of Christaller's mixed hierarchy perspective.

Second, Christaller (1966 : 71) recognized that the development of settlements as central places and as locations for industry could be sequential and complementary events. His discussion appears to emphasize situations where industrial entrepreneurs perceive commercially successful centres in a central place system as places where financial success in manufacturing is likely, that is, the prosperity of individual centres in a central place system can influence where factories locate. In a third and related point, Christaller considered the influence of a changing industrial labour force on the development of central places. He pointed out that the industrial labour force represents an important consumer group, and can contribute to the development of central places through increasing local consumption, complementary area consumption, or both (Christaller 1966 : 96-97).

Fourth, while discussing how the natural endowment of regions influence the consumption of central goods and services, and thus the importance of settlements as central places, Christaller (1966 : 46) considered briefly the relation between central place importance and the location of mineral production :

> As for minerals, their extraction usually occurs at definite points, therefore, the concentration of population occurs at definite points. These places of concentrated population have, purely because of this agglomeration, a higher demand for central goods and services ; and they frequently develop into central places.

This comment supplements Christaller's views on central places and the location of agricultural and forest product processing activities, and supports his conviction that settlements must develop into central places and that all do not necessarily acquire that status. His interpretation of the relationship between central place importance and the location of resource production towns, or of manufacturing towns for that matter, is straightforward. If a resource or industrial centre becomes a supply point for less developed production points, or for any type of complementary region, the place may become a central place. If a town, regardless of the nature of its economic base, fails to develop surplus central goods and services, then it will remain a deficit place, or at best become an auxiliary central place.

Despite these efforts by Christaller to forge links between his theory and industrial location, central place theory was not intended to account for all forms of industrial location. Parr (1973 : 193-194) has noted that : "many important locational considerations remain outside the scope of central place theory." And, that as a basis for explaining the influence on industrial location of such factors

> as localized material orientation, convenient access to manufactured inputs, the existence of skilled labour, or the advantages of industrial agglomeration, central place theory is of practically no utility.

Christaller's (1966 : 69) awareness of this situation is reflected in his observation that for his theoretical interpretation to grasp reality, factors that cause both change and variations in central place systems must be studied, and that one of these factors is industrial location. Understanding the degree of correspondence between recent locational trends in central place and industrial location offers potentially rewarding research opportunities.

Mixed hierarchies

An often cited fundamental difference between Christaller's and alternative views of the vertical organization of settlement systems is that the alternative views (e.g., Losch 1954) are more flexible. This is often the case, however, it must be emphasized that Christaller both recognized and attempted to operationalize the mixed hierarchy concept. It can even be argued that on at least conceptual grounds he attempted to integrate the concept into his theory.

Near the conclusion of step three of his theory, Christaller (1966 : 76, 80) emphasized that there is an ongoing competition among the forces driving the marketing, transportation, and administrative principles for predominance in a region. In step five, where dynamic central place systems in general are dealt with, and in the context of a consideration of circumstances causing deviations from, or preventing establishment of, central place systems corresponding to an assumed marketing scheme, Christaller (1966 : 113-121) explained how temporal competition between the three sets of forces can reshape the territorial organization of central place systems. Moreover, he emphasized that in real-world situations one of the principles will rarely win-out completely. Therefore, studies of evolving central place systems employing his theoretical framework may not produce clear-cut results, that is, the central place systems revealed can represent every kind of transitional situation, or mixed hierarchy

(Christaller, 1966 : 116). Also supporting his mixed hierarchical perspective was his description of the locational behaviour of industries dependent on non-ubiquitous materials that locate according to central place principles.

It is noteworthy, that in Christaller's theoretical discussions of landscapes generated by competition among his three principles, the landscapes were not ordered in a rigid chronological sequence. In later works, however, and in situations where he felt it appropriate to do so, he sometimes put the forces generating his three central place landscapes into a historical settlement sequence in which the pattern generated by the marketing principle represented the first phase (Christaller 1937 : 155-164, 197 ; 1938a : 122-125 ; 1938b ; 1942 : 53-55 ; 1950b : 11-12).

The need for a mixed hierarchy perspective in Christaller's central place theory was established in his basic work, and it was cited frequently in later publications (e.g., Christaller 1934 : 67 ; 1950a : 362 ; 1950b : 11-12, 160 ; 1962 : 9-10). Theoretical settlement progressions for mixed hierarchies were presented in at least two cases (Christaller, 1950a ; 1950b). However, the concept was developed most fully under the heading "Results : A Combined and Improved System of Central Places" (Christaller 1941 : 6-8). There, he attempted to create an ideal central place pattern exhibiting the advantages of the marketing, transportation, and administrative models without their disadvantages. It would appear, therefore, that his interpretation of central place hierarchies was not as rigid and inflexible as is widely reported. Development and application of a full-fledged mixed hierarchy principle could represent a significant improvement in the explanatory power of classical central place theory.

FOOTNOTES

1. In this study the term "Classical Central Place Theory" refers to Christaller's (1933 ; 1966) original contribution and not to either works which are inconsistent with the logical structure of his theory or to recent studies known as *Modern Central Place Theory.* Marked differences between classical theory and most of the central place research conducted over the last thirty years are found in both the operational definitions and the research procedure employed, while the scope of modern central place theory is much broader than that

of classical theory. Some of these differences are considered in this paper.

2. Existing descriptions present central place theory in two steps: one consisting of several operational definitions (Step 1 in Figure 1.1 in this paper) and the other consisting of a presentation of the marketing, transportation, and administrative models of central place organization (Step 3 in Figure 1.1).
3. Christaller (1966 : 22-23) pointed out that the operational definitions presented in the section on "Fundamental Meanings", were incomplete. Therefore, the definitions considered here represent an attempted synthesis of those presented under Fundamental Meanings, Static Relations, and in the "Connecting Part : Applications of the Theory to the Actual Geography of Settlements" (Christaller, 1966 : 14-27, 49-72, 139-151).

REFERENCES

Barnum, H.G., *Market Centres and Hinterlands in Baden-württemberg*, Department of Geography Research Paper No. 103, Chicago : University of Chicago, 1966.

Beaujeu-Garnier, J. and Chabot, G., *Urban Geography*, London : Longmans, 1967.

Beavon, K.S.O., *Central Place Theory : A Reinterpretation*, New York : Longman, 1977.

Berry, B.J.L. and Garrison, W.L., "Functional bases of the central place hierarchy", *Economic Geography*, 34, 1958a, 145-154.

Berry, B.J.L. and Garrison, W.L., "A note on central place theory and the range of a good", *Economic Geography*, 34, 1958b, 304-311.

Berry, B.J.L. and Garrison, W.L., "Recent developments of central place theory", *Papers and Proceedings of the Regional Science Association*, 4, 1958c, 107-120.

Berry, B.J.L., "Research frontiers in urban geography", in Hauser, P.M. and Schnore, L.F. (eds.), *The Study of Urbanization*, New York : John Wiley and Sons, 1965, 403-430.

Berry, B.J.L., and Barnum, H.G., "Aggregate relations and elemental components of central place systems", *Journal of Regional Science*, 4, 1962a, 35-68.

Berry, B.J.L., and Tennant, R.J., "Retail location and consumer behaviour", *Regional Science Association, Papers and Proceedings*, 9, 1962b, 65-106.

Berry, B.J.L., *Review of Central Place in Southern Germany*, by W. Christaller, translated by C.W. Baskin (Englewood Cliffs, N.J., Prentice Hall, 1966), *Economic Geography*, 43, 1967a, 275-276.

Berry, B.J.L., *Geography of Market Centres and Retail Distribution*, Englewood Cliffs, N.J. : Prentice Hall, 1967b.

Berry, B.J.L. and Harris, C.D., "Central Place", in D.L. Sills (ed.), *International Encyclopedia of the Social Sciences*, 1968.

Berry, B.J.L., and Pred, A., *Central Place Studies*, A Bibliography of Theory and Applications, Philadelphia : Regional Science Research Institute, 1961.

Beary, B.J.L., and Horton, F.E., *Geographic Perspectives on Urban Systems*, Englewood Cliffs, N.J., Prentice Hall, 1970.

Borchert, J., "American metropolitan evolution", *Geographical Review*, 57, 1967, 301-332.

Brush, J.E., "The hierarchy of central places in south-western Wisconsin", *Geographical Review*, 43, 1953, 380-402.

Carter, H., *The Study of Urban Geography*, London : Edward Arnold, 1975.

Christian, C.M. and Harper, R.A. (eds.), *Modern Urban Systems*, Columbus : Charles, E. Merrill, 1982.

Christaller, W., *Die zentralen Orte in Süddeutschland* : Eine ökonomisch geographische Untersuchung über die Gesetzmässigkeit der Verbreitung und Entwicklung der Siedlungen mit städischen Funktionen, Jena : Gustav Fischer Verlag, 1933.

Christaller, W., "Allgemeine geographische Vorausset-zungen der deutschen Verwaltungsgliederung", *Jahrbuch für kommunalwissenshaft*, 1 : 1934, 48-72.

Christaller, W., *Die ländliche Siedlungsweise im Deutschen Reich und ihre Beziehungen zur Gemeindeorganisation*, Berlin : Einzelschriften des Kommunalwissen-schaftlichen, Instituts an der Universität Berlin, VII, 1937.

Christaller, W., "Siedlungsgeographic und Kommunalwissenschaft", *Petermanns Geographische Mitteilungen*, 84, 1938a, 49-53.

Christaller, W., "Rapports fonctionnels entre Les agglomerations urbaines et les Campagnes", *Comptes Rendus de Congres Internationale Geographie Amsterdam*, 2, 1938b, 123-37.

Christaller, W., "Die Zentralen Orte In Den Cstgebieten Und Ihre Kultur-Und Marktbereiche", in Gemeinschaftswerk im Auftrage der Reichsarbeitsgemeinschaft für Raumforschung, *Struktur Und Gestaltung Der Zentralen Orte Des Deutschen Ostens*, Leipzig : K.F. Koehler Verlag, 1941, 2-22.

Christaller, W., "Wesen und Arten sozialraumlicher Landschaftseiheiten und ihre Darstellung in der Karte 1 : 200,000", *Berichte zur Deutschen Landeskunde*, 7, 1950a, 357-67.

Christaller, W., *Das Grundgerüst der räumlichen Ordnung in Europa* : *Die Systeme der europäischen zentralen Orte*, Frankfurter Geographische Hefte, Jg., 24, 1950b.

Christaller, W., "Die Hierarchie der Stadte", in K. Norborg (ed.), *Proceedings of the IGU Symposium in Urban Geography, Lund 1960*, Lund : C.W.K. Gleerup Pubs., 1962, 3-11.

Christaller, W., *Central Places in Southern Germany*, translated by Carlisle W. Baskin, Englewood Cliffs, N.J., Prentice Hall, Inc., 1966.

Christaller, W., "Wie Ich zu Der Theorie der zentralen Orte Gekommen Bin", *Geographische Zeitschrift*, 56 : 88-101. Translated as "How I discovered the theory of central places : a report about the origin of central places", in P.W. English and R.C. Mayfield (eds.) (1972), *Man, Space and Environment*, New York : Oxford University Press, 1968, 600-610.

Christaller, W., A comment following H. Bobeck, "Die Theorie Der Zentralen Crte im Industrielzeitalter," in Deutscher Geographentag, Bad Godesberg, 1967, *Tagunsberichte und Wissenschaftliche Abhandlungen*, 36, 1969, 198-213.

Dickinson, R.E., "The economic regions of Germany," *Geographical Review*, 28, 1938, 609-626.

Dickinson, R.E., *City Region and Regionalism*, A Geographical Contribution to Human Ecology, London : Routledge and Kegan Paul, 1947.

Dickinson, R.E., *City and Region : A Geographical Interpretation*, London : Routledge and Kegan Paul, 1964.

Dziewonski, K., "Analysis of settlement systems : the state of the art", *Papers of the Regional Science Association*, 40, 1978, 39-49.

Harris, C.D., "Patterns of cities", in J.D. Eyre, (ed.), *A Man for All Regions : The Contributions of Edward L. Ullman to Geography* (Chapel Hill : University of North Carolina at Chapel Hill, Department of Geography, Studies in Geography, No. 11, 1968, 66-79.

Hartshorn, T.A., *Interpreting the City : An Urban Geography*, New York : John Wiley and Sons, 1980.

King, L.J. and Golledge, R.G., *Cities, Space and Behaviour : The Elements of Regional Geography*, Englewood Cliffs, N.J., Prentice Hall.

Losch, A., *The Economics of Location*, New Haven : Yale University Press, 1954.

Murphy, R.E., *The American City : An Urban Geography*, New York: McGraw Hill, 1966.

Northam, R.M., *Urban Geography*, New York ; John Wiley and Sons, 1979.

Palm, R., *The Geography of American Cities*, New York : Oxford, 1981.

Parr, J.B., "Growth poles, regional development, and central place theory", *Papers and the Regional Science Association*, 31, 1973, 173-212.

Preston, R.E , "Two centrality models", *Year Book of the Association of Pacific Coast Geographers*, 22, 1970, 59-78.

Preston, R.E., "The structure of central place systems", *Economic Geography*, 47, 1971, 136-155.

Preston, R.E., "A comparison of five measures of central place importance and settlement size", *Tijdschrift Voor Economische en Sociale Geografie*, 66, 1975, 178-187.

Preston, R.E., "The recent evolution of Ontario central place systems in the light of Christaller's concept of centrality", *Canadian Geographer*, 23, 1979, 201-221.

Preston, R.E., "The dynamic component of Christaller's central place theory and the theme of change in his research", *Canadian Geographer*, 1983 (forthcoming Spring Issue).

Russwurm, L.H., "Systems stability and urban ecosystems", in R.E. Preston (ed.), *Applied Geography and the Human Environment*, Waterloo : University of Waterloo, Department of Geography Publication Series, No. 2, 1972, 126-139.

Rydell, C.P., Review of *Central Place in Southern Germany*, by W. Christaller, translated by C.W. Baskin (Englewood Cliffs, N.J., Prentice Hall, 1966), *Journal of the American Institute of Planners*, 33, 1967, 277.

Ullman, E.L., "A theory of location for cities", *American Journal of Sociology*, 46, 1941, 853-64.

Vance, J.E., *The Merchant's World : The Geography of Wholesaling*, Englewood Cliffs, N.J., Prentice Hall, 1970.

Vance, J.E., *This Scene of Man; The Role and Structure of the City in the Geography of Western Civilization*, New York : Harper and Row.

Wehrwein, G.S., "The rural-urban fringe", *Economic Geography*, 18, 1942, 217-28.

Yeats, M. and Garner, B., *The North American City*, New York : Harper and Row, 1980.

THREE

R. K. WILKINSON

THEORIES OF URBAN AREA SIZE

The question of what determines the size of an urban population has practical as well as theoretical interest. Policy makers at all levels adopt attitudes to the question of whether towns and cities are "too small" or "too big" and presume, in the formulation of measures to induce the migration of population and firms, that there are determinants of size which can be controlled. On the theoretical side, the existence of a pattern to the growth of individual areas and the apparent stability of a hierarchy of city sizes demand explanation.

There are two broad approaches to these questions. The first concentrates on the individual city and seeks to explain why the economic and technical factors which brought it into existence combine to determine its size and perhaps to indicate a best size. This type of analysis follows the concepts and approach of the neoclassical theory of the firm. The second approach is "macro" in concept and seeks to explain the hierarchy of urban sizes on the assumption that there is a "system" of urban areas or cities. This approach stems from Chrystaller's and Lösch's theories of the origin and growth of cities. An alternative method of analysis seeks to fit known statistical distributions to observed data on city size and to suggest reasons why these distributions are applicable. Such attempts to explain the system of city sizes have in common the need to explain the "rank-size rule". According to this rule the position of the city in the hierarcy (i.e., its rank) multiplied by its size is a constant. The population of a city of rank n, therefore, is equal to the population of the largest city times $\frac{1}{n}$. The explanation of the "rank-size rule" is the central theme of the work on urban systems. A second major question concerns the "optimum size" of an urban area. Views on what is meant by optimum size and whether the existence of an optimum is worth serious consideration are strongly divided. We shall deal with this question first.

THE QUESTION OF OPTIMAL SIZE

The definition of optimum

Theories of the origin and persistence or urban areas through time, suggest that the urban area located at some point where net advantages in terms of costs (or productivity) existed and the subsequent accumulation of population made it possible to take advantage of scale economies which existed at the current level of technological development. We argued further that there would be a tendency for population to accumulate while ever expected utilities outweighed the costs of movement. The existence and development of urban areas is attributed to the existence of scale economies and to agglomeration economies which, in turn, lead to the existence of public goods and positive externalities. However, after a point it is likely that scale economies will be exhausted and that increasing congestion will lead to the development of negative externalities and negative public goods and generally to high social costs and diseconomies of agglomeration. At any point in time, therefore, an individual urban area can be portrayed in terms of costs and benefit curves whose curvature represents the tendency, all other things being equal, for unit costs to fall and then to rise and for unit benefits to rise and then to fall. This situation is portrayed in Fig. 3.1(a) which can be seen to be no more than an adaptation of the cost and revenue curves used to describe the firm. In a perfectly competitive market the optimum output of a firm is defined by the minimum average cost of its output (X in Fig. 3.1(a)). At this point also the firm is in equilibrium because marginal cost equals marginal revenue and if all firms in the economy aim to achieve this position resources will ultimately be allocated in an optimal manner.

The conventional portrayal of optimum size for an individual

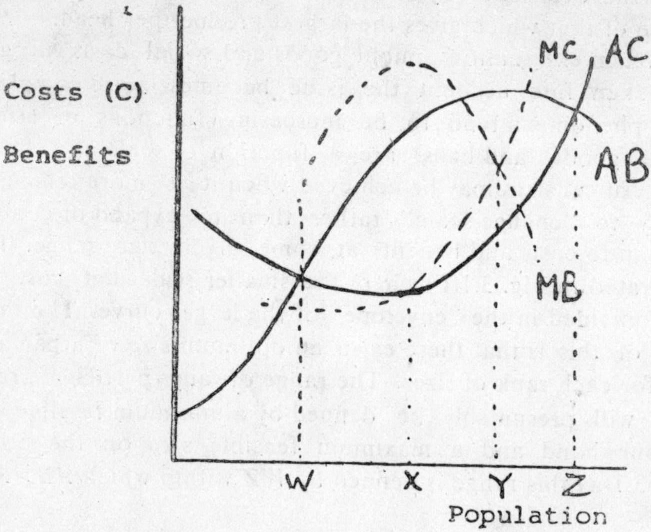

MC/*MB*=Marginal Costs/Benefits ;
AC/*AB*=Average Costs/Benefits.

FIG. 3.1 (*a*) : *Optimal city size—Costs and benefits*

city is equivalent to a firm in an imperfect economy where revenues (in this case benefits) begin to fall off after a point. Thus, there is a divergence between the minimum average cost point *X* and the maximum net benefit point (*MB*=*MC*), *Y*. In terms of city size this difference is usually defined as the difference between the optimum from the point of view of the residents of the city, i.e., Max (*AB*−*AC*), and the optimum from the viewpoint of the whole economy (*MB*=*MC*, *TB*>*TC*). This suggests a conflict of views which may be more apparent than real. The point where *MB*=*MC* will result in a larger city than that where average *net* benefits are maximised. A weakness of this argument is that the nature of costs and benefits are not usually clearly specified. The situation of purely private costs and benefits is straight forward. The citizen may be presumed to choose between the average product per head when size is that which maximises net benefits and that which optimises resource allocation in the economy. If citizens can be presumed to have the information to make this decision, they may also be presumed to make a rational choice of that which gives the largest product per head.

When externalities, public goods and social costs in general are taken into account the issue becomes more complex. All these phenomena tend to be increasing functions of size, and public goods (and bads) are a function of scale as well as size. Thus critical sizes may be achieved when it is more efficient for a city to "change scale" rather than to expand or contract in relation to costs and benefits at some given size range. This is illustrated in Fig. 3.1(b) where the smaller scale net cost curves are contained in the "envelope" of the larger curve. The implication of this is that there exists an optimum size of urban area or city for each rank of sizes. The range of any particular rank of sizes will presumably be defined by a minimum feasible size on the one hand and a maximum feasible size on the other. In Fig. 3.1(a) this range is defined by *WZ* within which $AB > AC$.

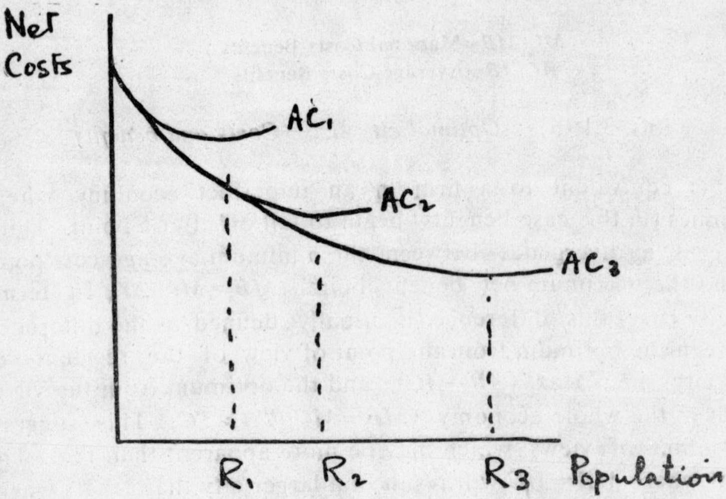

R_1=lowest rank
R_3=highest rank

FIG. 3.1 (*b*) : *Optimal size by rankings*

Evidence of optimality

If the urban area can fairly be treated as an economy then, at any

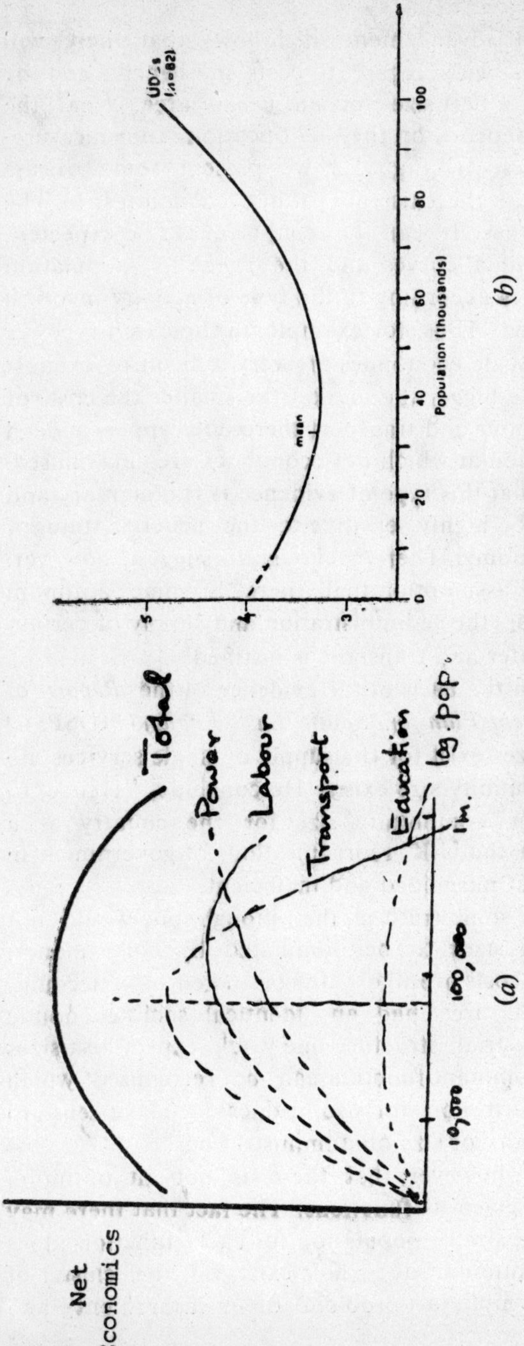

FIG. 3.2 (*a*) & (*b*) : *Net economies and city size*

(a) management of public housing in urban district councils, and
(b) central plant and equipment from bus systems in U.K.
(*Source* : Thring 1975).

given stage of technical advancement, it follows that there will be optimum positions with regard to costs and benefits and, by implication, therefore, a best size for an urban area. What the best size is obviously depends on the identification and measurement of net economies. In Fig. 3.2 we present some of the fragmentary evidence on the existence of net economies by the population size of areas. It can be seen, as might be expected, that the shape of individual curves and the range of population which they cover varies according to the type of activity involved and the service provided. Thus, for example, in the case of power it would appear that scale economies are very difficult to exhaust and, in other words, the bigger the market the smaller the cost of supply, whereas for labour and transport there does appear indeed to be a size of population at which net economies are maximised. It has to be stressed that this type of evidence is fragmentary and that, of course, it will be highly sensitive to the general state of technology in an economy. There is enough to suggest, however, that the common sense assumption that there is some optimum size of jurisdiction for the administration and supply of certain services like power, water and transport is justified.

Bennett[4] argues on the basis of the evidence of the *Report of the Strategic Development Plan for South East England* (DSPSE) that while optimum sizes exist for the supply of single services no single optimum community size exists. He concludes "Hence, to search for an optimum, community size for the country as a whole, as intended in the U.K. reorganisations of government in 1974, may be somewhat misguided and inefficient."

There is obviously some truth in this though one would not expect administration sizes to be dominated by costs alone; revenues and thus net costs are likely to be taken into account. However, unless each area had an identical socio-economic composition and industrial structure one would expect best sizes to vary. Unless one dominant function can be recognised which can act as a single criterion for size, it does not make sense to impose a rigid uniformity of size on administrations.

It does not follow, however, that there is not an optimum size for any one area given its functions. The fact that there may be a different optimum size of population for each function does not mean that an optimum does not exist for the cluster of functions. This is simply a problem of measurement and identification which might involve, for example, minimisation of the weighted average total net costs of providing the given cluster of services for the population. [See Figs. 3.2(b) and 3.2(d)]. In the diagrams the total net economy curve represents a weighted sum of the individual curves. For individual urban areas clearly the net economy curve will differ in terms of its shape and position according to the composition of the individual function which comprise it.

An evaluation of the concept and evidence

Thus net economies are likely to occur at different levels of population according to the nature of the urban area. This suggests that individual urban areas may have a best size but that there is not one best size for all urban areas. It is necessary to make this point because the character of some criticism and the interpretation on the existence of an optimum size for some authors has taken the form of assuming that there is one best size for all urban areas. It follows from what we have just said that the best size of any individual urban area will depend upon its character. This then pre-supposes individual urban areas have differing

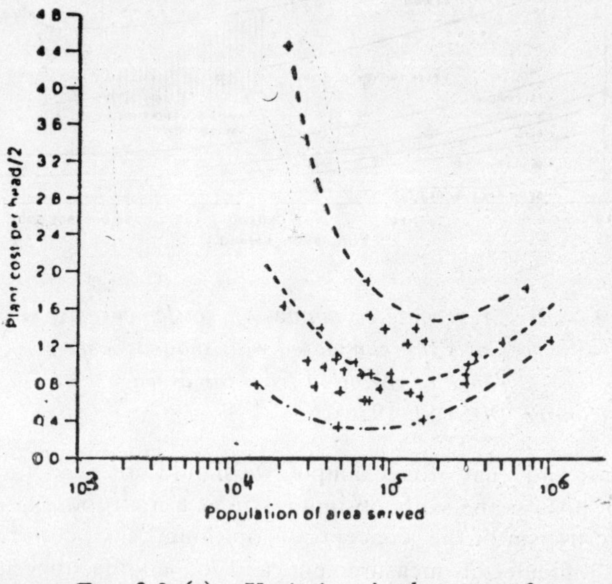

FIG. 3.2 (*c*) : *Variations in the costs of*

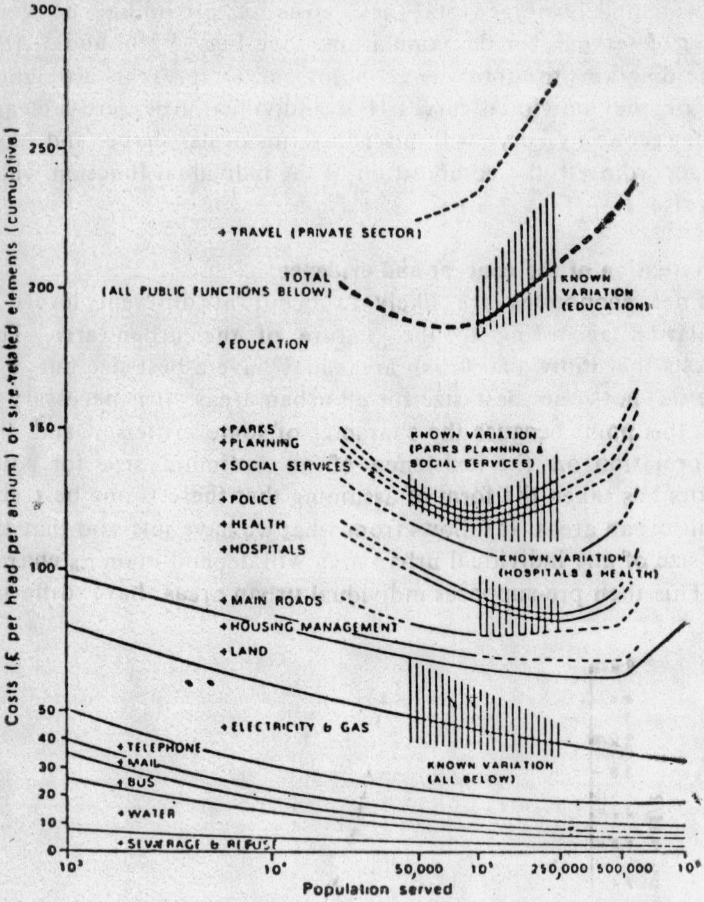

FIG. 3.2 (*d*) : *Aggregate economies of settlement size in the UK. Costs are cumulated with shaded area showing the range of variation from the average.*
(*Source* : *DSPSE* 1976).

functions and that, for example, we should not expect a market town to possess the same optimum size as a metropolitan area. A further criticism of the concept of optimum size concerns the possible difficulty of measurement and of adding together the optima of different services supplied within the urban area. In addition it is also argued that different economic agents (for example, firms and households) will have different perceptions of what constitutes an optimum. Without wishing to belittle either of these points they would appear to be no more serious than can be applied to the measurement of concepts such as the standard of living or the cost of living. Different people will have different conceptions of what constitutes a standard of living while its different components can only be roughly added together in terms of monetary values. Nonetheless, the idea of a standard of living is well established and does have meaning to those who live in an economy. The concept of optimum city size also, while being difficult to measure precisely, has some meaning both to policy makers and to ordinary citizens. Urban areas which would benefit from a reduction or an increase in size are relatively easy to recognise. New towns advertise the advantages of their infrastructure in order to attract industry and population. More ancient cities with social and economic problems find it difficult to hold on to their population and, in some cases, planners decant it to other areas. This suggests that at any given level of technology there is a perceived range of population size for any urban area which is regarded as in some sense desirable and, therefore, optimal.

The best size of an urban area is likely to change over time as the area moves through its life cycle and as the nation proceeds along a path of economic growth and development. The existence of such changes is a further reason why and how the function of an individual urban area may change over time. This, in turn, suggests the existence of an interdependent system of urban areas related to the stage of industrialisation and technical development of the economy in which each individual urban area has a particular place.

The normative model of resource allocation which forms the basis of welfare economies provides both a criterion for measuring efficiency and a set of prescriptions on how to achieve it. The fact that the criterion is impossible to recognise in practice does not prevent it from being used as an ideal worth achievement. This also applies in the case of spatial distributions. The fact that the optimum size of an urban area or city cannot be defined precisely in practice does not necessarily reduce the usefulness of the concept. The lessons of welfare economies are that if individual agents. seek to maximise in a way which can be described by the equation of marginal costs and benefits of their various activities then assuming no frictions an optimum resource allocation will be achieved. In the field of urban questions this points to the removal of obstacles to mobility for both capital and labour, the control of monopolies especially on land-use and the encouragement of spatial price competition.

The interdependence of city size provides a justification for examining the whole "system" of cities or urban areas. As we shall see there is strong evidence that there exists an urban hierarchy which implies that there must be a maximum and minimum to the size of urban areas in any rank of the hierarchy. Over time, areas which are ascending or descending in rank order will be found at the top or bottom of the range defining any particular rank and there will be an average and, in this sense, a best (or at least an equilibrium) size towards which areas will tend in this rank.

Tolley's model

One way of incorporating the concept of interdependence into a model of urban area size is demonstrated in Tolley's theory discussed by Richardson.[9] This is summarised in Fig. 3.3. The purpose of this model is to demonstrate the effects of negative externalities on urban area size and, in particular, to argue that the elimination of such externalities would lead to urban areas becoming bigger and this would be beneficial in terms of economic costs. These points are brought out in the diagram by having a continuous scale along which employment is measured. Measuring from the origin on the left shows the amount of employment in an individual urban area measuring from the origin on the right shows employment in the rest of the economy, so the whole scale shows total employment allocated between the urban area and the rest of the economy. The model is centred on the concept of the labour market and presumes that employment is flexible with respect to wages. Thus we can show the demand curves for labour in the urban area and in the rest of the economy. The curves on the extreme right show the marginal products without externalities, those on the left show the effects of adding externalities to private products and then to social products. Assuming that all externalities are negative and that social products lie below private marginal products, then accounting for social costs and externalities results in a contraction of the population in the particular urban area. It follows that any policies aimed at improving life in the urban area by removing negative externalities wlll have the effect of encouraging population to move back in by making the wage worth that much more and, therefore, of increasing the size of the area relative to the rest of the economy. We are less concerned here with the policy implications of the model and whether in fact the control of environmental pollution and congestion would achieve these effects or, indeed, whether the assumption that workers are sensitive to such wage differentials, than with the formulation of a model in which attention focuses on *relative* urban area size. As we indicated in the introduction, another approach to relative size is to attempt to explain the whole system of urban areas in the national economy.

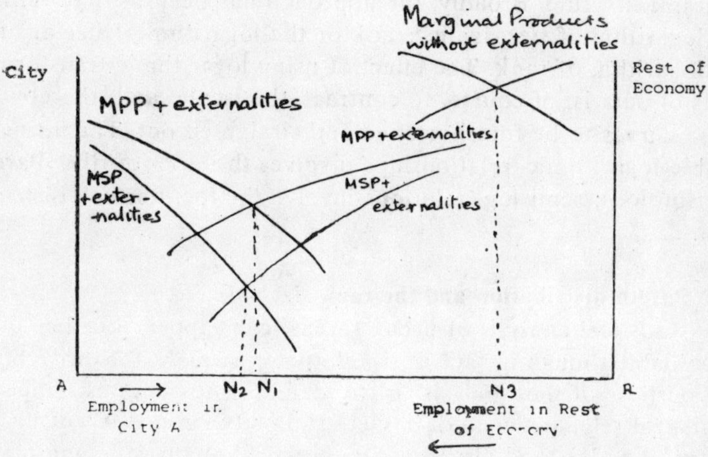

FIG. 3.3. *Tolley's theory of city size*

Comment on Fig. 3.3

The horizontal scale measures employment in the economy. Employment in city A is measured from A all other employment is measured from R. Thus

$$N \equiv NA + NR$$

If negative externalities increase with size the vertical distance between the Marginal Physical Product curves (MPP) and Marginal Social Product curves (MSP) increases with size. Since the rest of the economy includes *all* other cities i.e., those with few or no negative externalities, they will be flatter.

A policy of taxation and subsidies to bring wage levels in line with M.S.P.s would reduce the size of large cities (*A* falls from N_2 to N_1) as well as providing a more efficient allocation of resources. A legislative policy to remove negative externalities would have the same effect. (See Richardson, *The Economies of City Size*, pp. 15-17.)

THE URBAN SYSTEM

The satistical approach

As already indicated, the statistical approach to explaining the system of urban areas has been preoccupied with the question of the rank size rule. Broadly, the approach has been to plot either the logarithm of size against rank or the logarithm of size against the logarithm of rank. The effect of using logarithmic transformations of data is, of course, to contract the scale and thereby to cause curves to be foreshortened and straighten out. The fitting of double logarithmic relationships involves the use of the Pareto distribution ; semi log. relations involve the log. normal distribution.

The Pareto distribution and the rank size rule

The statistical analysis of urban areas can appear to be quite formidable though in fact, it is relatively straight-forward. Since the purpose of the analysis is to demonstrate the existence of statistical regularities in data measuring city sizes, it is worthwhile to try to understand just what the satistical analysis demonstrates.

A distribution function $f(x)$ shows the frequency with which a variable x takes the value x in a sample of n observations. If x is a continuous variable $f(x)\,dx$ shows the frequency of x within a given interval centred on x. Related to every distribution function is a cumulative distribution function $F(x)$ which shows the number of observations taking values on or below a given value and $G(x)$ the corresponding cumulative function showing the number of observations taking values on or beyond a given value of x. In other words, if x is urban area population, the distribution of the populations of urban areas can be shown as a relative frequency curve. $G(x)$ and $F(x)$ describe the cumulative frequency curves ("more than" and "less than" respectively) associated with this distribution.

If N is the total number of observations, $G(x)$ equals $N-f(x)$. Distributions in economics are characteristically positively skewed. Pareto used the cumulative distribution which bears his name to describe the upper tail of the personal income distribution. The Pareto distribution is usually written as follows :

$$G(x) = Ax^{-a} \qquad \ldots(1)$$

where $G(x)$ is the number of incomes greater than a particular value of X, and A and a are constants determined from that data. The former depends on the number of income recipients but a has been found to be about 1-5 in many studies.

Zipf's[10] rank size rule is a special case of the Pareto distribution where

$$G(x) = Ax^{-1} \qquad \ldots(2)$$

where $G(x)$ is the number of urban areas of at least x inhabitants. The rank size rule is obtained from this equation by multiplying both sides by x. Thus if we re-arrange equation (2) we have

$$G(x) = A. \qquad \ldots(3)$$

This says that the product of an urban area's rank and size is a constant. If $F(x)$ is equal to 1 then $x = A$, i.e., A is the size of the largest urban area.

We can summarise this final statement very simply. We know that the distribution of things like human height and weight and intelligence quotients can be described by characteristic formulae. Given such a formula we can predict the number of observations lying between given values of x, the variable under consideration. Thus, we could take the observations of urban area sizes for the U.K. and draw a frequency distribution which we could plot as a histogram. This histogram would approximate the frequency density curve of urban area sizes. From this we could obtain the cumulative frequency histograms. These lines show respectively the number of urban areas having populations on or below a given size or the number of urban areas having populations above a certain size (Fx and Gx respectively in Fig. 3.4). If we thought that in theory such distributions could be predicted from the Pareto formula then we could make such predictions and compare

If N is the total number of observations, $G(x)$ equals $N-f(x)$.

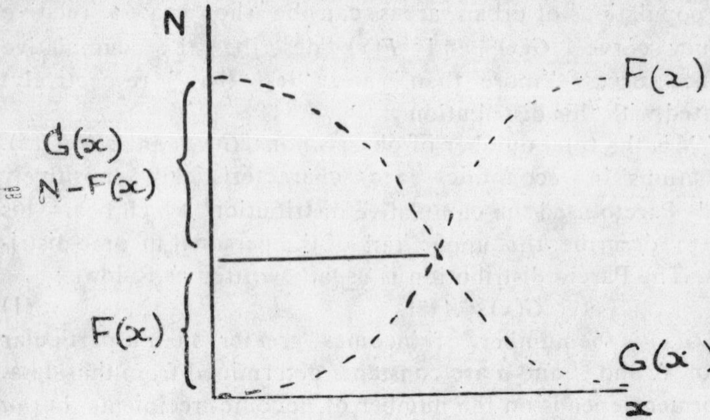

FIG. 3.4 : *Illustration of cumulative frequency curves. F(x) shows cities with population sizes less than a given number ; G(x) shows cities with population bigger than a given number*

them with the actual data. The best way of testing the rule is to fit the Pareto distribution in logarithms by means of least squares techniques. Alternatively, one can plot the data for urban size and distributions on logarithmic paper and if the data fit the distribution then the points plotted should lie along a straight line. This latter technique was used in the Department of Environment report with the results shown in the diagram. In the graph cities were ranked according to population and the logarithm of a city's population was plotted against the logarithm of its rank. The change in population rank order of S.M.L.A.s between 1951 and 1971 is shown in the attached figure. Figures 3.5. and 3.6 show a considerable degree of change in the rank ordering of individual cities especially at the lower end of the urban hierarchy where new towns began to make an impact. The diagram, on the other hand, shows relative stability in rank order among the top twenty or so S.M.L.A.s but the remaining 100 rarely sustained their rank position over time. In nearly all cases, cities that were climbing up or dropping down the hierarchy in the 1950's continued to follow this trend in the 1960's. This continuity of change in both decades is very striking. There were, of course, differences in the

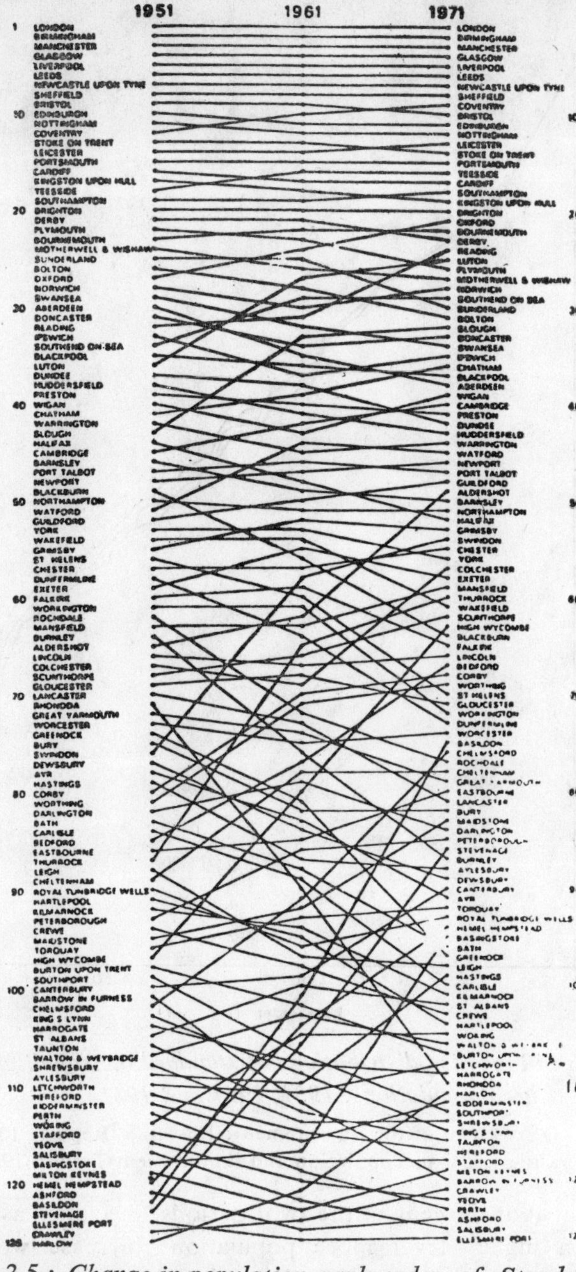

FIG. 3.5 : *Change in population rank-order of Standard Metropolitan Labour Areas, 1951, 1961 and 1971*

Source : Department of the Environment, Research Report 10, British Cities : Urban Population and Employment Trends, 1951-71.

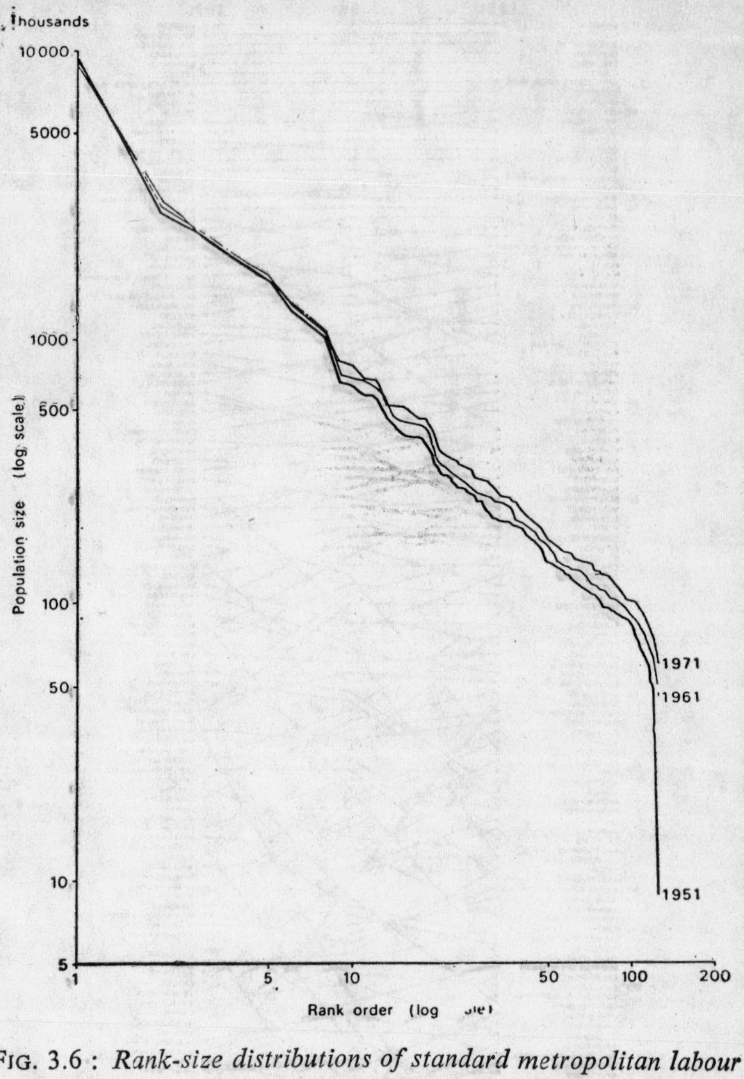

FIG. 3.6 : *Rank-size distributions of standard metropolitan labour area populations, 1951, 1961 and 1971*

Source : Department of the Environment, Research Report 10, British Cities : Urban Population and Employment Trends, 1951-71.

rate of ascent or descent in the two periods, because as a city reached a higher level more population increase would be required to produce a change in its rank order while the reverse would be true in the case of cities falling in the hierarchy, therefore the accelerating rate of decline in position recorded by many cities is observable in the second decade. In general, however, these dramatic changes in the rank ordering of individual cities tended to cancel each other out, making their impact on the hierarchical structure or urban Britain relatively limited. Britain continues to have an almost perfect hierarchy of city sizes, that is, a limited number of large cities and proportionately more with smaller populations. The general impression is that national population growth since 1951 has been spread proportionately over the cities of the nation resulting in a near parallel upward movement of the rank size distributions. There is a slight indication of a flattening out of the rank size distribution resulting from a shift of population away from the largest to intermediate size cities and the rapid growth of newly emergent cities at the bottom of the hierarchy. It nevertheless remains true that quite substantial movements of population to and from individual urban areas have had only a limited impact on the urban hierarchy in aggregate. This then would tend to suggest the existence of a relatively stable urban hierarchy or urban system.

There are many studies of other nations which also provide support for this rule though it has to be said that they apply mainly to advanced and mature nations where there has been sufficient time and development for an urban hierarchy to develop. In less developed nations there tends to be a system where we have a dominant city with a long tail of small settlements. This applies despite the different and varied definitions of urban areas which have been used. These studies have to be regarded with some caution because, apart from the varied definitions of urban area which have been used, the geographical coverage has also varied considerably and it needs emphasising that if the rule applies to two areas separately it cannot apply to them both collectively.

In an analysis of data for the U.S.A. Edwin Mills[8] fitted the equation

$$\log G(x) = \log A - a \log (x)$$

In this equation, log G obviously refers to the place in the hierarchy i.e., the rank, and x to the size of the urban area. Mills fitted this equation to a sample of urban areas for the U.S.A. with the following result

$$\log G(x) = 9.4540 - 0.9573 \log (x)$$
$$(0.1238) \quad (0.0223)$$
$$R^2 = 0.989$$

The coefficient of log x is nearly-1 and thus is reasonably consistent with the rank size rule. The value of R^2 (0.989)— suggests a very close association between the dependent variable rank and the independent variable size. The regression coefficient of less than minus one suggests that the line would have a slightly steeper slope as suggested in the diagram in Fig. 3.6 for England and Wales.

A similar exercise carried out on a random sample of urbanized areas in the U.S.A. in 1970 by Bish and Nourse[4] gave the following equation :

$$\log \text{Rank} = 4.09 - 0.92 \log \text{size}$$
$$(0.02)$$
$$R^2 = 0.987$$

The coefficient of log size can be seen to be close to the value obtained by Mills and to be statistically highly significant (being many times bigger than its standard error of 0.02).

The Simon model

The basis of Simon's model is the normal distribution or, what he refers to us the law of proportionate effect. Suppose z is a sum of random variables. If the factors acting on a particular variable are additive in their effects (then by the central limit theorem*) the variable will be normally distributed. If x is the variable we can write

$$x = wixi$$

If the effect of the factors is multiplicative (i.e., the effect is the product of n random variable) we have :

$$x = x_1^{w1}, x_2^{w^2}, x_3^{w^3} \ldots x_n^{wn}.$$

This means that the effect of any factor (w) on the values of x is multiplicative (or proportionate) rather than simply additive. The geometric sum of this equation may be written :

$$\log x = \sum^{n} w_i \log x_i$$

* See any statistical textbook—randomly drawn samples are normally distributed.

In this case the variable measured in logarithms is normally distributed, i.e., conforms to the log normal distribution. The Pareto and Log Normal distributions as applied to urban area size are compared in Fig. 3.7.

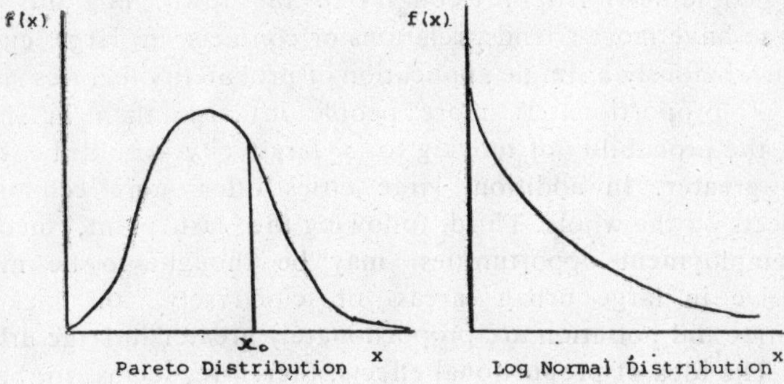

FIG. 3.7 : *Comparison of Pareto and Log Normal distribution*

Whereas the Pareto distribution has a mode of zero, the log normal distribution has a positive mode. However, beyond x_0 the log normal corresponds with the Pareto as shown in the above diagram. In fact, all urban data are "truncated" (i.e., cut-off) in this way because a minimum size of settlement is taken. For such data the log normal and the Pareto distributions approximate each other.

The equation above demonstrates the nature of proportionate effects and in this case it assumes that urban area sizes are determined by a large number of factors whose effects are multiplicative. Suppose also there is a certain probability of an urban area being born (i.e., reaching the value x_0). Simon has shown these assumptions to lead to a class of urban area size distributions of which the Pareto is a special case and a good approximation.

Like all such analyses this statistical work is essentially descriptive and does not explain how the distributions arise nor how they behave over time. The distribution of urban area sizes obviously depends on the nature of multiplicative effects. The question arises then, why should urban area sizes be subject to such effects?

Simon offers three possible explanations. First, many of the factors which affect birth and death rates affect large sectors of the population at once (for example, unemployment, birth control and progress in medicine) and, hence, affect cities in direct proportion to their population size. Second, it is argued that when people move from the country to the town, migrants are likely to have more friends, relations or contacts in large cities. This is obviously a simple application of probability theories since there are proportionately more people in large than in small cities, the probability of moving to a large city would be that much greater. In addition, large cities offer more economic prospects on the whole. Third, following the last point, income and employment opportunities may be thought to be more attractive in large urban areas or, conversely, the lack of amenities and pollution are proportionately greater in large urban areas. The idea of proportional effects, therefore, seems to be a plausible one and the only way in which we could cast doubt on it is to try to prove that such effects may not be observed. This would be rather a pointless exercise. What we need to know is whether this approach provides a satisfactory *explanation* of urban area size instead, as it might appear, of simply being a description.

The system of urban areas : The economic approach

The economic approach to the explanation of the system of urban areas is illustrated most readily by the work of Beckman.[1, 2] As we shall see, this work is a direct development of the Christaller model for urban areas but, unfortunately, its exposition involves some mathematics which while elementary in technique is complex. A complete summary of the model is given in the Appendix. Here we shall simply outline its main features.

The origin of urban areas has been attributed to differential cost or productivity advantages in space. This both leads to and feeds on the concentration of population. In the Christaller model the existence of urban areas is related directly to a hierarchy of demands or hinterlands. In the Beckman model P refers to the population of an urban area, P is the population served by that urban area. We can, therefore, think of the population of a town working and producing a surplus which it supplies to surrounding population. If we take the population of any town in the hierarchy of urban areas and refer to it as of size *m*, we can represent this in the form of a simple equation where $P_{m'}$ the urban area, is a fraction *k* of $P_{m'}$ the total population. These two equations are represented below. *k* is the fraction of a worker, presumably measured in manhours, required to supply one person in the area constituting the hinterland of any one town. $\frac{1}{k}$ therefore represents productivity of a worker. Thus the population of an urban area multiplied by its productivity represents the total number of people who can be supplied by that urban area. This is written below :

$$P_m \times \frac{1}{k} = P_m$$

In order to simplify matters it will be convenient to modify the notation at this point. In what follows *D* represents the demand on an urban area. It replaces *P* in the Beckman model, the total population served by an urban area. Insofar as total population measures total demand, *D* is equivalent to *P*.

Thus the previous expression

$$P_m \times \frac{1}{k} = P_m$$

may be rewritten as follows

$$P_m \,.\, f = D_m, \text{ where } f = \frac{1}{k}$$

the population of P_m multiplied by its average productivity, *f*, supplies the demands of D_m. The relationship between the size of an urban area and its hinterland can now be written as

$$P_m = kD_m \qquad \ldots(4)$$

$k = \frac{P_m}{D_m}$, the fraction of a worker (measured in manhours) required to supply one unit of demand.

$\frac{1}{k}$, is, therefore, the average productivity of workers.

In a hierarchical structure such as the Christaller model, the population served or the demand on a given urban area will come from both its own population and that of urban areas below it in the hierarchy. Supposing that any one area can supply *s* smaller areas in the next rank below in the hierarchy we can define the total demand on an urban area as follows.

$$D_m = P_m + sD_{m-1} \qquad \ldots(5)$$

This equation says that the total demand comprises that coming from the residents of the given urban area, P_m plus that of 3 areas in the next rank below.

For simplicity all these areas are assumed to be the same size. If we substitute equation (4) into (5) we obtain

$$D_m = kD_m + sD_{m-1}$$

$$D_m = \frac{s}{1-k} D_{m-1} \qquad \ldots(6)$$

This equation defines the relationship between different levels of the hierarchy. The constant $\frac{s}{1-k}$ represents the average level of productivity in the economy.

The smallest urban areas in the urban hierarchy have hinterlands comprised of rural population by definition. So the population of the smallest area P_1 comprises the population of that area P_1 plus the fraction of the rural population it serves, r.

$$D_1 = P_1 + r \qquad \ldots(7)$$

Since we know from (4) that $P_1 = kD_1$ then we can substitute for P_1 in (7) to obtain

$$D_1 = kD_1 + r$$

$$D_1 = \frac{r}{1-k} \qquad \ldots(8)$$

This defines the relationship between demand in the lowest level of the hierarchy and the non-urban population.

From equation (b) above we can write

$$\frac{D_m}{D_{m-1}} = \frac{s}{1-k}$$

and since we have from equation (4) a proportionality between p_m and D_m we have

$$\frac{P_m}{P_{m-1}} = \frac{s}{1-k} \qquad \ldots(9)$$

We know that $s>1$ and $0<k<1$ therefore $\frac{s}{1-k} > 1$. It follows that $P_{m'}$ the urban area or city size will increase exponentially with m, the level in the hierarchy. Equation (9) means that an urban area of any size must be $\frac{s}{1-k}$% as big as urban areas of the next smallest size. If $s=3$ and $k=0.5$, P_m would be 6 times as big as $P_m - 1$. We can show this in terms of a simple diagram as follows.

In Fig. 3.8, the top three ranks of a hierarchy are shown. Since $s=3$, there are three areas in the second rank and, given

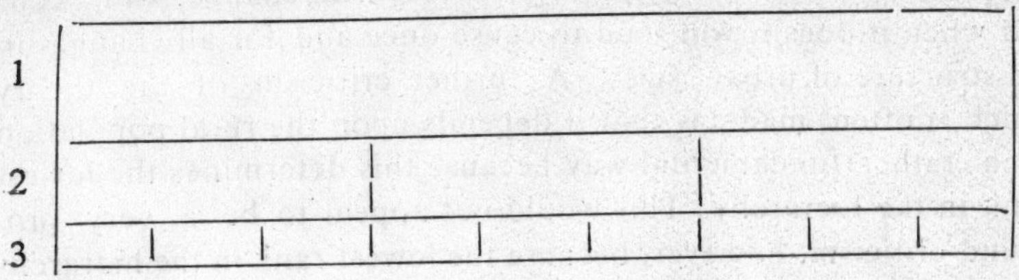

FIG. 3.8 : *A hierarchy or urban areas*

that $k=0.5$, these are each $\frac{1}{6}$ of the size of the top ranking area, or city. Correspondingly, there are three satellites for each of the second rank areas or cities, and each of these is $\frac{1}{6}$ of its size. Thus, 3 determines the number of sub-divisions in each rank and k determines their relative area.

The underlying idea of Beckman's theory is a very simple one which fits in very neatly with the rationalisation given for the existence of urban areas. Of course, it says nothing about the mechanism by which particular sizes are achieved, presumably the alteration in size distribution and the achievement of any particular size by an individual urban area could be explained in terms of the factors which we have already considered which would motivate the movement of households and firms in particular directions. With only slight modification the theory gives rise to a distribution of urban areas within each rank of the hierarchy so that in any particular rank of the hierarchy urban areas may well differ in size. They do not have to be exactly the same size but they will, nonetheless, be a typical size. Geographical irregularities like the availability of resources and amenities which determine comparative advantages for particular areas are not encompassed in this theory. They, presumably, determine indirectly the values of k and s, as well as determining the location of particular areas. The theory obviously presumes a very simple production function in which cost curves are not smooth but rather L-shaped and in which labour is the only input.

However, this does not seem to be a very weak assumption particularly as this is a static theory ; it merely indicates that there is no tendency towards smooth changes in the structure of the hierarchy in the short-term. Technological change will occur and when it does it will tend to cause once and for all changes in the structure of urban sizes. A further criticism of the theory which is often made is that it depends upon the rural population in a rather fundamental way because this determines the lowest rank in the hierarchy. This would not appear to be a very profound criticism, however, because the lowest rank in the hierarchy has to be determined in some arbitrary way and this seems to be as good as any other rationalisation.

CONCLUSIONS

Government, business and commercial organisations all have different kinds of hierarchies and it is not surprising that urban areas can be characterised in much the same way. Similarly, just as there would appear to be optimum units for administration and production, it would seem feasible to expect there to be similar optimum size units for urban areas. As we have seen above, sufficient theory exists to rationalise the observed structure of the urban system and to relate the size of individual urban areas to economic forces. Therefore, the attempt to define an optimum size and to explain the observed urban hierarchy would seem to be neither pointless nor futile. On the other hand, however, in the current state of knowledge the theory has a negative rather than a positive operational use. It serves to define what may be possible in trying to influence the size of urban areas rather than what are likely to be desirable lines of policy to pursue.

All this is to relate the size of urban areas to mainly outside influences. Of course, k, the productivity factor, may also be related to the industrial structure of an urban area and it would seem likely that there is an intimate relationship between the size and structure of urban areas. Certainly, size is likely to influence structure via the demand for particular industries and services. How far structure can influence size is a matter for speculation. In order to consider these questions however, we need to understand the determinants of the structure of urban areas and this is the subject of a further discussion.

FOOTNOTES

1. M.J. Beckman, "City Hierarchies and the Distribution of City Size", *Economic Development and Cultural Change*, Vol. 6, 1958, pp. 243-248.
2. M.J. Beckman, and J. McPherson, "City Size Distributions in a Central Place Hierarchy : An Alternative Approach", *Journal of Regional Science*, Vol. 10, 1970, pp. 25-33.
3. R.J. Bennett, *The Geography of Public Finance*, Methuen, 1980.
4. R.L. Bish and H.O. Nourse, *Urban Economics and Policy Analysis*, McGraw Hill, 1975.
5. E.E. Lampard, "The Evolving System of Cities in the United States", in H.S. Perloff and L. Wingo, *Issues in Urban Economics*, 1968.
6. A. Lösch, *The Economics of Location*, 1954.
7. C. Madden, "On Some Indications of Stability in the Growth of Cities in the U.S.", *Economic Development and Cultural Change*, Vol. 14, 1956.
8. E.S. Mills, *Urban Economics*, Scott, Foresman, 1972.
9. H.W. Richardson, *The Economics of Urban Size*, Saxon House, 1973.
10. G. Zipf, *Human Behaviour and the Principle of Least Effort*, 1949.
11. B. Walker, Welfare Economics and Urban Problems, Hutchinson, 1982.

APPENDIX

THE BECKMAN MODEL OF URBAN SIZE : AN EXPOSITION

1. P_m is the population of an urban area of the mth size.
   P_m is the population *served by* an urban area of the mth size.

$$P_m = kP_m \qquad \ldots(1)$$

$k = \frac{P_m}{P_m}$ the fraction of a worker who performs the function(s) for one person.

$\frac{1}{k}$ Persons served by one worker.

2. Workers in the smallest urban areas satisfy their own needs and those of r, rural residents. The total population served by the smallest urban areas is therefore

$P_1 = r + P_1$ and from (1) we have

$$P_1 = k(r + P_1)$$

$$P_1 = \frac{kr}{1-k} \qquad \ldots(2)$$

$$[P_1 = kr + kP_1$$
$$P_1 - kP_1 = kr$$
$$P_1(1-k) = kr]$$

Thus, $$P_1 = \frac{r}{1-k} \qquad \ldots(3)$$

$$[P_1 = r + \frac{kr}{1-k}$$
$$P_1(1-k) = r\,(1-k) + kr$$
$$P_1(1-k) = r - rk + kr$$
$$P_1(1-k) = r]$$

3. An urban area of a given size can serve s urban areas of the next smallest size. Thus,

$$P_m = P_m + sP_{m-1} \qquad \ldots(4)$$

The population served by an urban area of size P_m is the population of that area plus s areas of the next smallest size where $s > 1$.

Substitute RHS of (1) into (4)

$$P_m = kP_m + sP_{m-1}$$

$$[P_m - kP_m = sP_{m-1}$$

$$P_m(1-k) = sP_{m-1}]$$

$$P_m = \frac{sP_{m-1}}{1-k} \qquad \ldots(5)$$

This is a difference equation relating P_m to P_{m-1}. P_{m-1} is related to P_{m-2} in exactly the same way. Thus,

$$P_m = \frac{s}{1-k}\left(\frac{s}{1-k}\, P_{m-2}\right)$$

$$= \left(\frac{s}{1-k}\right)^2 P_{m-2}$$

4. Similarly, the population served by an area of any size is related to the population served by an urban area of the next smallest size. So,

$$P_m = \left(\frac{s}{1-k}\right)^3 P_{m-3} = \ldots = \left(\frac{s}{1-k}\right)^{m-1} P_1$$

The value of P_1 is known from equation (3). Thus,

$$P_m = \left(\frac{s}{1-k}\right)^{m-1} \frac{r}{1-k}$$

$$\left[\frac{s^{m-1}}{(1-k)^{m-1}}\ \frac{r}{1-k}\right.$$

$$\left.\frac{rs^{m-1}}{(1-k)^m}\right]$$

$$P_m = \frac{rs^{m-1}}{(1-k)^m}$$

This is the solution of the indifference equation for P_m. Substituting for P_m in (1) gives,

$$P_m = \frac{krs^{m-1}}{(1-k)^m} = \frac{kr}{s}\left(\frac{s}{1-k}\right)^m \qquad \ldots(6)$$

$$\left[\frac{skrs^{m-1}}{s(1-k)^m} = \frac{skrs^m}{s(1-k)^m} = \frac{kr}{s}\left(\frac{s}{1-k}\right)^m\right]$$

Since $s > 1$, and $o < k < 1$,

then $\frac{s}{1-k} > 1$. Thus equation (6) says that urban area size increases geometrically with m. Dividing P_m by P_{m-1} gives

$$\frac{P_m}{P_{m-1}} = \frac{s}{1-k}$$

$$\left(\frac{P_m}{P_{m-1}}=\frac{\frac{kr}{s}\left(\frac{s}{1-k}\right)^m}{\frac{kr}{s}\left(\frac{s}{1-k}\right)^{m-1}}\right)$$

This equation says that an urban area of any size is $\left(\frac{s}{1-k}\right)$% as big as urban areas of the next smallest size. Thus, if

$$s=2k=0.2, \frac{s}{1-k}=2.2.$$

5. The Rank-size rule.

Rank	No. of U. Area
1st	1
2nd	s
3rd	s^2
4th	s^3
n^{th}	s^{n1}

Beckman's development of this rule depends on the rule for the sum of a geometric series.

The sum of the term of a geometric progression.

S is the sum of the nth terms of a GP whose first term is A and whose common ratio is r.

$$S=a+ar+ar^2+\ldots+ar^{n-1}$$

Multiply this equation by $-r$

$$-rs=-ar-ar^2=ar^3-\ldots-ar^n$$

Whereas the first equation contains terms of every power from 1 to $n-1$, the second contains terms with every power of r from 1 to n.

Add the two equations to obtain

$$S=rs=a+ar^n$$

$$S(1-r)=a(1+r^n)$$

$$S=\frac{ar^{arn}}{1+r} \text{ or } \frac{ar^n-a}{r-1}$$

In the analysis of urban size $a=1$. Thus,

$$S=\frac{1+r^n}{1+r}$$

and since S refers to the number of urban areas in each rank we can write

$$S=\frac{1+s^n}{1+s}$$

Since we start from the largest and proceed to the smallest urban area we have

$$S=\frac{1-s^n}{1-s}$$

which gives the sum of the series to the nth class.

If there are S^n urban areas in the nth size class the middle one in the class will have the rank $s^{n/2}$ and the sum of terms to this point will be

$$S=\frac{1-s^n}{1-s}+\frac{s^n}{2}$$

If s^n is much larger than $\frac{1}{s-1}$ we can approximate the previous expression by

$$s^n\left(\frac{1}{s-1}+\frac{1}{2}\right) \qquad \ldots(7)$$

Equation (6) gives the *population* of an urban area in the middle of the nth smallest class, whereas (7) gives the *rank* of an urban area in the nth largest class.

If there are N size classes altogether, the equations will refer to the same urban area if we put $m=N-n$.

The product of the rank and populations for an urban area in the middle of the mth smallest or n^{th} largest class is

$$\frac{kr}{s}\left(\frac{s}{1-k}\right)^{N_{-n}} s^n\left(\frac{1}{s-1}+\frac{1}{2}\right)$$

[i.e. (6)×(7)]

$$=\frac{kr}{s}\left(\frac{1}{s-1}+\frac{1}{2}\right)\left(\frac{s}{1-k}\right)^N$$

$$\times(1-k)^n=C(1-k)^n$$

[Cross multiply the terms

$$\frac{kr}{s}\left(\frac{1}{s-1}+\frac{1}{2}\right)s^n\left(\frac{s}{1-k}\right)^{N_{-n}}$$

This says that the product of rank and size is a constant times $(1-k)^n$.

Operate on the second term

$$\left[\frac{s^n s^m}{1-km} = \frac{s^N}{1-k^m}\right.$$

Multiply by $1-k^n$

$$\left.\frac{S^N}{(1-k)^m}\;\frac{(1-k)^n}{(1-k)^m} = \frac{S^N}{(1-k)^m}(1-k)^n\right]$$

If k is close to zero, $(1-k)^n$ will be *close* to 1 and rank times size will be nearly constant.

The equation suggests that the product of rank and size will decrease somewhat as n decreases, a result which is consistent with both U.K. and U.S.A. data.

FOUR

JIN HWAN LEE

KOREAN CITY-SIZE DISTRIBUTION BASED ON THE RANK-SIZE RELATIONSHIPS

INTRODUCTION

GROUPS of cities in regions, countries, or the world, usually distribute a consistent regularity in size. The rank-size rule sometimes referred to as "Zifp's Rule", is an example of an organizing principle that helps account for this regularity. The rank-size concept was first discussed in the literature in the 1920s.[1] Since that time, the rank-size distribution has been studied in many areas of the world for many years. The early testing of the rank-size concept is G.K. Zifp's work in 1949. According to him, widespread attention to the fact that the distribution of all cities by rank and size in many countries is such that the population of any city multiplied by its rank is a constant.[2] In other words, the rank-size rule states that the size of a given city can be predicted by simply knowing its population rank among all cities in the area studied and the size of the largest city.

The distribution of city-size based on population have been studied in Korea. However, there have been few studies to survey the recent rank-size distributions of Korean cities. Therefore, it is significant to survey the recent distributions of the rank-size of Korean cities.

Purpose of the study

Geographers have studied the distribution of city-size in Korea. Brian J.L. Berry (1961) and William L. Garrison (1958) described the rank-size distribution adopted to Korean cities.[3] Truman Sea Hartshorn (1980) recognized their works as follows : "Some less developed countries such as Korea and El Salvador were found to follow the rank-size relationships.[4] However, they used the data on population of Korean cities before 1960. Now, the question is : How has the distribution of city-size in Korea after 1960 appeared ?

Therefore, the purpose of this study is two fold : First, to survey the changes in the distribution of city-sizes in Korea over time. Secondly, to show the interrelationships between the distribution of city-sizes in Korea and that of the rank-size rule.

Methodology

In order to examine the changes of city-size distributions over time, all cities with population of more than fifty-thousand will be divided into four categories : small-size city (50,000-100,000), medium-size city (100,000-500,000), large medium-size city (500,000-1,000,000), and large-size city (more than 1,000,000). There is a criterion for setting up the population of fifty-thousand. Fifty-thousand urban residents are usually needed to constitute a city in Korea. The change of city-size distribution will be surveyed.

In order to show the lognormal distribution, the cumulative percentages of city-sizes changing from small-size cities to large-size cities will be used over time. The cumulative percentages will represent the trend of the distribution of recent Korean cities.

In order to investigate the rank-size rule for Korean cities, the distribution curves of city-sizes will be plotted on double-logarithm papers. At the same time, regression equations for four periods will be derived in order to compare the slopes of rank-size lines between the actual distribution of city-size and the theoretical rank-size rule. That is, the slopes of the lines of Korean cities will be compared with the slope of the rank-size rule (—1.0). These regression equations will show whether the population of Korean city is larger than that of the rank-size rule or not.

The data of 1966 census, 1970 census, 1975 census, and 1979 temporary census in Korea will be used for this study. The distribution of Korean city-sizes in four periods, 1966, 1970, 1975, and 1979 will be studied.

LITERATURE REVIEW

The problems in rank-size distribution are posed comparisons of city populations and ranks. In any area, when cities are ranked from the largest to the smallest according to population, the largest city would rank number 1, the second largest number 2, and so on. If these ranks are plotted against city population size, the rank-size relationship emerges. There are few large cities and many small ones, and there is an apparent empirically regular relationship between the rank of a city and its population (Berry and Garrison, 1958).

City-size relations have been noted by a number of persons. The distribution of city-size was first studied by Auerbach in 1913, and Lotka developed the idea of city-size distribution.[5] However, the best-known elaboration of rank-size regularities was developed by G.K. Zifp (1949). He presented the rank frequency distribution of the 100 largest metropolitan districts in the United States in 1940. He yielded the best-fitting equation as follows.

$$R=(P^{-1})\ 10{,}000{,}000 \qquad \ldots(1)$$

where P is city size and R is city rank. He indicated that $k=10{,}000{,}000$, and was approximately equal to the population of the largest metropolitan district. He drew the line calculated by least squares. This was a simple regression line with a negative slope. He produced the equation as :

$$\log Y = -0.98\ \log X + 7.05 \qquad \ldots(2)$$

where Y is population and X is city rank. In this equation, the slope is —0.98 which is not significantly different from —1.0.[6]

Berry (1961) argued that rank-size regularities had been associated with the existence of integrated systems of cities in economically advanced countries, whereas primate cities had been associated with colonial economies in underdeveloped countries. He divided 37 countries into three categories using the lognormal distribution of cities with over 20,000 people : rank size, intermediate, and primate distribution including Korea into the "rank-size" category. Rank-size distribution was found when many forces affected the urban pattern in many ways because of complexity of economic and political life and age of the system of cities. Intermediate city-size distribution included countries of a variety of sizes and at a variety of levels of development. Intermediate distributions were arranged on the scale from primacy to rank-size. Primate cities were either political and administrative capitals or empire capitals. According to him, countries with the lowest primacy indices had rank-size distribution, and countries with the highest had primate city-size distribution.[7]

He also investigated that there was no relationships between type of city-size distribution and the degree to which a country was urbanized. He tried to explore the relationship between economic development and city-size distribution by using a principal component analysis of a data matrix composing the ranks of 95 countries on each of 43 proposed indices to economic development. From this result, he presented four basic patterns : technological scale, demographic scale, external relations, and a group of large countries with high per capita and of small countries with low per capita. The 37 city-size distributions had been classified on the basis of the four patterns.[8]

Berry proposed seven developmental models of city-size distribution from the first stage to the fourth stage according to the city-size and the cumulative percentage. These simple models are as follows :

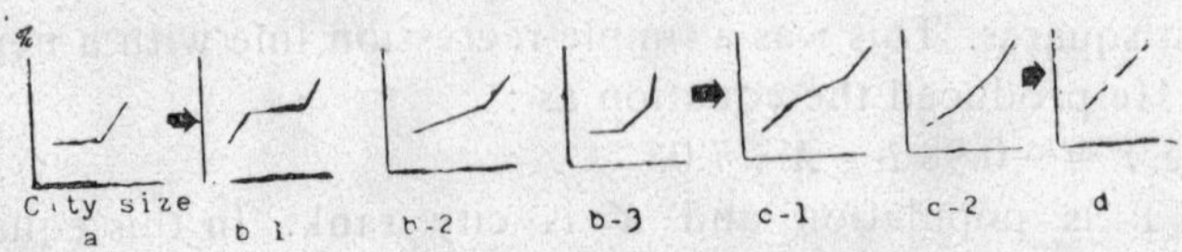

FIG. 4.1 : *Developmental models of city-size distribution*[9]

Cesar A. Vapnarsky (1969) examined the Argentine rank-size distribution of cities over time. He defined "closure" as :

> the proportion of all existing interactions beginning or terminating within a particular system which are also completed within the same system. That is, closure is a

> quotient which varies between 0 and 1. Closure is 1 if no interaction occurs between the system and the external world and closure is 0 if all interactions initiated or terminated within the system are completed outside it.[10]

He described that countries differed in their degree of closure, as well as in their degree of interdependence. Four logical possibilities proposed by him were : [11] (1) High closure and low interdependence ; this combination would characterize a very underdeveloped area. (2) Low closure and low interdependence ; the primacy of the city establishing the main link with the external world was expected in this case. (3) Low closure and high interdependence ; while the largest city tended to show primacy, the rest of the distribution would be expected to fulfil the rank-size rule such as Argentina. (4) High closure and high interdependence ; the condition for the fulfilment of the rank-size rule by the whole distribution of cities, including the largest one, were accomplished such as the United States.

City-size distribution for the Egyptian urban system was presented by Gary L. Fowler (1972). He attempted to test Berry's model of the lognormal distribution. The best-fitting curves for the city-size distribution at each census time from 1897 to 1960 were plotted on lognormal probability paper. Each plot was of cumulative frequencies so that a distribution was lognormal if it assumed the form of a straight line. He found that the relatively simple (primate) structure of the 1897 distribution gradually became more complex (lognormal) as the size of the urban system increased and cities of medium-size began to grow rapidly. He concluded that the curves showing the distribution of Egyptian city sizes followed the general progressions outlined in Berry's model mentioned before.[12]

Harry W. Richardson (1973) described the similarities and differences among lognormal, Pareto, and rank-size distributions. He illustrated similarities of the three distributions by using three equations. According to him, if the frequency distribution of city sizes was convex and positively skewed, the lognormal distribution might yield a good fit. The equation of lognormal distribution is as :

$$N = \log P \qquad \cdots(3)$$

where N is cumulative percentage of cities and P is city size. The lognormal distribution represents the whole range of city size, whereas Pareto distribution deals with the upper tail. The equation of Pareto distribution is as :

$$\log N(\bar{p}) = \log A - q \log p \qquad \ldots(4)$$

where $N(\bar{p})$ is cumulative percentage of cities above the threshold level, $\bar{p}$, and A and q are constants. This is similar to the equation of the lognormal distribution. The equation of rank-size distribution is as :

$$R \cdot P^q = k \qquad \ldots(5)$$

where R is city rank, and q and k are constants. The rank of city used in rank-size distribution instead of cumulative percentage of cities in Pareto distribution. A special case of the rank-size distribution is $q=1$. This case is called rank-size rule, i.e. :

$$R \cdot P = k = P_1 \qquad \ldots(6)$$

where P_1 is the size of the largest city. He described that rank-size distribution might instead be interpreted as a general model according to the value of the exponent. If $q=1$ implies the rank size, $q>1$ represents metropolitan dominance, whereas $q<1$ accounts for an urban system in which intermediate cities are large.[13] This method is similar to Malecki's work which follows.

The change in rank-size systems of cities was also examined by Edward J. Malecki (1975). He presented a critique of some past empirical research on city sizes and criticized that Zifp created many problems which persisted in empirical rank-size research. Because his data were for political or administrative cities, most subsequent research had failed to define rigorously the boundaries of the settlements. According to him, empirical studies of the type did not appear to give any consideration to the significance of these changes in the coefficients. He suggested several ways for an examination of intercept and slope changes over time.[14] First, the intercept value could change because of a uniform rate of increase or decrease in the populations of all places in the settlement system like Fig. 4.2(a). In this case, all places were attracting migrants in proportion to their population and were experiencing equal rates of natural growth.

Second, the slope of the regional rank-size distribution changed because smaller settlements were not growing at as rapid a rate as larger ones, forcing the tail of the distribution to

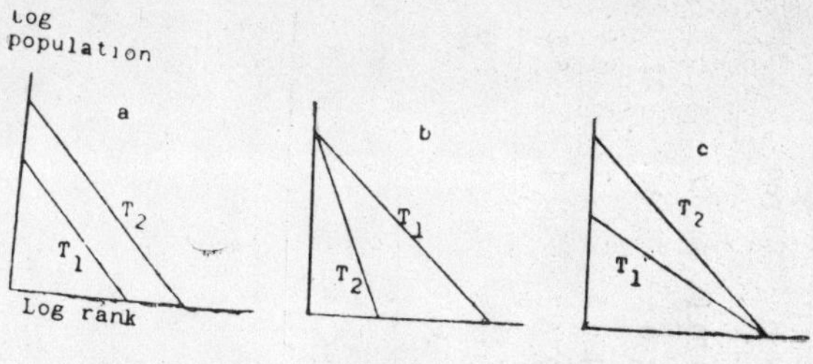

(*a*) (*b*) (*c*)

FIG. 4.2 : *Models for changes in intercepts and slopes from T_1 to T_2*

the left as Fig. 4.2(b). This situation may be seen in the recent rapid growth of metropolitan areas and the concomitant de-population of small towns.

Third, the slope of the rank-size distribution changed because the population of the largest cities had increased to force the slope of the distribution to steepen to meet the increased intercept as Fig. 4.2(c). This case may occur when the most rapid population growth takes place in the larger centres in a region, but without an actual decline in small place population.

DISTRIBUTION OF RANK-SIZE OF CITIES IN KOREA

The description of changes in urban concentration which have taken place with the development of Korea into a complex urbanized country is suggested as a surveying city-size distribution. In this study, the data on population after 1960 is used for Korean cities which have a population of more than 50,000.

There were 44 cities with a population of more than 50,000 in 1966, 46 cities in 1970, 50 cities in 1975, and 51 cities in 1979. The number of cities with more than 50,000 residents slightly increased over the last fifteen years. In the Table 4.1, all cities at each census are arbitrarily divided into four categories based on population size of cities as mentioned before.

The proportion of the level of urbanization which is total urban population divided by total national population is 35.9 per cent in 1966. The per cent of a country's population living in cities is "urbanization". The proportion in 1979 is 56.5 per cent.

TABLE 4.1 : Classification of population

(Population in ten thousand)

Class	1966			1970			1975			1979		
	Pop.	Freq.	%	Pop.	Freq.	%	Pop.	Freq.	%	Pop.	Freq.	%
5—10	1750.1	27	16.7	199.0	27	14.3	148.9	22	8.5	120.1	19	5.7
10—50	213.9	13	20.4	221.4	14	16.0	368.3	22	21.0	480.5	26	22.7
50—100	137.7	2	13.1	114.5	2	8.3	191.3	3	10.9	134.5	2	6.4
More than 100	522.7	2	49.8	849.3	3	61.4	1045.0	3	59.6	1376.7	4	65.2
Total	1049.4	44	100	1384.2	46	100	1753.5	50	100	2111.8	51	100
National Pop.	2919.3			3143.5			3470.9			3735.5		
Level of Urbanization	35.9%			44.0%			50.5%			56.6%		

The great increase of the level of urbanization among the four periods appeared between 1966 and 1970, and the smallest increase was between 1975 and 1979. The urban population had gradually increased from 35.9 per cent in 1966 to 56.5 per cent in 1979. This is an increase of 1.6 times for the last fifteen years. These figures about the level of urbanization indicate that the increase of population in urban areas has been significant in Korea.

This rapid growth of urban areas is based on urban industrialisation. In the middle of the 1960s, Korean government began to emphasize urban industrialization. The Government set up the Second Economic Development Plan (1967-1971). The major goals of the plan were : (1) to progress heavy industries, and (2) to expand trade in quantity and regions. Based on this plan, many industrial facilities were built in urban areas such as The Steel Manufacturing Company in Pohang, The Oil Refineries in Ulsan and Yochon, Electronic Manufacturing Industries in Buchon, an industrial district in Seoul, and The Free Trade Centre in Masan.

Seoul, Pusan, Daegu, and Inchon with populations of 8.1 million, 3.0 million, 1.6 million, and 1.0 million respectively are the largest cities in Korea. The primate city, Seoul, was much larger than any other city in each population census. Seoul is an old city and traditionally known as capital of Korea. Today, the capital has become the hub of Korea. Industrial facilities, administrative functions, transportation networks, educational facilities, cultural heritage, and sight-seeing facilities are concentrated in Seoul.

The city-size distribution in Korea

The curves in Fig. 4.3 for the distribution of city size at each census time are plotted on lognormal probability paper according to Berry's model. In some respects, this paper uses Berry's model as developed in his work "City-Size Distributions and Economic Development (1961)". Each plot is a cumulative percentage of cities with over 50,000 people so that if a distribution is lognormal, or rank-size, it assumes the form of a straight line. The vertical axis represents the cumulative percentage of city population, and the horizontal axis shows the city size.

The 1966 distribution in Fig. 4.3 is similar to Berry's model b-2 in Fig. 4.1. The population of small-size cities was minimal, but the number of cities was large. The proportion of small-size, medium-size, and large medium-size cities is 50.2 per cent which is almost one-half of the total population of cities in comparison with a large number of cities, 42 among 44 cities. Only two cities, Seoul and Pusan, had 49.8 per cent of the total city population in 1966 as shown in Fig. 4.3. The 1966 curve gradually goes up with slow slope to the city size of 1,000,000 and suddenly

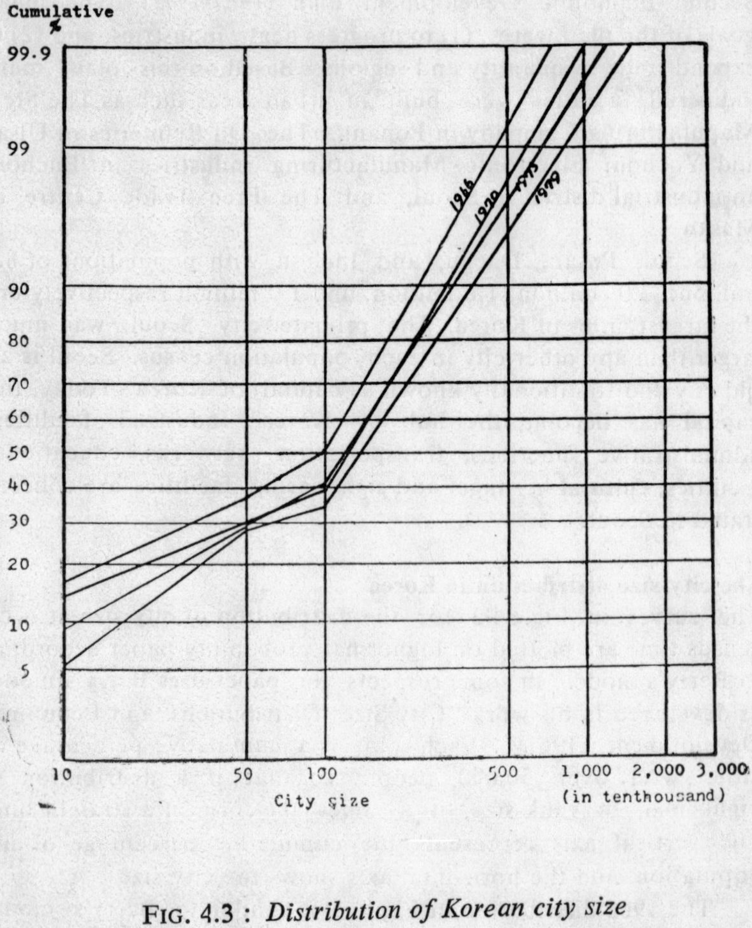

FIG. 4.3 : *Distribution of Korean city size*

increases with a large slope from the point of city size of 1,000,000. This curve is far the lognormal distribution.

The 1970 curve is similar to the 1966 curve in shape. The percentages of small-size cities, medium-size cities, and large medium-size cities decreased. However, population of large-size cities increased from 49.8 per cent of total city population in 1966 to 61.4 per cent in 1970. The cumulative percentages of small, medium, and large medium-size cities in 1970 were smaller than those in 1966. This means that the population had moved into larger cities. In addition to Seoul and Pusan, Daegu was included into the category of large-size city and its population reached one million in 1970.

The city-size distribution for 1975 was slightly different from those of 1966 and 1970. Urban systems in 1975 were developing toward a lognormal distribution. However, the shape of the curve is still similar to Berry's model b-2. The 1975 curve becomes entangled with the 1970 curve. This indicates that the proportion of population of large medium-size cities increased, as the proportion of population of small-size cities decreased. The cumulative percentage between 50,000 and one million in 1975 was slightly higher than that of 1970. Population of medium-size cities had increased since 1970, whereas population of small-size cities had decreased since 1966.

The 1979 city-size distribution was also developing toward the lognormal distribution. It is similar to Berry's model 3-a of Fig. 4.1. Slightly different characteristics between the 1975 curve and the 1979 curve were an increase of proportion of large-size cities and a decrease of proportion of large medium-size cities. The percentage of population of large-size cities was the greater because the city of Inchon was added to the category with population of more than one million. The population of Inchon reached 1.04 million in 1979. Only four largest cities had 65.2 per cent of the total city population in Korea. Thus, the sequence of change for the Korean urban system indicated strength in fast growth of larger cities.

The rate of industrial growth has accelerated the concentration of population in urban areas has severely produced many problems in pollution, housing, transportation, and sewage systems. Therefore, one major goal by the Korean Government is to disperse the crowded population to small-size cities and rural areas.

Rank-size distribution

According to the rank-size rule, the following formula applies to the settlements in a given area.

$$P_i \cdot R^q = C \qquad \ldots(7)$$

where P_i is the population of a city of rank R, and q and C are constants. The formula can be converted into a logarithmic form

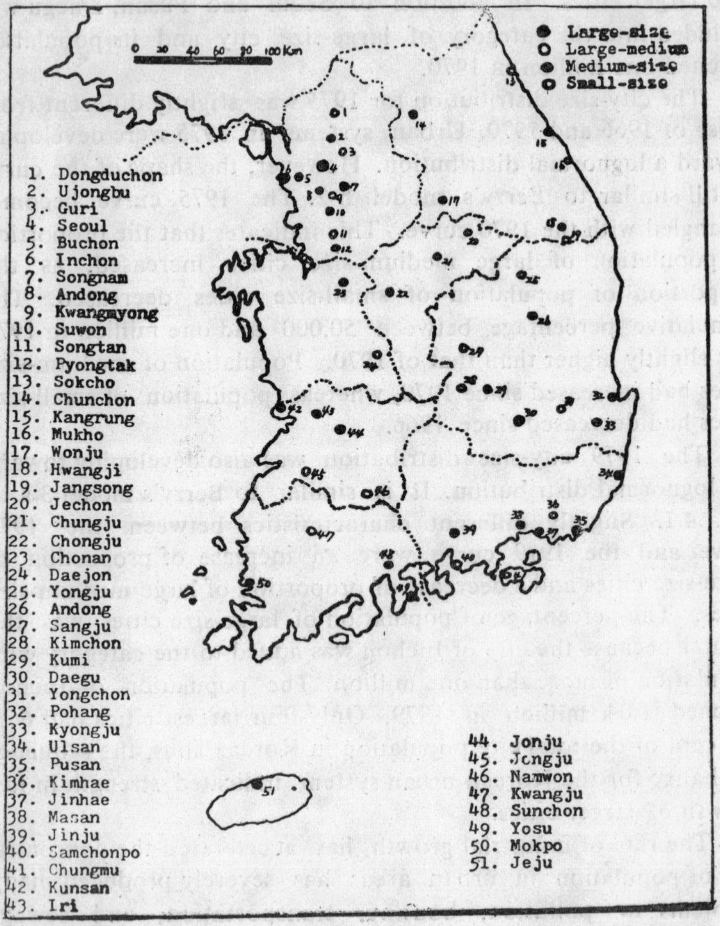

FIG. 4.4 : *Location of Korean cities*

as follows.

$$\log P_i - q \log R = \log C \qquad \ldots(8)$$

This implies that the rank of any city, when modified by some exponent and multiplied by the size of that city, is equal to a constant which represents the population of the largest city.

The deviation of actual distribution is compared with the straight line of slope —1 that corresponds to the rank-size rule by using q value in the equation of the simple regression. The deviation of the actual distribution of cities from the rank-size rule is cleared by plotting on a double-logarithm paper. Since the model postulates a slope of —1 as the most probable steady state, deviations of individual cities are measured with respect to a line of slope —1.

The rank-size distributions of cities corresponding to four national census in Korea have been plotted in Figs. 4.5, 4.6, 4.7, and 4.8. These figures are the graphical representation of the actual distribution of cities at each census compared to a line with slope of —1.

Four equations of simple regression from the computer print-out are in Table 4.2. There are high associations between populations and ranks in these equations. This table shows that the actual distributions of city-size of four periods are inconsistent with those of the rank-size rule. The value of q in 1966 is 1.0186 which is the smallest in four periods, whereas that of 1979 is the largest, 1.2144. This means that the distribution of rank-size of cities in 1966 is the closest to the distribution of the rank-size rule, while the distribution of cities in 1979 is the farthest distribution from the distribution of the rank-size rule. For example, the values of q in 1966, 1970, 1975, and 1979 are 1.0186, 1.0740, 1.1412, and 1.2144 respectively which are larger than the value of q in the rank-size rule, 1.0. Therefore, all slopes of four periods are steeper than the slope of the rank-size rule. This

TABLE 4.2 : **Equations of regressions**

Year	Regression equation	R^2	T-value
1966	log Pop.=2.3046—1.0186 log Rank	.9426	—26.27
1970	log Pop.=2.4411—1.0740 log Rank	.9511	—29.24
1975	log Pop.=2.6120—1.1412 log Rank	.9816	—50.62
1979	log Pop.=2.7656—1.2144 log Rank	.9915	—75.58

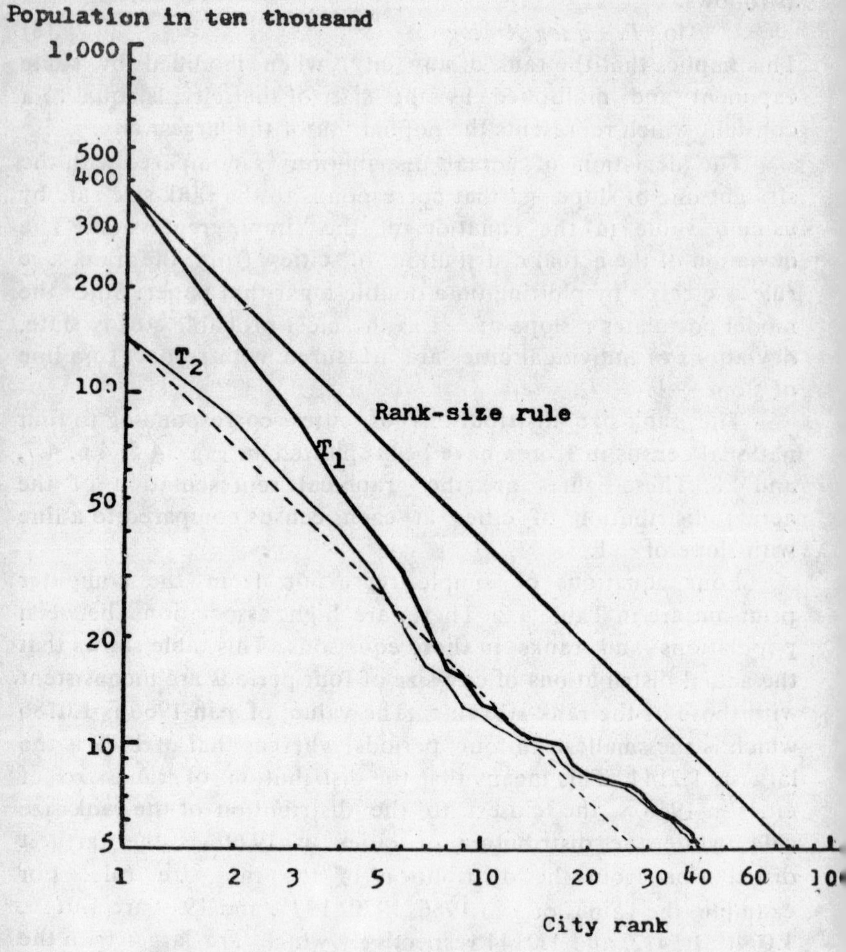

FIG. 4.5 : *Distribution of rank-size of cities (1966)*

result denotes that the expected city-sizes based on the rank-size rule are larger than the real sizes of cities in Korea. Since all q values in actual distributions of cities are larger than 1.0, these models represent the metropolitan dominance, as pointed by Richardson in Fig. 4.2(b) and 4.2(c). The values of slope in actual distribution of cities have been larger and larger over time. Therefore, the adoption of rank-size rule to the distribution of

Korean city-size seems to be less adequate over time. The result of *T*-test rejects the null hypothesis that there is no relationship between city population and city rank at 0.05 significant level.

The graphic representations of city-size distributions are in Figs. 4.5, 4.6, 4.7, and 4.8. The metropolitan dominance is also shown in these figures because the slopes of lines (T_1) are $q>1$. The distribution of rank-size of cities shows concave-shaped curves. The deviation of medium-size cities from the line of slope —1 is larger than those of small and large-size cities. According to this result, population in medium-size cities are much less than the expected population size by the rank-size rule.

If the second largest city, Pusan, is just assumed as the largest city, the curves will be different from the curves in which Seoul

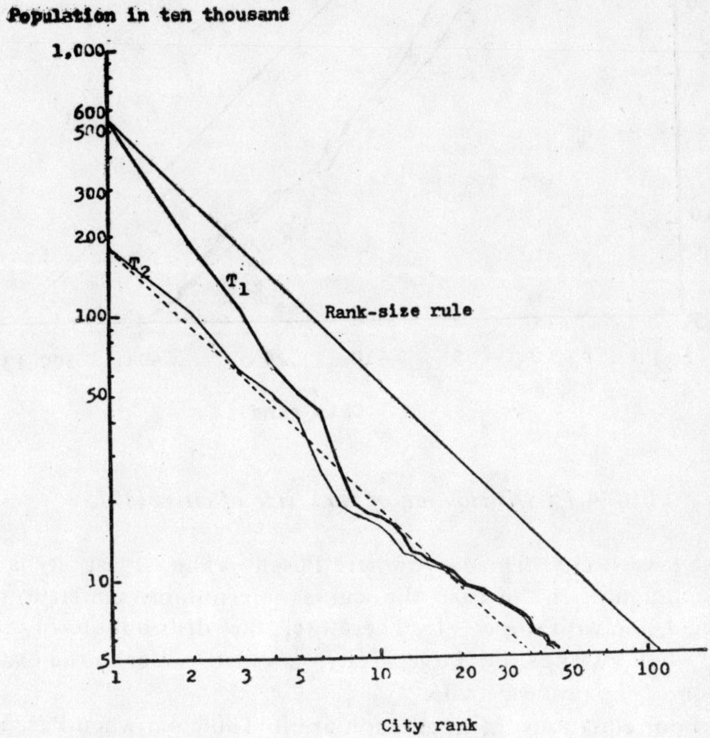

FIG. 4.6 : *Distribution of rank-size of cities (1970)*

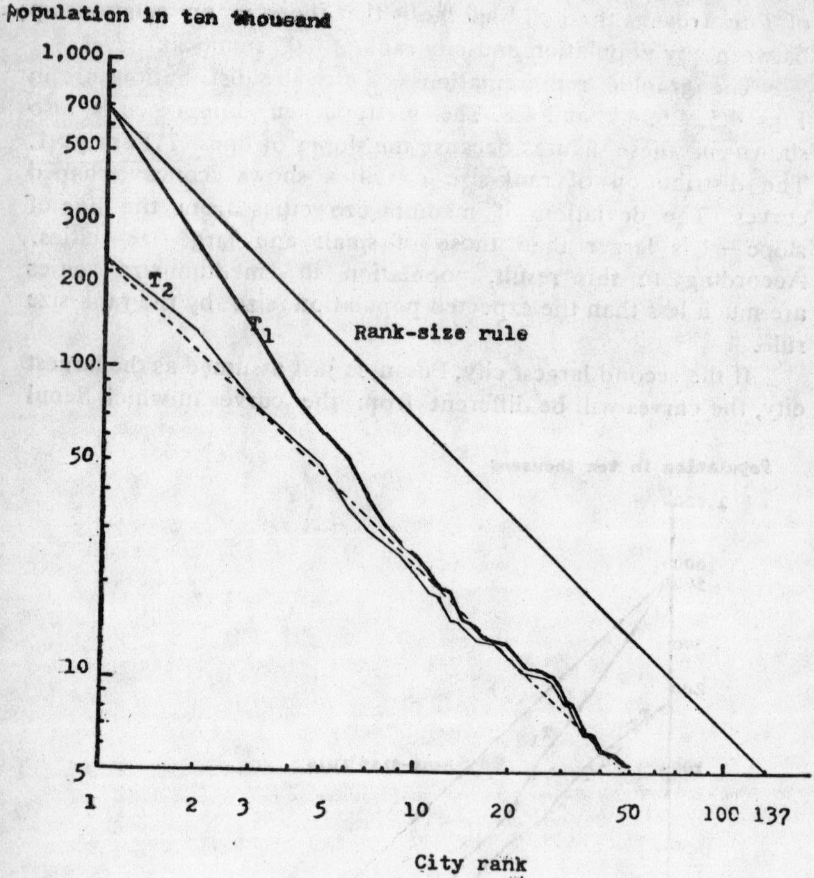

FIG. 4.7 : *Distribution of rank size of cities (1975)*

is the largest city. The curve where Pusan is the largest city is T_2 in each figure. In this case, the curves are notably similar to the straight line with slope —1. Therefore, the distribution of city-size, when Pusan is the largest city, is much closer to the distribution of the rank-size rule.

Four equations of regression are in Table 4.3 when Pusan is assumed as the largest city. The q values in regression relationships in 1966, 1970, 1975, and 1979 are very close to —1.0.

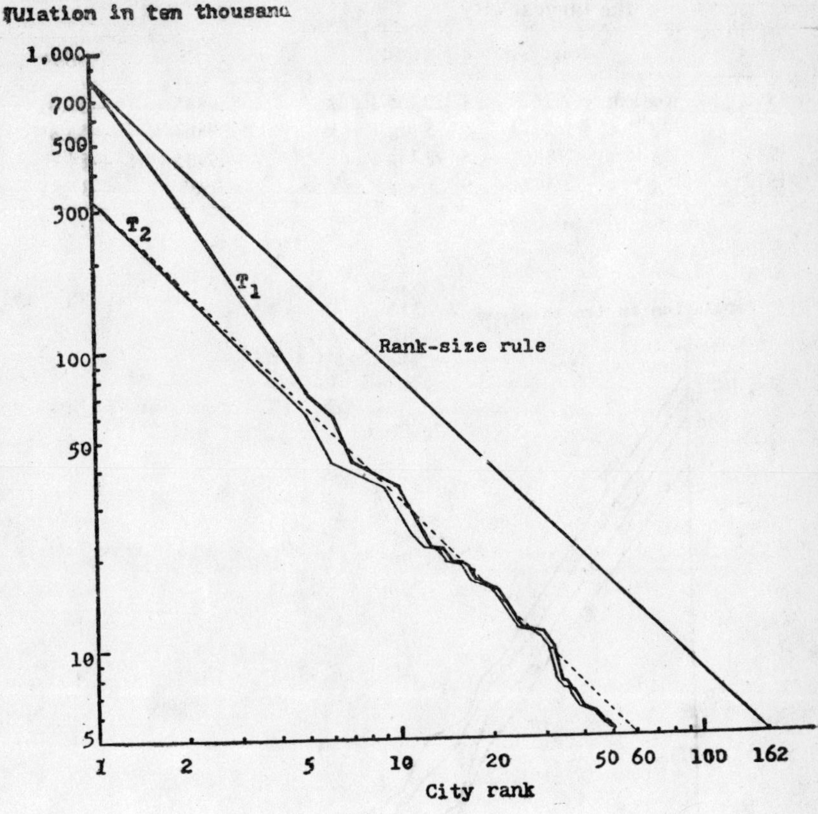

FIG. 4.8 : *Distribution of rank-size of cities (1979)*

These regression lines are almost consistent with the line of rank-size rule. Therefore, if Seoul is removed from the distribution of Korean cities, the city-size distribution will follow the rank-size rule. This implies that the Korean city-size distribution still has primacy. The result of *T*-test rejects the null hypothesis that there is no relationship between city population and city rank at 0.05 significant level.

In Fig. 4.9, the changes of curves are upward over time. These changes follow Malecki's model *A*, as shown in Fig. 4.2. However, the growth of the upper-tail of the line in each census

TABLE 4.3 : **Equations of regression when Pusan is assumed as the largest city**

Year	Regression equation	R^2	*T*-value
1966	log Pop.=2.1629—1.0022 log Rank	.9845	—51.04
1970	log Pop.=2.2324— .9775 log Rank	.9864	—55.83
1975	log Pop.=2.3568— .9792 log Rank	.9935	—84.79
1979	log Pop.=2.4424— .9823 log Rank	.9938	—87.85

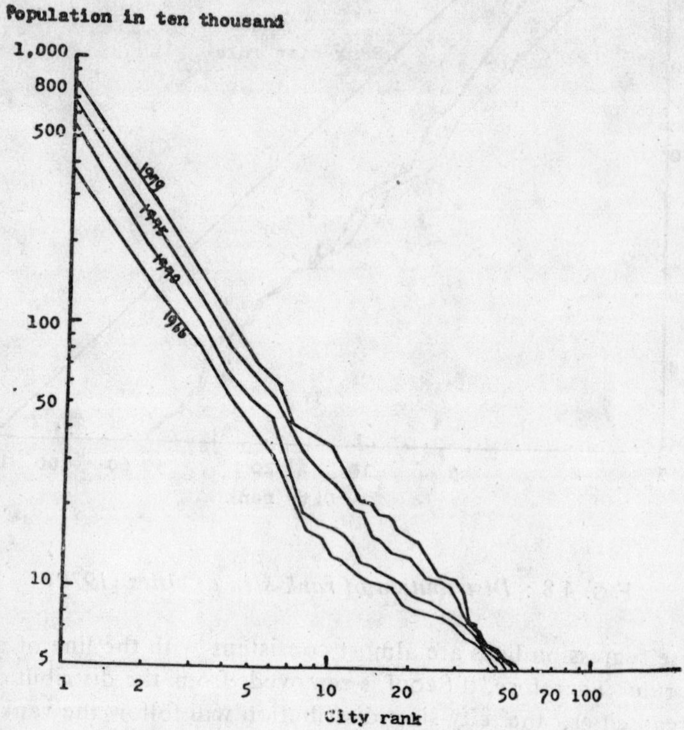

FIG. 4.9 : *Distribution of Korean cities (1966-79)*

is larger than that of the down-tail of the line. This result supports that the population growth in big cities is larger than that of small cities.

CONCLUSION

The distribution of Korean city-sizes was surveyed on the basis of the rank-size relationships. The distribution of Korean city-size has several dominant characteristics. First, more than sixty per cent of the urban population is concentrated in the four largest cities : Seoul, Pusan, Daegu, and Inchon. All these cities have more than one million people. At the same time, the population growth of large cities far exceeds that of small cities over a period of time.

Second, the distribution of Korean city-sizes is developing toward the lognormal distribution over time. According to Berry's model, there are four stage in development of city-size distribution (Fig. 4.1). Here the distribution of Korean city-sizes is approaching the last stage.

Third, the distribution of Korean city-sizes was inconsistent with the distribution of the rank-size rule. The distribution of Korean city-sizes was dominant in primate characteristics. Because of rapid growth of the primate city, it has been more inadequate to adopt the rank-size rule to the distribution of city-size in Korea over time.

Fourth, in comparison with the distribution of the large and small-size cities, the distribution of medium-size cities in each census is the most inconsistent with that of the rank-size rule. In general, the real population sizes in cities in each census are smaller than the expected population sizes of rank-size rule. Particularly, the real population sizes in medium-size cities are much smaller than the expected population size in medium-size of the rank-size rule.

Finally, if the second largest city, Pusan, is assumed as the largest city, the distribution of Korean city-size will be similar to that of the rank-size rule. This result also supports the primate dominance in city-size distribution.

FOOTNOTES

1. Truman A. Hartshorn, *Interpreting The Cities : An Urban Geography*, New York : John Wiley and Sons, 1980, p. 90.
2. George K. Zifp, *Human Behaviour and The Principle of Least Effort*,

New York : Addison-Wesley Press, 1949, p. 359.

3. Brian J.L. Berry and W.L. Garrison, "Alternate Explanations of Urban-Size Relationships", *Annals of Association of American Geographer*, Vol. 48, March, 1958, 83-87.
4. Truman A. Hartshon, *op. cit.*, p. 91.
5. K. Dziewonski, "General Theory of Rank-Size Distribution in Regional Settlement Systems : Reappraisal and Reformulation of the Rank-Size Rule", *Papers of the Regional Science Association*, Vol. 29, 1972, p. 73.
6. G.K. Zifp, *op. cit.*, p. 375.
7. Brian J.L. Berry, "City-Size Distributions and Economic Development", *Economic Development and Cultural Change*, Vol. 9, July, 1961, p. 575.
8. *Ibid.*, pp. 584-585.
9. *Ibid.*, p. 583.
10. Cesar A. Vapnarsky, "On Rank-Size Distributions of Cities : An Ecological Approach", *Economic Development and Cultural Change*, Vol. 17, July, 1969, pp. 584-585.
11. *Ibid.*, p. 585.
12. Gary L. Fowler, "Development of City-Size Distributions for the Egyptian Urban System, 1897-1960", *The Professional Geographer*, Vol. 24, November, 1972, pp. 317-319.
13. Harry W. Richardson, "Theory of the Distribution of City-Size : Review and Prospects", in L.S. Bourne and J.W. Simmons, (eds.), *System of Cities*, New York : Oxford University Press, 1978, pp. 169-171.
14. Edward J. Malecki, "Examining Change in Rank-Size Systems of Cities", *The Professional Geographer*, Vol. 27, February, 1975, pp. 44-45.

FIVE

N. DAMSON M'TIZWA-MANGIZA

THE HIERARCHICAL STRUCTURE AND SPATIAL DISTRIBUTION OF SUBURBAN SHOPPING CENTRES IN HARARE, ZIMBABWE

INTRODUCTION

UNTIL recently, the administration and planning of Harare, the capital of Zimbabwe, has been characterised by fragmentation and discriminatory practices based mainly on racial grounds (Smout 1977, 1974 ; Gargett 1977). Consequently, the development of suburban shopping centres, like other sectors of urban activity, has lacked on overall planning policy. Further, past research work on suburban shopping centres, has concentrated on centres located in the Low Density Residential Areas (LDRAs) which are high income areas, and until recently, predominantly white (Smout 1971, 1974, & 1977). However, since Zimbabwe's independence in 1980, urban planning policy has shifted substant ally, with the expressed desire to improve the long neglected High Density Residential Areas (HDRAs) which accommodate the majority of black people who constitute over 70 per cent of the total population of the city. In view of this, there is, therefore, a need for a critical appraisal of the structure of urban activity in Harare. The specific aims of this study then are as follows :

(1) To investigate the hierarchical structure and spatial distribution of suburban shopping centres in Harare ;
(2) To analyse the functional composition of the centres ; and

(3) Generally, to provide a comprehensive picture of the whole city with respect to suburban shopping centres, with the ultimate view of furnishing much needed data for planners in particular, and for all those cencerned with urban analysis in general.

The rest of the study is divided, sequentially, into the following subsections : Conceptual framework of analysis ; Area of study ; Data collection ; Analysis and discussion of results ; and conclusions.

CONCEPTUAL FRAMEWORK OF ANALYSIS

The study of shopping centres and shopping patterns has been conducted mainly in the context of four theoretical approaches : location theory formulations originating from Christaller's central place theory (Christaller 1933) ; spatial interaction concepts derived from the gravity model (Huff 1962, 1963) ; the cognitive-behavioural approach (Downs 1970) ; and the structural approach (Davies 1968, 1972). The applications and limitations of these theoretical approaches have already been thoroughly analysed by Davies (1976) and the British National Economic Development Office (NEDO, 1970), among others, and are generally understood. Nevertheless, because for the purpose of this study, central place theory has been chosen as a conceptual framework, it is necessary to dwell on it a little longer.

Central place theory assumes an equilibrium between demand and supply for any given good, where demand is a function of disposable income available for purchasing the good and for transport to the point of supply (range of good), and supply is a function of the minimum size of market necessary for profitable operation (threshold of good). In terms of location, goods of similar thresholds, or orders, group together. The end result is a locational landscape and vertical hierarchy characterised by large numbers of low order central places and smaller numbers of higher order central places. With respect to consumers, their behaviour is that of economic men whose objective is to maximise utility, in this case, by visiting the nearest central place in which the desired good is offered. Christaller's original model has been criticised principally on the following grounds : Firstly, the non-dynamic and deterministic nature of the model ; secondly, the unrealistic assumptions underlying the model ; and thirdly, certain logical inconsistencies characterising the internal structure of the model (Carter 1975 ; Davies 1973, 1976). Apart from these criticisms, there also have been several additions to and modifications of the original model, namely by Losch (1944), Berry and Garrison (1958) and by Isard (1956). Of particular relevance to the present study are the modifications by Berry and Garrison. In their numerous studies in the USA, Berry and Garrison demonstrated that hierarchies of centres may be observed inside individual urban areas. These hierarchies are comprised of nucleated shopping centres typified by the following five-tier structure :

(i) isolated corner stores ;
(ii) neighbourhood shopping centres ;
(iii) community or district shopping centres :
(iv) regional shopping centres ; and
(v) the central business district (CBD).

Berry and Garrison further suggested a theory of *tertiary activity* based, essentially on the two concepts of *threshold* and *range* of good, that is the minimum level of demand necessary to support the profitable operation of a business enterprise, and the maximum distance customers will be prepared to travel to the supplier, respectively. The interrelationship between these two variables exhibits enough regularity to lead to a hierarchical differentiation of centres, though not to a formal arrangement of nested hexagonal market areas (as Christaller would have it) because of differential mobility of residents and uneven population densities characterising urban areas. This more flexible interpretation of central place theory appears to be generally more useful, as suggested by Davies (1976) in commenting on the unnecessarily severe criticism of the abstract nature of central place theory.

With respect to the present study, central place theory, as modified by Berry and Garrison, provides a good organisational framework for analysing systematic regularities of shopping centres in Harare. The concept of hierarchy is particularly useful in this regard.

AREA OF STUDY

Harare, then Salisbury, was founded in September 1890 by the Pioneer Column and the British South Africa Company Police Force (BSAP) who had trekked north from South Africa to establish a new colony on the authority of a royal charter granted by the British Crown in 1889. Harare was proclaimed the capital of Mashonaland, and later the capital of Rhodesia when that country emerged. Fig. 5.1 is a map of present day Zimbabwe showing the provinces and major towns of the country. Fig. 5.2 shows Harare and its environs in 1900 : In the middle was established the city centre itself, surrounded by the 'townlands' or 'commonage', originally reserved for horse and cattle grazing (Christopher 1977). A cadastral plan was prepared between 1890 and 1894 for the central grid and the townlands, as illustrated in Fig. 5.3 which shows Harare's cadastral framework in 1930. Surrounding the central grid and the townlands were farms, 15,000 morgen or 1,250 hectares each in area, which had been staked out by members of the pioneer column according to their agreed entitlements (See Fig. 5.2). These farms were later to be

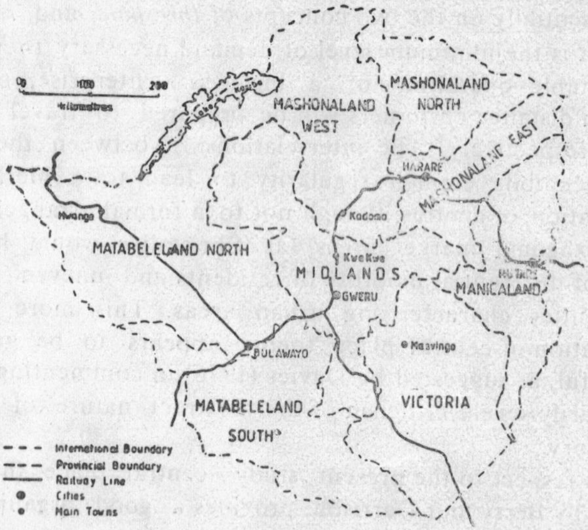

FIG. 5.1 : *Zimbabwe : Towns and provinces mentioned instudy*

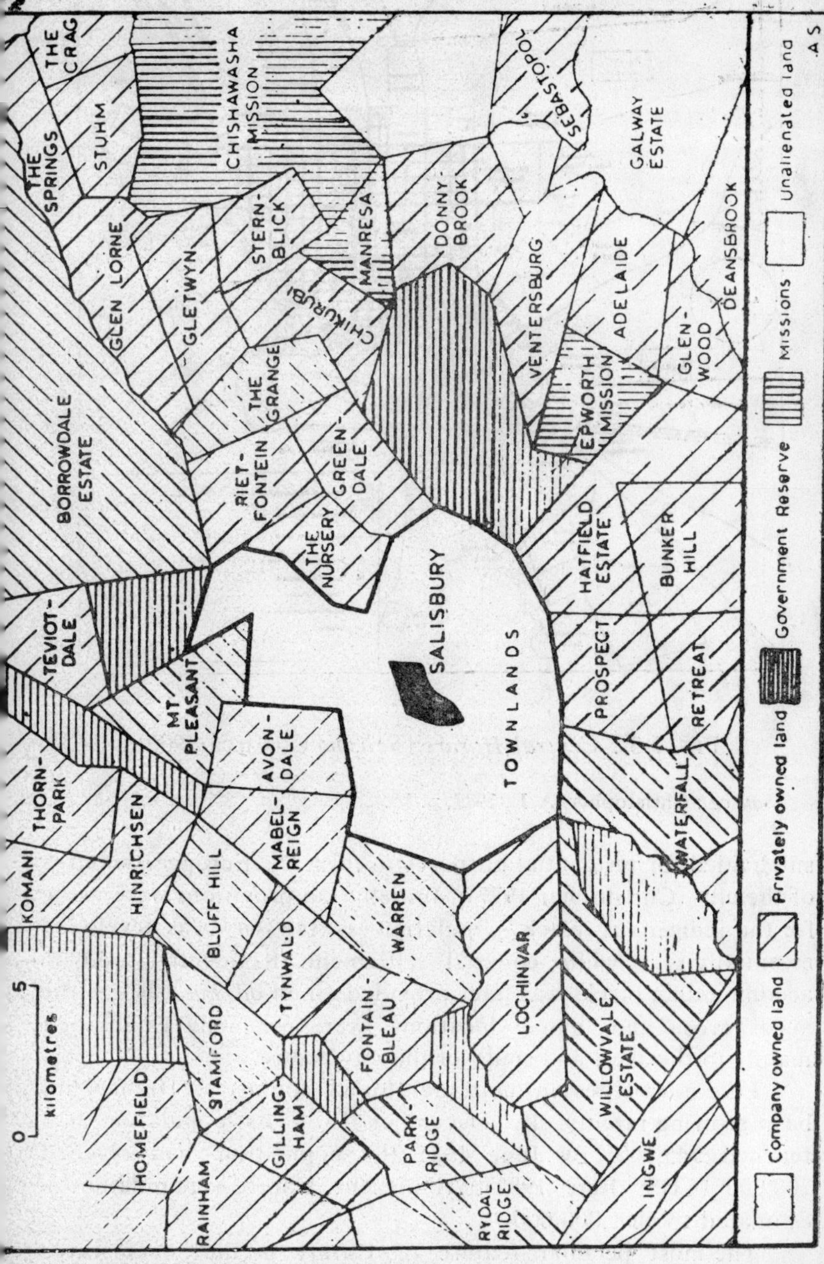

FIG. 5.2 : *Harare (Salisbury) and Environs* (Circa 1900)

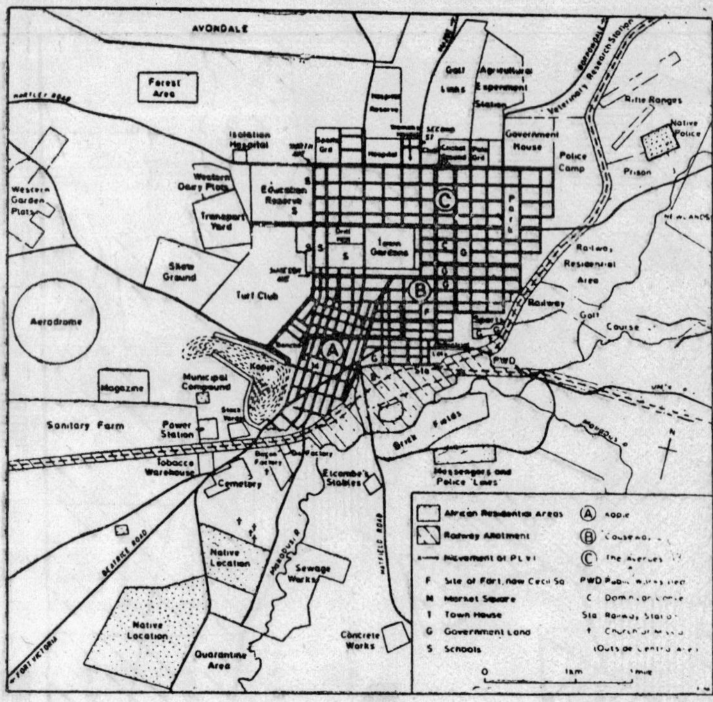

FIG. 5.3 : *Central Harare* (*Salisbury*) (Circa *1900*)

Source : Christopher, A.J., 1977, p. 15.

subdivided for residential purposes to form the European suburbs of the city (Christopher 1977). Initially no provisions were made for the indigenous black population as the city was developed essentially as a white colonial settlement. Residential land to accommodate blacks was later provided on an *ad hoc* basis as the needs arose and 'native locations' were gradually established mainly to the west and south of the city centre.

Like most cities in underdeveloped countries, Harare has been growing rapidly. By December 1974, its population had reached 545,000. By June 1981 the population had reached 700,000 (COS, June 1981). At present Harare's population is estimated to be 1,000,000.

The most peculiar feature of Harare is the deep-seated

racial division and the consequent spatial segregation by race. Although, with the coming of independence, the institutionalised racial discrimination system is now obsolete, its effect on the spatial form of the city is phenomenally evident, to the extent that it is difficult to make any demographic and socio-economic generalisation about the city as a whole. The predominantly white LDRAs (former 'European Areas') reflect the privileged socio-political position of the past and the much higher incomes which the whites are used to, while the HDRAs (former 'African Townships'), which have been described as "products of poverty and paternalism" (Smout 1974, p. 17), reflect years of political repression and neglect. Fig. 5.4 is a land-use map of Harare showing, among other things the location of LDRAs and HDRAs.

With respect to characteristics relevant to shopping centres, that is, development density, household incomes and mobility, there are marked differences between LDRAs and HDRAs. The development density in HDRAs is generally of the order of thirty houses per hectare or 12 houses per acre, as compared to one house or less per acre in most LDRAs. Table 5.1 gives the most recent data on HDRA household incomes and Table 5.2 gives the same kind of data for LDRAs. In general, LDRA household incomes, as compared with HDRA households, are seven times higher. In terms of mobility, ownership of private cars is much higher in LDRAs than in HDRAs. In 1977 it was estimated that the average level of ownership was 1.99 cars per white household (Hardwick 1977, p. 96). On the other hand, the current level of car ownership among HDRA households is estimated to be 18.38 per cent or 0.18 car per household, a figure which is 11.1 times less than that of LDRA households (Mutizwa 1982, p. 228).

Clearly then, the nature of suburban shopping centres in Harare is bound to be influenced by the dual socio-economic structure of the city, and any problems and solutions have to be viewed within this contextual framework.

DATA COLLECTION

Past studies have measured functional size of shopping centres either by simply counting the number of proprietary establish-

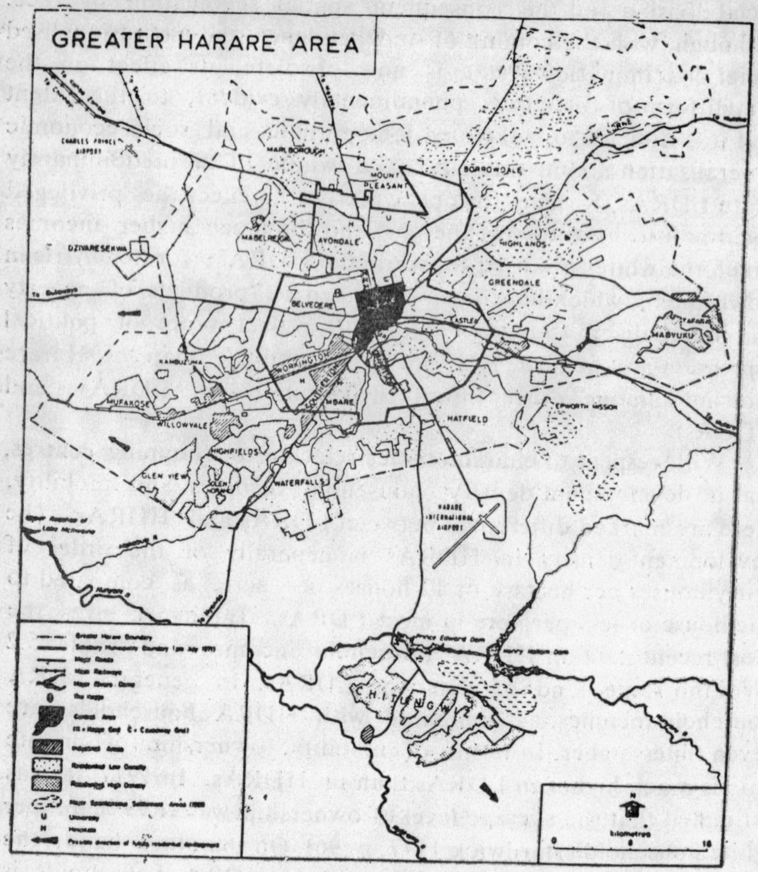

FIG. 5.4 : *Harare* : *Land use* (*1982*)

By courtesy of D. Hywel Davies, *University of Zimbabwe, Geography Department.*

ments per centre or by calculating the combined floorspace of the proprietary establishments in the centre. The latter method has been employed extensively, particularly in studies concerned with forecasting and allocation techniques for the planning of shopping centres (Cripps 1969 ; McClelland 1966 ; Diamond and Gibb 1962). Smout (1971) has devised an alternative method for measuring functional size of shopping centres, consisting

TABLE 5.1 : High density residential areas—Household incomes (1982)

Z $ per month	%	Cumulative %
<10	3	3
11-30	2	5
31-50	4	9
51-70	6	15
71-90	3	18
91-110	14	32
111-130	16	48
131-150	11	59
151-200	15	74
201-250	9	83
251-300	5	88
301-350	3	91
351-400	2	93
401-450	1	94
451-500	1	95
501-550	1	96
551-600	1	97
>600	3	100

Z $ 100 = U.S. $ 1.3023

Source : Hoek-Smith, M.C., *Socio-Economic Survey* : *Harare* (*High Density Areas*), June 1982.

essentially of three stages :

(i) Compilation of an inventory of functions : This involves identifying all suburban shopping centres in the city and visiting them to record all existing types and quantities of functions.

(ii) Grouping of functions and allocation of points : All the functions recorded above are ranked according to the frequency of their occurrence, from the lowest to the highest frequency. The functions are then exhaustively classified using Clark's group concept which, simply put, is based on the idea that "every member of a group should be closer to some other member of the group than some other point" (Smout 1971, p. 144). Finally, each of the different groups is allocated points such that the least frequency group will have the highest points

TABLE 5.2 : **Low density residential areas—Household incomes (1977/78)***

Z $ per month	%	Cumulative %
<400	8	8
400-499	9	17
500-599	12	29
600-699	13	42
700-799	14	56
800-899	8	64
900-999	10	74
1000-1399	19	93
>1400	7	100

Z $ 1,00 = U.S. $ 1.3023

Source : Zimbabwe Central Statistical Office, *Higher Income Expenditure Survey, 1977/78*, p. 36.

* Present day income levels are definitely higher than those presented in this table, in view of adjustments for inflation. This means that the gap between LDRA and HDRA household incomes is actually higher than the one suggested by Tables 5.1 and 5.2.

and the highest frequency group will have the lowest points. The logic of this ties in with central place theory where it is assumed that lower order functions are more abundant than higher order functions. The functional classes actually derived by Smout and used in the present study are given in Table 5.3.

TABLE 5.3 : **Measuring size of shopping centres—Individual function points**

Function	Points
Food Shops	
—Baker	4
—Butcher	1
—General Food	1
—Supermarket—large	4
—Supermarket—medium	3
—Supermarket—small	2
—Others	4
Other Shops	
—General dealer—large	4
—General dealer—small	2
—Bottle store	3

—Chemist	3
—Clothing	2
—Electrical	4
—Florist	4
—Gifts and Stationery	4
—Garden requisites	3
—Hardware	3
—Household soft goods	4
—Shoes	4
—Others	4
Financial Offices	
—Bank branch	4
—Bank agency	3
—Building Society branch	5
—Building Society agency	3
—Insurance Company branch	5
—Insurance Company agency	4
Other Offices	
—General business	4
—Surgery	3
—Estate agents	3
—Others	5
Services	
—Service station (automotive)	1
—Vehicle hire and sales	4
—Dry cleaners	2
—Hairdresser	2
—Restaurant	4
—Licensed premises	5
—Shoe repair agency	4
—Sports pools	1
—Others	4
Social and Administrative	
—Clinic	5
—Library	5
—Police station	5
—Post Office branch	4
—Post Office agency	3
—Town Council Hall/office	4
—Others	5

N.B.—All functions above fall into 5 classes with function points ranging from 1 to 5 as follows : class 1=5 ; class 2 = 4 ; class 3 =3 ; class 4 = 2 ; class 5 = 1. It shouıd also be noted that the 6 function types used by Smout above (Food shops ; Other shops ; Financial offices ; Other offices ; Services ; Social and Administrative) are slightly different from the seven function types used in this study (see Table 5.6). Thus the table above was used for measuring size of shopping centres only, and not for classifying functional types.

(iii) Calculation of individual centre functional scores : For any given centre, this involves recording all functions provided in the centre, and determining the total score by considering the functional classes to which they belong.

This particular method outlined above has the advantage that it enables a distinction to be drawn, firstly between different types of function ; and secondly, between functions of the same type with different capacities for attracting custom. In effect, this approach puts more weight on higher order functions, with the result that both quantity and functional order of services are more accurately reflected in the total shopping centre score than would be the case with the two alternative methods mentioned earlier.

Returning to the present study, all suburban shopping centres were first located on a large scale map of the city after an exhaustive search procedure involving map analysis and visits to new and unmapped areas of the city. The centres were then all visited, their functions recorded and total functional scores calculated using the method outlined above.

ANALYSIS AND DISCUSSION OF RESULTS

Within the whole of Harare, 108 suburban shopping centres were identified. Fig. 5.5 is a map of Harare showing the spatial distribution of all the shopping centres identified and Fig. 5.6 shows the rank-size hierarchy of the centres. The names, functional sizes and ranks of the centres are given in Table 5.4, which also gives the functional composition of each centre (which will be discussed later).

Clearly, the rank-size hierarchy shows no evidence of distinct orders of centres, that is, it is not a stepped hierarchy but rather more of a continuum. This confirms one general conclusion of earlier central place studies, that within the intra-urban context the stepped hierarchy of centres envisaged by Christaller is difficult to authenticate and that more often than not the distribution of centres forms a continuum (Losch 1944 ; Davies 1976).

Figs. 5.7 and 5.8 show the rank-size hierarchies of LDRAs and HDRAs separately. In the LDRAs, 70 shopping centres were identified and in HDRAs 38 centres were identified. Clearly, even

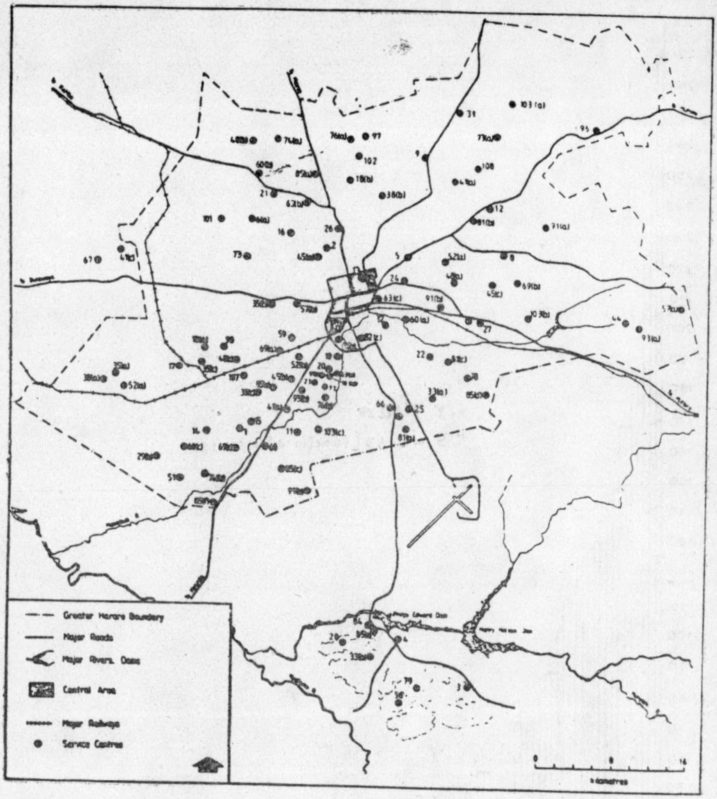

FIG. 5.5 : *Spatial distribution of shopping centres in Harare*

though the HDRAs carry more than 70 per cent of the total population of the city, their shopping centres are, in terms of quantity, by far outnumbered by those in the LDRAs. Undoubtedly, this is a result of the dual socio-economic structure of the city outlined earlier : The LDRAs are much more affluent, which means that they can afford to support a large number of centres. Even so, it appears that some of the LDRA shopping centres are superfluous and uneconomic, as concluded by Smout in 1974, and as shall be demonstrated in the consideration of vacant premises in all centres. It should be noted that both LDRA and HDRA rank-size hierarchies, like the combined city hierarchy, take the

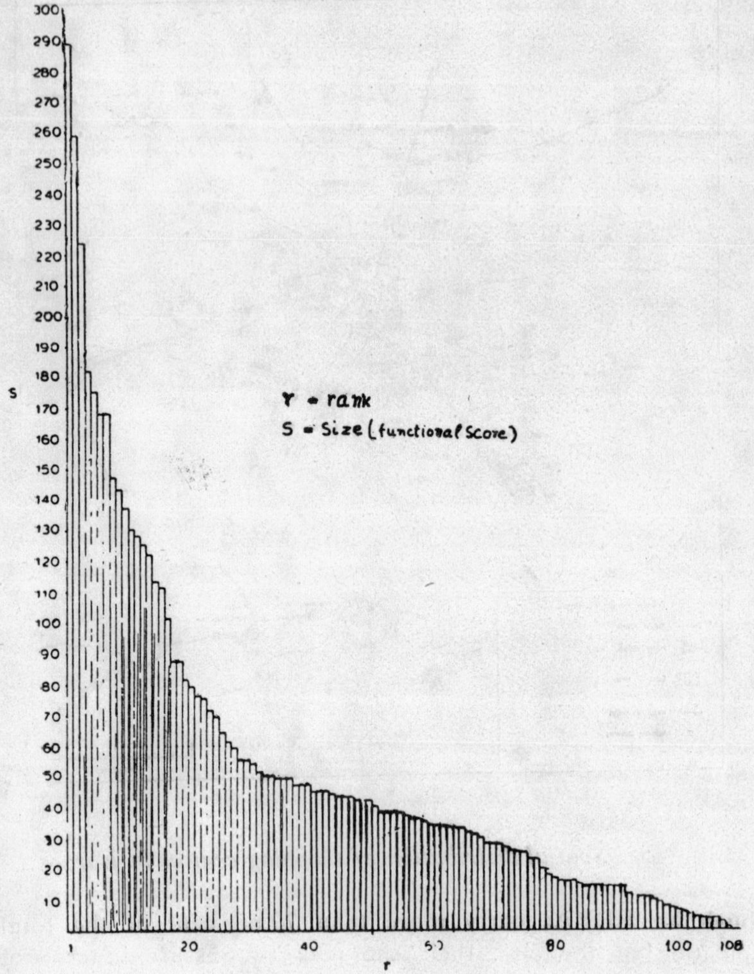

FIG. 5.6 : *Harare suburban shopping centres—Combined rank-size hierarchy*

form of a continuum rather than a stepped distribution.

One aspect considered important to test is the relationship between the quantity of service centre functions (as measured by the total functional score for that area, *Y*) and the size of the residential area (as measured by total population and total number

TABLE ˁ.4 : **Harare suburban shopping centres—Rank-size hierarchy and functional composition**

	Centre	*s*	*a*	*b*	*c*	*d*	*e*	*f*	*g*
1	Machipisa	289	39.9	3.0	15.2	4.6	5.3	26.1	5.9
2	Avondale	259	0	3.6	50.2	9.5	7.1	22.5	7.1
3	Makoni	224	24.2	5.1	38.5	0	1.3	17.5	13.3
4	Chikwanha	182	29.3	7.3	24.0	0	6	30.7	2.7
5	Newlands	175	6.9	6.3	54.3	10.9	1.7	17.7	2.3
6a	Mabelreign	168	0.6	5.7	40.6	13.1	3.6	19.6	16.7
6b	Magaba	168	19.6	2.5	41.7	0	8	23.9	4.3
8	Kamfinsa	147	9.5	5.4	49.6	11.6	8.8	12.2	2.7
9	Borrowdale	143	3.5	4.3	41.1	24.1	0	17	9.9
10	Matapi	137	18.2	3.6	11.7	0	16.1	38.7	11.7
11	Parktown	130	3.8	6.2	57.7	4.6	6.2	10.8	10.8
12	Chisipite	128	6.9	3.5	56.1	11.5	2.6	12.3	7.4
13	Fife Avenue	125	2.4	10.5	56.8	11.2	0	15.2	4
14	Western Triangle	122	28.3	0	36.5	0	5.7	26.2	3.3
15	Old Highfields	113	36.2	2.7	19.5	0	3.5	25.7	12.4
16	Stratheven	111	0.8	5.6	50.3	4.3	14.4	8.1	16.2
17	Kambuzuma 5 & 6	101	19.4	3.2	26.9	0	3.0	38.6	8.9
18a	Kambuzuma 2	87	24.1	2.3	32.2	0	4.6	26.4	10.3
18b	Mt. Pleasant	87	1.2	6.9	40.3	9.2	0	16.1	26.4
20	Musika	81	21.0	7.4	30.9	0	9.9	25.9	4.9
21	Avlonlea/Greencroft	79	2.8	11.1	55.4	6.4	0	12.8	11.5
22	Queensdale	76	9.2	5.3	55.2	6.6	0	17.1	6.6
23	Community Centre	75	32.1	0	11.9	0	9.3	22.6	24.0
24	Samora Machel Av.	71	3.1	13.8	63.1	12.3	0	7.7	0
25	Queensway	69	1.5	8.8	50.0	11.8	4.4	8.8	14.7
26	Second Street	64	4.8	6.4	30.2	12.7	0	23.8	22.7

TABLE 5.4 (*Contd.*)

	Centre	*s*	*a*	*b*	*c*	*d*	*e*	*f*	*g*
27	Beverley	61	3.3	4.9	62.3	4.9	0	13.1	11.5
28	Huruyadzo	59	30.0	6.0	30.0	0	0	8	26
29a	Chidziva	55	24.0	16.0	24.0	0	7.3	10.9	38.2
29b	Makomva	55	18.6	13.5	32.0	0	7.5	11.3	17.0
31	Crowhill Road	54	17.7	0	39.9	0	13.5	19.2	9.6
32	Braeside	51	5.9	11.8	52.9	5.9	5.9	9.8	7.8
32a	Hatfield	50	14.3	10.2	38.7	16.3	0	4.1	16.3
33b	Zengeza 2	50	30.0	3.5	26.5	0	0	8.0	32.0
35a	Msasa Road	49	8.1	0	26.5	28.6	0	18.4	18.4
35b	Marimba	49	8.2	14.3	75.5	0	0	2.0	0
35c	Kambuzuma	49	16.3	0	14.3	0	14.3	16.3	38.0
38a	Samuriwo	47	24.0	0	31.3	0	6.4	29.8	8.5
38b	Groombridge	47	2.1	8.5	61.7	6.4	0	10.6	10.6
38c	Lochinvar	47	6.4	8.5	36.2	0	8.5	29.8	10.6
41a	Houghton Park	45	15.6	6.7	37.8	0	0	28.9	11.1
41b	Balantyne Park	45	6.7	4.4	40.0	6.7	17.8	15.6	8.9
41c	Tsimba	45	21.0	0	12.3	0	0	26.7	40.0
44	Chaminuka Street	44	37.8	0	7.6	0	9.1	4.5	40.9
45a	Kensington	43	2.3	13.6	67.9	0	0	16.3	0
45b	Craster Road	43	11.6	7.0	34.9	0	0	46.5	0
45c	Greendale	43	16.3	9.3	44.1	0	0	20.9	9.3
48a	Rhodesville	42	7.1	9.5	52.4	0	0	21.4	9.5
48b	Marlborough Town	42	0	8.1	56.9	16.2	0	8.1	10.8
48c	Rugare	42	22.5	0	13.2	0	0	19.0	45.2
51	Chitubu	40	27.3	0	25.2	0	0	37.5	10.0
52a	Glen Roy	38	5.3	5.3	23.7	15.8	0	26.3	23.7

52b	Southerton Industrial	38	10.5	7.9	34.2	0	10.5	36.8	0
52c	Arcadia	38	10.5	10.5	39.5	0	10.5	15.8	13.2
52d	Muriranyenze Street	38	28.3	0	21.7	0	0	26.3	23.7
56	Dongo Road	37	16.5	7.1	49.4	0	0	16.2	10.8
57a	Tafara	36	50.0	0	8.3	0	0	27.8	13.9
57b	Belvedere	36	2.8	22.2	36.1	0	0	13.9	25
59	Workington	35	2.9	0	28.0	0	11.4	42.9	0
60a	Hillside	34	2.9	11.8	85.3	0	0	0	0
60b	Bluff Hill	34	11.9	5.9	20.7	0	11.5	50.0	0
60c	Epaceman	34	28.4	11.0	28.4	0	0	20.6	11.8
63a	Joburg Lines	33	3.4	5.1	6.8	0	21.2	36.4	27.3
63b	Avondale West	33	4.6	0	63.7	0	0	22.0	9.8
63c	Estlea	33	11.6	11.6	46.5	0	0	30.3	0
66	Caledon	32	12.1	6.1	60.6	0	0	21.2	0
67	Chishamiso	31	16.9	0	21.8	0	0	32.3	29.0
68	Tait Cresent	30	23.3	0	46.7	0	13.3	16.7	0
69a	Lytton Road	28	14.3	10.7	25.0	0	0	50	0
69b	Athlone	28	7.1	25.0	39.3	17.9	10.7	10.7	0
69c	Lusaka	28	17.9	0	39.3	0	10.7	32.1	0
72	Marowa	25	81.5	0	0	0	0	18.5	0
73	Meyrick Park	26	4.5	9.5	38.1	0	0	42.9	0
74a	Marlborough	25	4.0	32.0	36.0	0	0	28.0	0
74b	Glen Norah B	27	40.0	0	24.0	0	0	0	36.0
76a	Pendennis Road	23	4.3	26.1	17.4	0	13.0	39.1	0
76b	Ardbennie	23	21.7	0	69.6	0	0	8.7	0
78	St. Patrick's Road	20	5.0	20.0	65.0	0	0	10.0	0
79	Mrewa	18	29.4	17.7	41.2	0	0	11.8	0
80	New Mabvuku	17	58.8	11.8	17.6	0	0	11.8	0
81a	Logan Park	15	12.5	0	43.7	0	0	43.8	0
81b	Lewisam	16	35.7	14.3	42.8	0	0	7.1	0

TABLE 5.4_(*Contd.*)

	Centre	*s*	*a*	*b*	*c*	*d*	*e*	*f*	*g*
81c	Chadcombe	16	18.7	0	25.0	0	0	56.3	0
84	Zanamwe	15	46.6	0	0	0	0	53.3	0
85a	Mwazha	14	7.1	21.4	21.4	0	0	14.3	35.7
85b	Ashbrittle	14	0	35.7	50.0	0	0	14.3	0
85c	Cheviot	14	35.7	21.4	35.7	0	0	7.1	0
85d	Park Meadowlands	14	46.1	23.1	23.1	0	0	7.7	0
85e	Southerton	14	21.4	21.4	28.6	0	0	28.6	0
85f	Lyndale	14	7.1	14.3	42.9	0	0	35.7	0
91a	Mandara	12	8.3	0	50.0	0	0	41.7	0
91b	Clyde	12	16.8	16.8	58.4	0	0	8.3	0
93a	Greystone Park	11	27.3	0	72.3	0	0	0	0
93b	Bassopo	11	54.5	0	0	0	0	0	45.5
93c	Nehanda Street	11	18.2	18.2	27.3	0	0	36.2	0
96	Glen Lorne	10	30.0	0	70.0	0	0	0	0
97	Northwood	9	33.3	0	33.3	0	0	33.3	0
98	Westwood	8	62.5	0	37.5	0	0	0	0
99a	Midlands	7	57.1	0	42.9	0	0	0	0
99b	New Location	7	57.1	0	42.9	0	0	0	0
101	Ashdown Park	6	0	33.3	66.7	0	0	0	0
102	Quorn Avenue	5	100.0	0	0	0	0	0	0

103a	Helensvale	4	0	75.0	0	0	0	25.0	0
103b	Cleveland	4	0	100.0	0	0	0	0	0
103c	Montgomery Drive	4	25.0	50.0	0	0	0	25.0	0
103d	Tsiga and Chikore	4	100.0	0	0	0	0	0	0
107	Cedrella	3	33.3	66.7	0	0	0	0	0
108	Rolfe Valley	1	0	0	0	0	0	100.0	0

s=functional score of the centre (a measure of size)
a=general dealers and food shops
b=supermarkets and department stores
c=specialist retail shops
d=financial establishments
e=general offices
f=personal services
g=social service and administrative establishments.
function types a to g are expressed as a percentages of s.

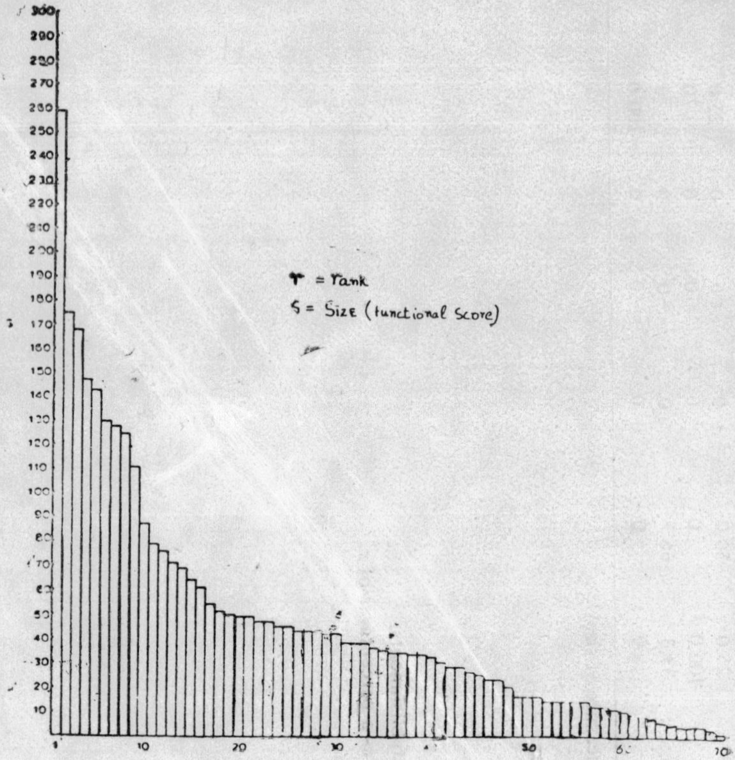

FIG. 5.7 : *HDRA shopping centres—Rank size hierarchy*

Key to Fig. 5.7

Rank	*Name of Centre*
1	Avondale
2	Newlands
3	Mabelreign
4	Kamfinsa
5	Borrowdale
6	Parktown
7	Chisipite
8	Five Avenue
9	Strathaven
10	Mount Pleasant
11	Avonlea/Greencroft
12	Queensdale

Rank	*Name of Centre*
13	Jameson/Samora Machel Avenue
14	Queensway
15	Second Street
16	Beverley
17	Crowhill Road
18	Braeside
19	Hatfield
20(a)	Msasa Road
20(b)	Marimba
22(a)	Groombridge
22(b)	Lochinvar
24(a)	Houghton Park
24(b)	Ballantyne Park
26(a)	Kensington
26(b)	Craster Road
26(c)	Greendale
29(a)	Rhodesville
29(b)	Marlborough Town
31(a)	Glen Roy
31(b)	Southerton Industrial
31(c)	Arcadia
34	Belvedere
35	Workington
36(a)	Hillside
36(b)	Bluff Hill
38(a)	Avondale West
38(b)	Eastlea
40	Caledon
41	Tait Crescent
42(a)	Lytton Road
42(b)	Athlone
44	Meyrick Park
45	Marlborough
46(a)	Pendennis Road
46(b)	Ardbennie
48	St. Patrick's Road
49(a)	Logan Park
49(b)	Lewisam
49(c)	Chadcombe
52(a)	Ashbrittle
52(b)	Cheviot
52(c)	Park Meadowlands
52(d)	Southerton
52(e)	Lyndale
57(a)	Mandara
57(b)	Clyde

Rank	*Name of Centre*
59	Greystone Park
60	Glen Lorne
61	Northwood
62	Westwood
63	Midlands
64	Ashdown Park
65	Quorn Avenue
66(a)	Helensvale
66(b)	Cleveland
66(c)	Montgomery Drive
69	Cedrella
70	Rolfe Valley

of households, X_1 and X_2 respectively). Unfortunately, the nature of the secondary data on population and housing units available was such that the testing could only be done for HDRAs.

In theory, it is expected that larger residential areas should have larger functional scores. Table 5.5 gives population (X_1) and households (X_2) data for all HDRAs as well as the total functional scores for the individual areas (Y). Figs. 5.9 and 5.10 are scattergrams of the data in Table 5.5, that is Y against X_1 and Y against X_2, respectively. Both scattergrams illustrate the absence of an overall relationship between total functional scores and size of residential areas. Both scattergrams also illustrate that Mbare and Highfield, the two oldest HDRAs, are by far the best serviced, and that the newer HDRAs like Glen View and Seke are comparatively poorly serviced. This situation is a result of the absence of an overall policy for the provision of social services—including shopping centres—in newly developed HDRAs. The Harare city council has often been criticised for placing priority on the development of beerhalls at the expense of other much needed social service facilities like shops, schools and clinics. The most recent evidence of this pattern of development is the new Warren Park HDRA which has a large, lavishly decorated beerhall, but no shops, schools or clinics (The Herald, 12 July 1982, p. 5). The lack of concern and of an overall policy is also reflected by the absence of development on many sites in HDRAs which were reserved for shopping centres a long time ago. Clearly, this situation has to be rectified soon if the objectives of social equality are to be realised.

The rank-size hierarchy is useful for determining the relative functional size of shopping centres, but it says little about the composition of individual centres. To get more detail on the functional composition of shopping centres, the list of functions identified in all centres was divided into seven function types as under :

(a) general dealers and food shops
(b) supermarkets and department stores
(c) specialist retail shops
(d) financial establishments
(e) general offices
(f) personal services

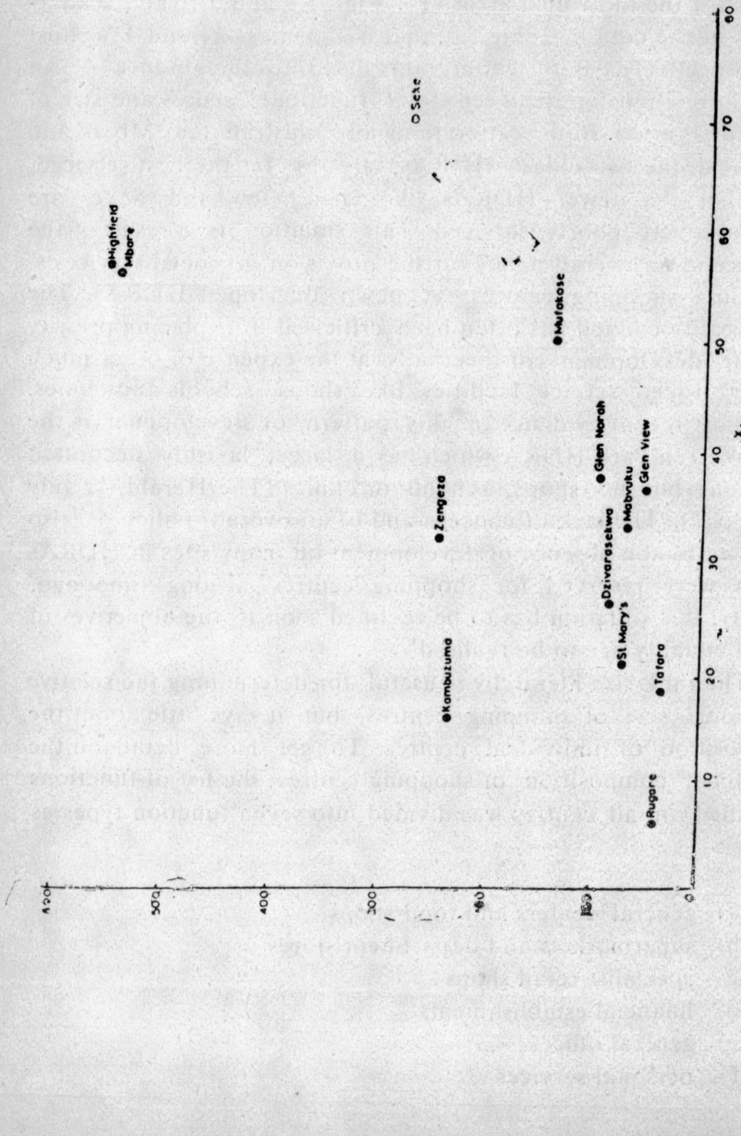

FIG. 5.9 : *HDRAs : Scattergram of total functional score (Y) against total population (X_1)*

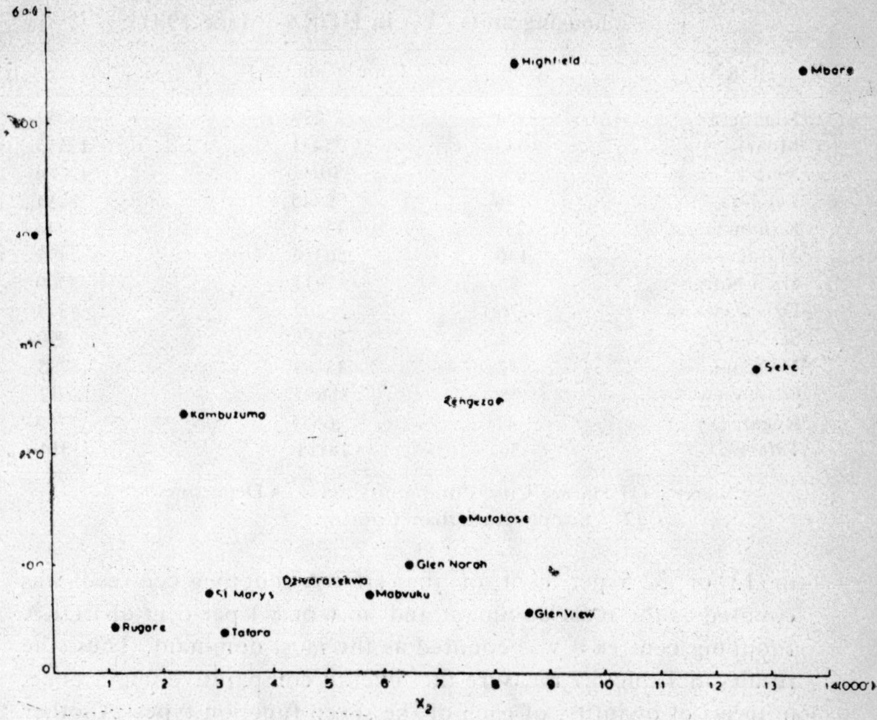

FIG. 5.10 : *HDRAs—Scattergram of total functional score* (*Y*) *against total population* (X_2)

(g) social services and administrative establishments.

The detailed composition of each of these seven function types is shown in Table 5.6. Table 5.4 shows all suburban shopping centres in rank order, and the functional composition of each of the 108 centres. In the table *s* represents the total functional score for each centre and the quantities of function types (*a*) to (*g*) in each centre are shown as percentages of *s*. For each centre the most dominant function type is underlined. Table 5.7 shows, for both HDRAs and LDRAs, the number of centres in which each of the seven function types was counted as the most dominant, that is the number of times each of (*a*) to (*g*) is underlined in Table 5.4. Taking function type (*a*) as an example,

TABLE 5.5 : **Total functional scores (Y), population (X_1) and housing units (X_2) in HDRAs (June 1981)**

HDRA	Score (Y)	Population (X_1)	Housing Units (X_2)
Highfield	552	57229	8457
Mbare	543	55431	13535
Seke	279	70190	12764
Zengeza	246	32345	8151
Kambuzuma	237	15687	2444
Mufakose	140	50350	7495
Glen Norah	99	37933	6500
Dzivarasekwa	76	26202	4348
St. Mary's	74	20569	2899
Mabvuku	72	33169	5795
Glen View	55	36652	8652
Rugare	42	6155	1182
Tafara	36	18181	3314

Source : (1) Harare City, Community Services Department
(2) Chitungwiza Urban Council.

in 13 or 32.5 per cent of the HDRA shopping centres it was counted as the most dominant and in 6 or 8.1 per cent of LDRA shopping centres it was counted as the most dominant. Thus the results in Table 5.7 measure the overall comparative importance, in terms of quantity, of each of the seven function types. Another way of measuring the overall importance of each of the seven function types in HDRA and LDRA shopping centres is by adding up all the total functional scores, s, for individual shopping centres to get the total functional score for all HDRA or LDRA centres, T ($\Sigma s = T$), and then calculating the percentages of T accounted for by each of function types (a) to (g). The results of this procedure are shown in Table 5.8.

The results in Tables 5.4, 5.7 and 5.8 show that the majority (68.9 per cent) of LDRA shopping centres are dominated by function type (c), that is specialist retail shops. On the other hand function type (a), general dealers and food shops, is the most dominant in HDRA shopping centres (32.5 per cent of the centres). These results suggest that LDRA shopping centres are specialist, providing individual high order retail functions in separate establishments or shops, while HDRA centres are more generalist, combining several functions under single premises or

TABLE 5.6 : **Functional composition of centres—Function types**

(a) General dealers and food shops.
—General dealer—large
—General dealer—small
—General food
—Butcher

(b) Supermarkets and department stores
—Supermarket—large
—Supermarket—medium
—Supermarket—small

(c) Specialist retail shops
—Bottlestore
—Chemist
—Clothing
—Electrical
—Florist
—Gifts and stationery
—Garden requisites
—Hardware
—Household soft goods
—Shoes

(d) Financial establishments
—Bank branch
—Bank agency
—Building society branch
—Building society agency
—Insurance company branch
—Insurance company agency
—Estate agents

(e) General Offices
—General business
—Surgery

(f) Personal Services
—Service station (automotive)
—Vehicle hire and sales
—Dry cleaners
—Hairdresser
—Restaurant
—Licensed premises
—Shoe repair agency
—Sports pools

(g) Social service and administrative establishments
—Clinic
—Library
—Police Station
—Post office branch
—Post office agency
—Town council hall/office

TEBLE 5.7 : **HDRA versus LDRA shopping centres—Dominant function types**

t	HDRA *n*(%)	LDRA *n*(%)
a	13(32.5)	6(8.1)
b	0(0)	4(5.4)
c	11(27.5)	51(68.9)
d	0(0)	0(0)
e	0(0)	0(0)
f	10(25.0)	13(17.6)
g	6(15.0)	0(0)

t = function types (a) to (g) (see text)
n(%)=number and percentage of centres in which that function is dominant.

TABLE 5.8 : **HDRA versus LDRA shopping centres : Average functional composition**

t	HDRA %	LDRA %
a	31.5	13.1
b	4.4	12.8
c	22.5	42.5
d	0.1	4.0
e	3.9	2.5
f	21.4	19.8
g	16.6	5.2

t=function types (a) and (g) (see text)

shops. This conforms with Davies' (1972) conclusion regarding the effect of socio-economic structure (income differences) on business provisions in shopping centres that high income area centres tend to be more specialised than centres of low income areas. The reason for this pattern, undoubtedly, is that low income residential areas cannot provide the requisite thresholds for specialised retail shops because of their low purchasing power, so that the only means by which entrepreneurs can realise profit is by combining several retail functions with different thresholds under single general dealer premises.

A significant characteristic also emerging from the results

in Tables 5.4, 5.7 and 5.8 is the absence of financial establishments in HDRAs. Although there are a few Post Office Savings Bank branches in HDRAs, the majority of residents rely on the CBD for banking, real estate and other financial transactions. On the other hand, LDRA shopping centres, particularly the larger ones, are well serviced in terms of financial establishments as shown in Table 5.4. The major commercial banks (Barclays and Standard) and major building societies (Central African Building Society—CABS—and Beverley) have branches and agencies spread all over the LDRAs. This pattern is only to be expected, given the much higher incomes of LDRA households. However, in view of the rising incomes of HDRA households (on account of the recently introduced statutory minimum wages) financial establishments in HDRA shopping centres are going to be increasingly necessary (RAL Merchant Bank, June, 1981). If the thresholds of financial functions are considered to be too high at present and in the near future, then it might be worthwhile to consider mobile agencies as an alternative solution.

In addition to functions offered, the number of vacant premises in each shopping centre were also counted. The purpose of this was to determine the level of space-efficiency, thereby reassessing Smout's (1974) contention that some of the suburban shopping centres located in LDRAs are uneconomic, and superfluous. The logic behind this is simply that where business is healthy and economic, all premises tend to be utilised, but where business is marginally economic, a lot of premises tend to become vacant. For this purpose, both LDRA and HDRA shopping centre hierarchies were divided into quartle classes as illustrated in Figs. 5.11 and 5.12. For each of the two hierarchies, the following were determined by quartile :

(i) number and percentage of centres with at least one vacant premise ; and
(ii) total number and percentage of premises vacant.

Tables 5.9 and 5.10 give the results of this exercise. In the case of LDRAs, 45.7 per cent of the 70 centres had at least one vacant premise, while the comparable figure for HDRAs was only 18.42 per cent. Of the total number of premises identified in LDRAs 8.15 per cent of them were vacant, while only 3.83 per

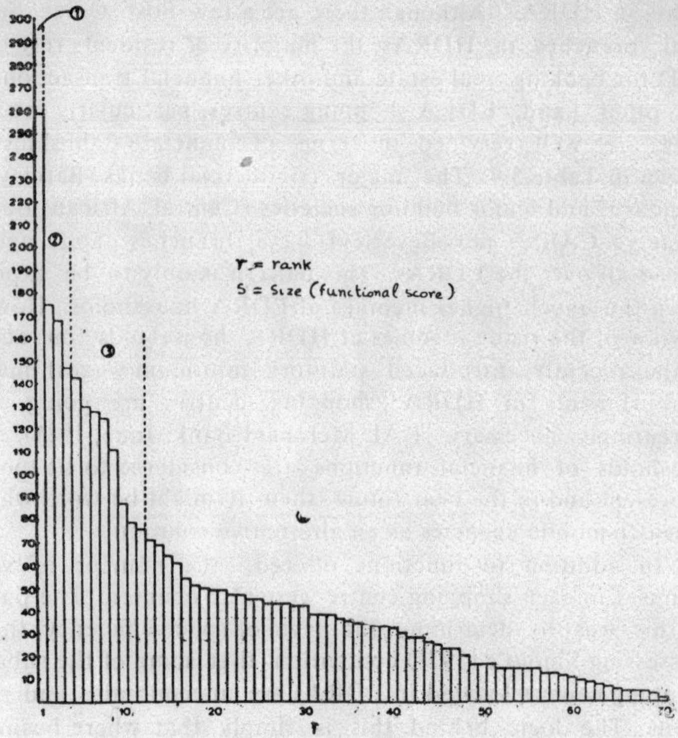

FIG. 5.11 : *LDRA centres—Quartile classes*

cent were vacant in HDRA centres. Another characteristic emerging from the data is that in the case of HDRAs, inefficient use of space (as measured by quantity of vacant premises) occurs only in the few very large centres at the upper end of the hierarchy, while there is not even a single vacant premise in quartile class 4 centres which in fact constitute 71.5 per cent of all the centres there. The opposite is true in the case of centres located in the LDRAs : Here class 4 (the smallest centres), account for most of the inefficient use of space, as evidenced by the fact that 46.55 per cent of them had at least one vacant premise, compared with zero (0) per cent in HDRA centres. From this data, it may be concluded that the LDRAs are characterised by an over provision of small space-inefficient and economically

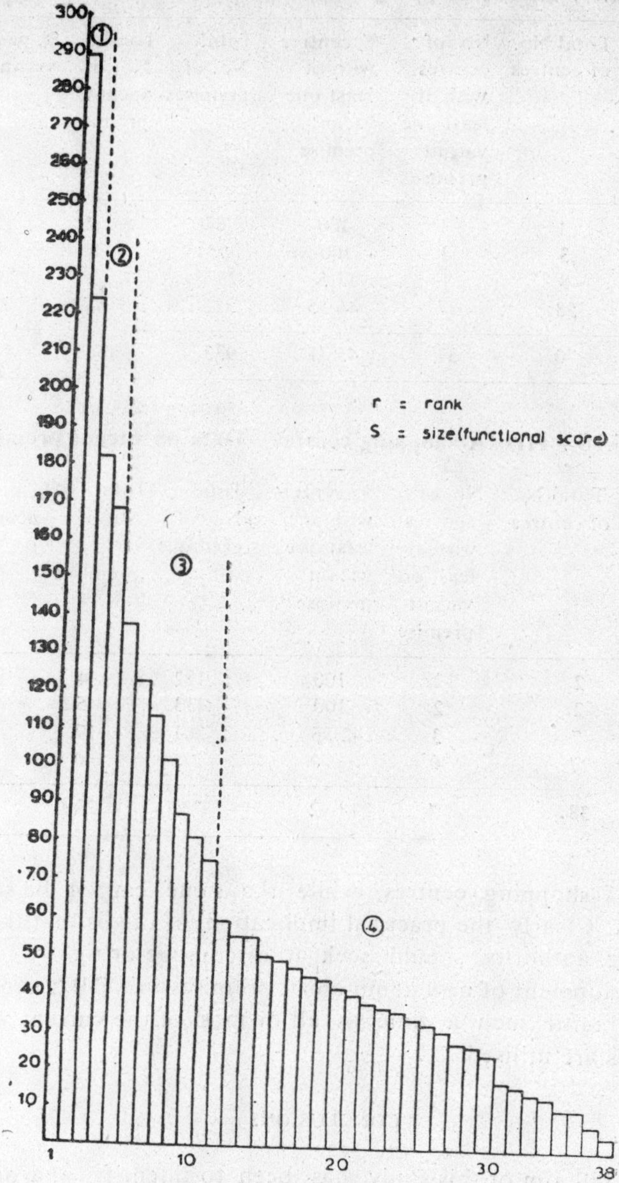

FIG. 5.12 : *HDRA centres—Quartile classes*

TABLE 5.9 : **LDRA shopping centres—Data on vacant premises**

Percentile Class	Total No. of centres	No. of centres with at least one vacant premise	% centres with at least one vacant premise	Total No. of premises	Total No. of vacant premises	% premises vacant
1	1	1	100	67	2	2.99
2	3	3	100	97	8	8.25
3	8	1	12.5	237	2	0.84
4	58	27	46.55	532	64	12.03
Total	70	32	45.71	933	76	8.15

TABLE 5.10 : **HDRA shopping centres—Data on vacant premises**

Percentile Class	Total No. of centres	No. of centres with at least one vacant premise	% centres with at least one vacant premise	Total No. of premises	Total No. of vacant premises	% premises vacant
1	2	2	100	182	4	2.2
2	2	2	100	113	5	4.42
3	7	3	42.86	201	19	9.45
4	27	0	0	236	0	0
Total	38	7	18.42	732	28	3.83

marginal shopping centres, while the same cannot be said of HDRAs. Clearly the practical implication of this is that the city planning authority should seek to discourage or tightly control the development of new commercial premises in LDRA shopping centres, until such a time as all or most of the current vacant premises are utilised.

CONCLUSIONS

The overall aim of this study has been to identify and analyse the rank-size hierarchical structure and spatial distribution characteristics of suburban shopping centres in Harare. Central place theory, as modified by Berry and Garrison, has provided the conceptual framework for analysis. The following are the major conclusions of the study, together with some of their practical implications :

(1) The hierarchy of suburban shopping centres in Harare forms a continuum rather than a stepped distribution. This confirms earlier interpretations of central place theory in the context of intra-urban locational studies, that rank size hierarchies tend to take the form of a continuum and not the stepped distribution suggested by Christaller.

(2) In spite of the fact that HDRAs carry more than 70 per cent of the city's total population shopping centre provisions in these areas are by far outnumbered by those in LDRAs. However, this disparity becomes understandable in the light of the dual socio-economic structure which characterises the city.

(3) There is a remarkable absence of financial establishments in HDRAs. This means that residents of these areas have no ready access to banks, building societies and estate agents. In view of changing economic circumstances, planning authorities and entrepreneurs alike may have much to gain by starting to disperse these functions into HDRAs. It has been suggested that if thresholds for these financial functions are too high at present, the use of mobile agencies may be a worthwhile consideration. Further, in terms of functional composition, LDRA shopping centres tend to be more specialised (as evidenced by the predominance of specialised retail shops), while HDRA centres tend to be more generalist (as evidenced by the pre-ponderance of general dealers and general food shops).

(4) In LDRA shopping centres, particularly the smaller ones, there is a higher percentage of vacant premises than in comparable HDRA centres, confirming Smout's (1974) conclusion that some of the LDRA centres are superfluous and only economically marginal. The practical implication of this, it has been suggested is that the city planning authority may have to tightly control the development of new commercial premises in the foreseeable future to enable full utilization of the current vacant premises.

(5) With regard to HDRAs, there is currently no systematic relationship between the size of residential areas (as measured by total population and total number of households) and the quantity of shopping centre provisions (as measured by total

functional score for the area). This situation appears to be a result of firstly, the absence of locational planning policy and, secondly, the absence of plan implementation strategies. With regard to locational planning policy, it is suggested that the central place theory concept of hierarchy may be a useful guide-line, as has been found to be the case in the U.K. (Szumeluk 1967 ; Davies 1976). The absence of shopping centre plan implementation strategies is a particular instance of a more general problem in urban development—the limited and sometimes counterproductive view that *Planners plan and developers develop.* As Lichfield and Darin-Drabkin comment, the result of this traditional attitude is "that much more attention has been given, in theory and in practice, to plan making as opposed to plan implementation" (Lichfield and Darin-Drabkin 1980, p. 22). An urban planning authority is, in theory, supposed to perform the following roles : (a) Policy making role ; (b) Control-regulative role (through land use plans and building regulations) ; (c) Managerial role (managing urban change through co-ordination of the different components of the urban system and seeing to the day-to-day maintenance of utilities on behalf of the public) ; and (d) Promotional role (promoting development through mechanisms designed to facilitate timely implementation of plans). In general, planners have tended to concentrate on (a) and (b), through physical development regulations and land zoning, to the detriment of (c) and (d). The first two functions (a and b) constitute what may be termed *negative-reactive* planning while the last two (c and d) constitute what may be termed '*positive-proactive*' *planning*. As suggested by Lichfield and Darin-Drabkin (1980) urban planning authorities can achieve positive-proactive planning by the following means :

(i) Ensuring that land is made available for development in the right place at the right time and at the right price and tenure ;
(ii) Taking over the development function itself, either on their own or as land owners in association with private property developers and financiers in order to have not only landlord control of building development but also that of a partner.

With regard to the implementation of HDRA shopping centre plans, it is suggested that in future proper measures must be taken to ensure that basic shopping centre facilities together with other public facilities like schools and clinics, become available at roughly the same time as the houses of a new residential development are occupied. To facilitate this, the city planning authority may consider direct involvement in shopping centre property development in the manner outlined above. This recommendation is scarcely a radical departure, in view of the fact that such participation is already taking place in the provision of one function of shopping centres—beer and liquor drinking facilities. It should be noted, however, that such direct participation entails a widening of local authority financial resources. Timely implementation of plans also demands a clear exposition of the roles and responsibilities, individual or shared, of the three usual plan implementation agencies--the city planning authority, central government and private entrepreneurs.

REFERENCES

Berry, B.J.L. and Garrison, W.L., "Recent Developments of Central Place Theory", *Papers and Proceedings of the Regional Science Association*, 4, 1958, pp. 107-20.

Berry, B.J.L. and Garrison, W.L., "Functional Bases of the Central Place Hierarchy", *Economic Geography*, 34, 1958, pp. 145-54.

Berry, B.J.L. and Garrison, W.L., "A Note on Central Place Theory and the Range of Good", *Economic Geography*, 34, 1958, pp. 304-11.

Christaller, W., *Central Places in Southern Germany*, Prentice Hall, 1966 (translated from German into English by Baskin, C).

Christopher, A.J., "Early Settlement and the Cadastral Framework", in Kay G. and Smout M. (eds.), *Salisbury : A Geographical Survey of the Cap'tal of Rhodesia*, Hodder and Stoughton, 1977.

Davies, R.L., "Structural Models of Retail Distribution", *Transactions of the Institute of British Geographers*, 57, 1972, pp. 59-82.

Davies, R.L., *Marketing Geography : With Special Reference to Retailing*, Methuen, 1976.

Downs, R.M., "The Cognitive Structure of an Urban Shopping Centre", *Environment and Behaviour*, 2, 1970, pp. 13-39.

Gargett, E., *The Administration of Transition : African Urban Settlement in Rhodesia*, Mambo Press, 1977.

Hoek-Smit, M.C., *Socio-Economic Survey : Harare (High Density Areas)*, June, 1982.

Huff, D.L., *Determination of Intra-Urban Retail Trade Areas*, University of California, Los Angeles, Real Estate Programme, 1962.

Huff, D.L., "A Probabilistic Analysis of Shopping Centre Trade Areas", *Land Economics*, 39, 1963, pp. 81-90.

Isard, W., *Location and Space Economy*, MIT, 1956.

Lichfield, N. and Darin-Drabkin, H., *Land Policy in Planning*, George Allen and Unwin, 1980.

Mutizwa, Damson, N., *Planning Suburban Service Centres in Harare : A Study of Structure, Use Patterns and Needs with Special Reference to Retailing in High Density Residential Areas*, Regional and Urban Planning Centre, University of Zimbabwe, 1982.

National Economic Development Office (NEDO), *Urban Models in Shopping Studies*, N.E.D.O. (London), 1970.

Ral Merchant Bank Ltd., *Executive Guide to the Economy*, Zimbabwe, Harare, June, 1981.

Smout, M.A.H., *Service Centres in Greater Salisbury, Rhodesia*, Ph. D. Thesis, University of London, 1971.

Smout M.A.H., *Commercial Growth and Consumer Behaviour in Suburban Salisbury, Rhodesia*, M.A. Thesis, University of Newcastle-Upon-Tyne, 1974.

Smout, M.A.H. "The Suburban Shopping Centres", in Kay, G. and Smout, M. (eds.), *Salisbury : A Geographical Survey of the Capital of Rhodesia*. Hodder and Stoughton, 1977.

Szumeluk, K., *Central Place Theory : Its Role in Planning with Particular Reference to Retailing*, Centre for Environmental Studies, Working Paper 9, 1967.

The Herald, Monday, July, 1982, p. 5.

Zimbabwe Central Statistical Office, *Higher Income Expenditure Survey*, 1977/78.

Zimbabwe Central Statistical Office, *Monthly Digest of Statistics*, June, 1981.

SIX

JAWAHAR LAL JAIN

URBAN SYSTEM OF MALWA
An Approach to Structure and Organisation of Urban Hierarchy

INTRODUCTION

An holistic perspective

GEOGRAPHICAL studies of individual towns, whatever their depth and detail of treatment, constitute merely a piecemeal treatment, unless they lead to the general picture of urban situation of a region as a whole. This is particularly so because geography seeks to discern regions with an unmistakable degree of unity and coherence within each region. This intrinsic unity and coherence may relate to 'anatomical homogeneity'—as in the case of a formal region characterised by uniformity of basic elements and components that make the geographical personality of the region ; or, much more importantly, it may relate to 'physiological wholeness', i.e., completeness of functional organisation of the region as a spatial system as in the case of what has come to be known as a functional or nodal region. This point of view, a holistic, panoramic perspective of regions, for an urban geographer can be realised only when he can conceive out of the entities of individual towns a fabric of inter-woven components and elements, which together, and through their complementary functioning, comprise an urban system. Through this role, they, in fact, render the region an operational entity and functional whole. Set amid the rural populace, these towns of various sizes and orders, make the cardinal points of the functional regional system, where its key functions are discharged so that the whole engine of the regional system keeps rolling. In essence, the towns, in this approach, are looked upon as 'parts of a whole', as functional centres of a system. It is the way the regional spatial system is organised and keeps its life apace that is emphasized, i.e., its structural and operational aspects. This conceptualisation of regional urban system, or of the spatial organisation of a whole society, takes geography closest to the 'organic theory of society'. No wonder then that although Walter Christaller (1933) is the celebrated pioneer who gave a theory of the organisational structure of such a system with a sound field example (his classical Central Place Theory), the rudiments of these ideas are traceable in the works of certain sociologists, such as Lalaune (1863), Galpin (1915) and Kolb (1923), much before Christaller.

Though a hierarchical taxonomy can be applied to any type of regions, it is most fruitfully applied to functional or nodal regions. Granting that a higher order town has functional complexes appropriate to all the lower orders also, apart, of course, from that of its own specific order, it is obvious that towns of various rank orders as well as their hinterlands of various orders should inherently group themselves with or within one or the other of higher order hinterlands.

This nesting pattern of hinterlands (nodal regions) and the grouping or alignment pattern of towns, with specific size, spacing and functional characteristics comprise the structural elements of central place hierarchy. It is through such an organisation that a set of towns distributed over a certain territory functions as an urban system.

Rank-size relationship

A parallel approach

In the meanwhile, there has evolved another parallel approach towards discerning a coherent system in a spatial organisation. It is represented by studies on what has popularly come to be known as the 'Rank-Size Relationship'. This is, in fact, a diagnostic analysis which verifies the existence of a system of cities in only a very subtle manner. Vertical distribution of city sizes, in fact, forms yet another dimension of an urban system. As obviously derives from fundamental logic, there occur progressively fewer towns of larger size and the vice-versa, so that city size distributions are strongly skewed positively (Richardson 1973, p. 239). As later substantiated through the hierarchical analysis of towns, the rank size curve for Malwa also clearly attests to the fact that towns of Malwa together comprise an urban system, and the city size curve stands in good harmony with the 'Rank-Size Rule' of Zipf (1941), as well as the stepped curve of city size distribution postulated by the Christaller-Loschian model of central place theory. It stands, in fact, between these two rather radically different curves of city size distribution (Jain 1980).*

DEFINING URBAN HIERARCHY

Assessment of methodological problem

The methodological problem is complex and multi-dimensional. One aspect is the determination of the centrality status and breaking the array of towns into discrete groups. Another aspect is the delimitation of hinterlands of towns of different orders of central services. Both of them involve further problems. For the first, there is no single yardstick to measure the general or total centrality of places. No single function is so all important, and no two functions have perfect correlation between them so that any one of them might be taken. Therefore, one is forced to select a number of significant criteria, which corners the worker to subjective decisions regarding this selection. Then again, there is the fundamental problem of combining them into a single index giving the total or general centrality status of towns. Unless the functions are valued in terms of a common unit, they cannot be combined. Also it involves the problem of weighting the functions before they can be rationally combined. To this effect one has first to convert the counts of each function in some index of score points, then give them appropriate relative

* For explanations for this apparently incompatible situation, see Jain (1980) 'Spatial Structure of Urban Settlement System of Malwa Plateau, M.P. : Distribution and Connectivity of Towns' paper read at the National Seminar on 'Settlement Systems of India', Hyderabad ; Robson, B.T. (1973) 'Urban Growth : An Approach', pages 27-37, London, and Jain (1979) 'The Growth and Distribution of Towns in the Malwa Plateau, M.P., Unpublished Doctoral Dissertation, University of Saugar, Sagar, M.P.

weightage, before they can finally be summed up to get total centrality index of each town. Giving proper relative weight to each function, in an objective way, is, however, a very tentalising and elluding problem. Deriving from this there appears the problem of hinterland delimitation. Each of the central services selected draws its clientage from territories which coincide with those for other services only very approximately and roughly, and some adjustment of hinterland boundaries becomes an indispensable manipulation, in order to outline a composite or general hinterland boundary. Moreover, as is implicit in the central placed theory, while each high order town has a correspondingly larger hinterland, it also has smaller hinterlands for each successively lower order of function. 'No such thing (hinterland) exists without appropriate qualification as to the level at which it is being considered' (Carter 1972, p. 101).

Nevertheless, the rationality of such a hierarchical scheme derives from the general experience which leads to the contention that 'certain functions will become associated in distinctive complexes, each complex in turn associated with a fairly clearly marked grade or rank in the hierarchy' (Carter 1972, p. 101). The same contention holds also for the hinterlands of these functional complexes or 'trait complexes'. Related with the problem of adjustment of hinterland boundaries is also, sometimes, the problem of their nesting.

The present method of town ranking

The method employed for the present study consists of selecting a set of significant criteria of centrality, hereafter called the central functions or services, for all towns of the region, giving them some relative weightages, and summing up these weighted values for all functions for each town—the general centrality score. The towns are then grouped into hierarchical orders of centrality on the basis of this total centrality score by locating natural breaks in the array of this score. Hinterlands are, however, delimited by single, most significant criterion—the predominant orientation of bus service linkages, the bus service nodality.

Key criteria

Selected Central Services—Criteria selected for the present study are divisible into 3 groups :

(1) (a) Administration, (b) Education, (c) Postal services, (d) Hospitals, (e) Hospital beds, (f) Banks and credit societies, (g) Cinemas, (h) Number of telephones.
(2) Bus service nodality—number of total and qualifying daily bus services.
(3) Population size of towns.

Bus services nodality is treated separately because :

(1) it is much more important than any other single function ;
(2) whereas other criteria are only institutional symptoms of presence of a function, bus service directly is a flow link between town and country ; and
(3) hinterlands are delimited by this criterion ; therefore, it was imperative to work out a separate hierarchy by this criterion alone also.

Population size is first treated as a yardstick against which the total score of central services, and that of bus nodality of towns were examined, and correlated. Then population itself was treated as a third group of traits of centrality, because not only is population size a good indicator of general status of towns, particularly in a region where most of towns are essentially central places such as Malwa is, but also because population—whether in central or non-central sectors—provides market for rural population around through its needs for essential services such as daily supply of milk, vegetables, foodgrains, general labour and other maintenance services, etc.

Weighting the central services

In order to work out total centrality of towns, centrality values given to a town by each function needed to be summed up. A fundamental prerequisite of any combination of different functions is that they should be properly weighted and converted into a common unit. In the want of a simple and yet sound method of weighting, a method was devised, partly deriving from Aboidun (1967) and Davies (1967). In the first stage, two sub-groups of central services were recognised :

(a) Those, that were given in the form of total numbers,

like telephone connections, banks, cinemas, and number of hospital beds. These numbers are very large.

(b) those in which certain conventional categories are recognised, and units of each category are separately given, such as university, college, and schools, or state headquarters, divisional headquarters, district headquarters and tahsil headquarters, etc. For this latter class of functions, higher categories were given higher score points, in a geometric progression, such that each higher category was given double the score points than the immediately lower category. Thus, if a town had one head post office, three sub-post offices, and seven branch post offices, each of which bore 20, 10 and 5 score points, respectively then the total score in postal services in that town would be

$$(1 \times 20)+(3 \times 10)+(7 \times 5)=20+30+35=85 \text{ points };$$

similarly for other towns.

Whereas the common sense rationality of this scoring on the basis of general categorisation of such services, prevalent in the region, recommends itself, the procedure involves some critical decisions, such as follows :

(1) The value of lowest category—there is only a limited danger of subjective arbitration in this, because it would affect all the towns similarly, so that their relative position would not be disturbed. Even if some other value were selected there is no reason, notes Aboidun (1967, p. 181) why same order of hierarchy should not reproduce.

(2) Number of categories recognised—this is an extremely critical decision, and with immense caution the conventional division was followed.

(3) The manner of progression of score points to successively higher categories—a common knowledge of usual relative number of functional units in each category, and their relative status, suggests that this progression should be geometrical. But, again the critical decision was as to the multiplying constant. To avoid amplification of implicit complications, this was kept at the lowest whole number that could give a progression, i.e., 2.

Obviously, the whole procedure involves certain critical decisions. To reduce to the minimum the subjective element, the same score —5— of lowest category and same progression with the same multiplying constant-2 was adopted for all functions concerned. Number of categories was also kept at 3 for postal and hospital services, and at 4 for educational services.

In the second stage of weighting, these score points for second sub-groups, and original numbers for the first sub-group were arranged in a common table. Now proceeding along the line of Davies (1967, p. 63), these values were weighted in the inverse proportion of the total of respective functions, i.e., larger the total smaller proportionately will be value of its each unit. To effect this, each function was summed up and the mean of the sums worked out as follows :

$$\bar{f} = \frac{f_1 + f_2 + \ldots . fn}{n}$$

Where n is number of functions ; f =function ; and

$\bar{f}$=the mean sum.

Then ratio of mean sum to the total of each function was worked out :

$$Rf_1 = \frac{\bar{f}}{f_1} \; ; \; Rf_2 = \frac{\bar{f}}{f_2} \; ; \; Rf_n = \frac{\bar{f}}{f_n}$$

Where, Rf is the ratio of corresponding function to the mean sum $\bar{f}$.

TABLE 6.1 : **Ratios of $\frac{\text{Mean sum}}{\text{Actual sum}}$ or $\frac{\bar{f}}{f}$ for various functions**

Rf_1	$\frac{\bar{f}}{f_1}$	Administration	5.951
Rf_2	$\frac{\bar{f}}{f_2}$	Education	1.136
Rf_3	$\frac{\bar{f}}{f_3}$	Postal Service	0.838
Rf_4	$\frac{\bar{f}}{f_4}$	Hospitals	1.562
Rf_5	$\frac{\bar{f}}{f_5}$	Hospitals Beds	0.487
Rf_6	$\frac{\bar{f}}{f_6}$	Banking & Credit Service	0.543
Rf_7	$\frac{\bar{f}}{f_7}$	Cinemas	2.160
Rf_8	$\frac{\bar{f}}{f_8}$	Telephones	1.137

These Rf values are the weights of each function relative to the mean sum. The values of all towns for each function were then reduced by the corresponding ratios—its *Rf* values—and re-arranged in the final table.

By summing up these weighted values of all functions for each town, the total centrality score was arrived at. Plotting these values against population size of towns (Fig 6.3a) hierarchical orders can be identified easily.

Results of the analysis

Figure 6.3(a) showing centrality score of towns plotted against their population sizes on a log-log scale, clearly reveals 5 discrete hierarchical orders. Of them first two are quite obvious, and the third one also fairly discrete, but the fourth order containing the bulk of small towns, is rather much diffused, both in range of central score as well as in the population sizes it covers. The lower most class with less than 50 score and below 8 thousand population size, and containing only 6 towns, is pretty insignificant. The number of towns in each class, and their progression for the rank orders is as follows :

TABLE 6.2 : **Malwa —Hierarchical classes of towns based on centrality scores**

Class	I		II		III		IV		V
Number of towns	2		3		11		62		6
Co-efficient of progression ('K' values)		1.5		4		5.5		0.1	

An important excercise in most of the central place studies has been to show correspondence between centrality and population of centres. In the case of Malwa, which has much fewer and lesser cases of non-central place towns, the present study shows a fairly high positive correlation, $r = (+)\ 0.70$, between them. Also, there are fairly discrete and diagnostic population ranges corresponding to each rank order of the hierarchy, which are given in Table 6.3 (barring only 2 or 3 obvious and notable deviants).

At this juncture, it would be an immensely interesting exercise to compare the characteristic population ranges with

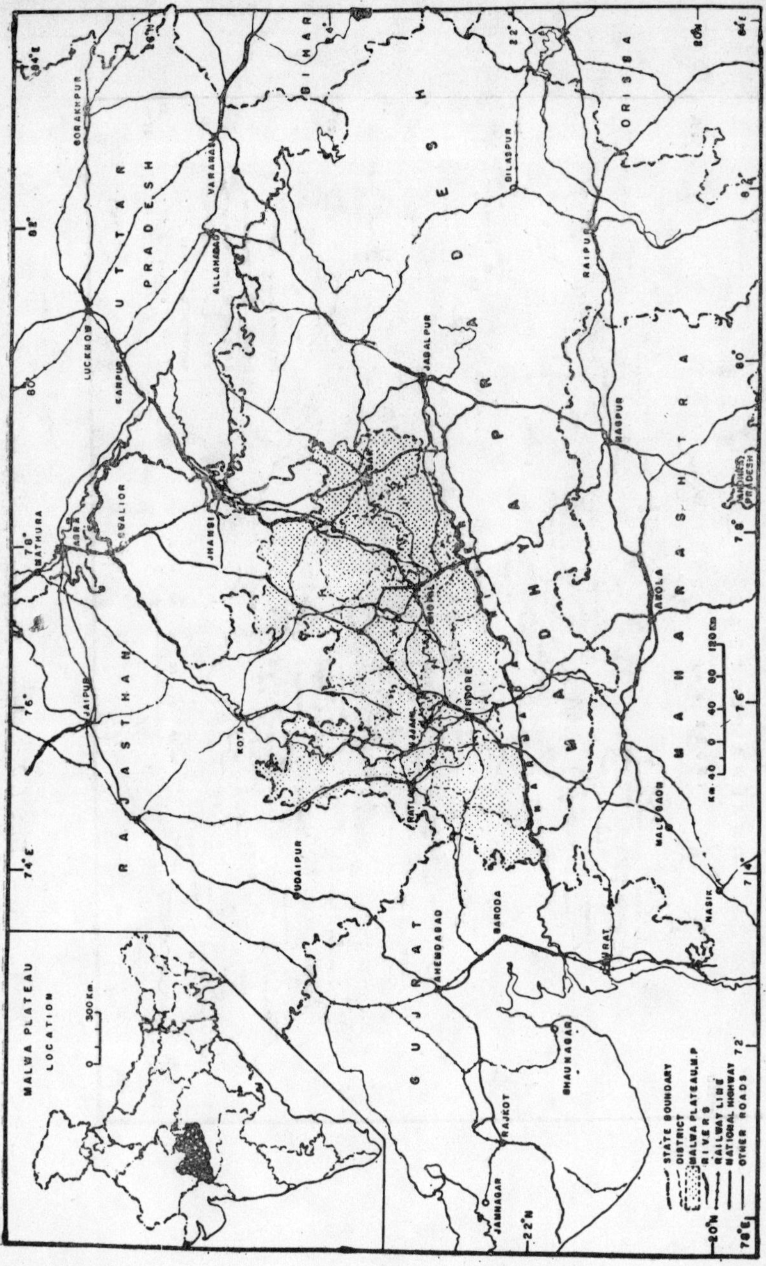

FIG. 6.1 : *Malwa Plateau—Regional setting*

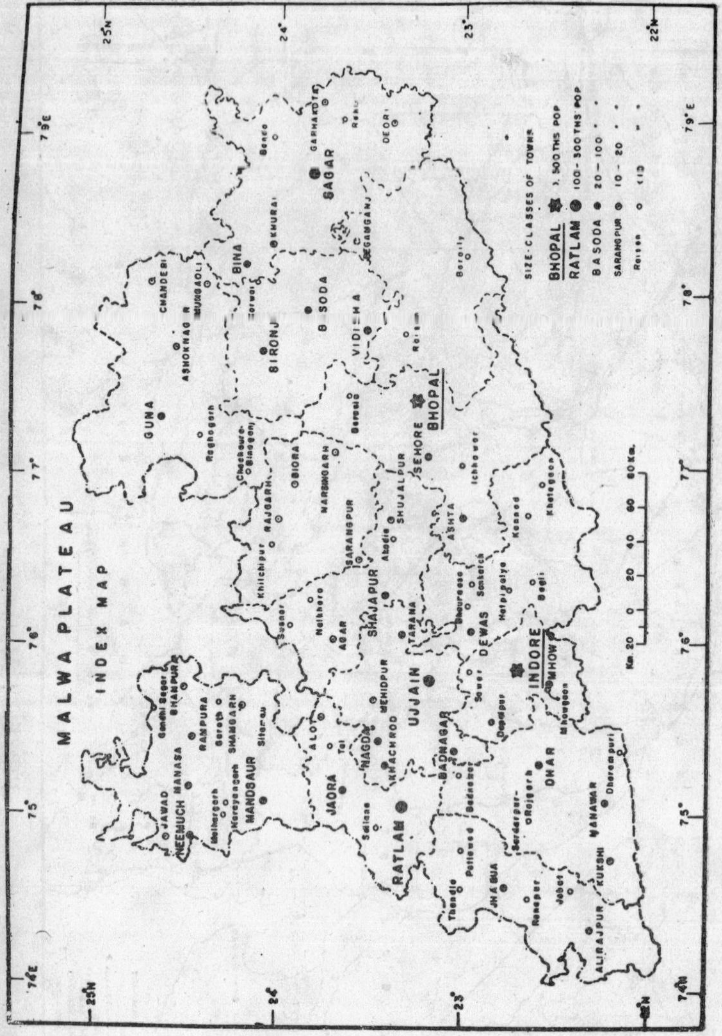

FIG. 6.2 : *Malwa Plateau—Index Map*

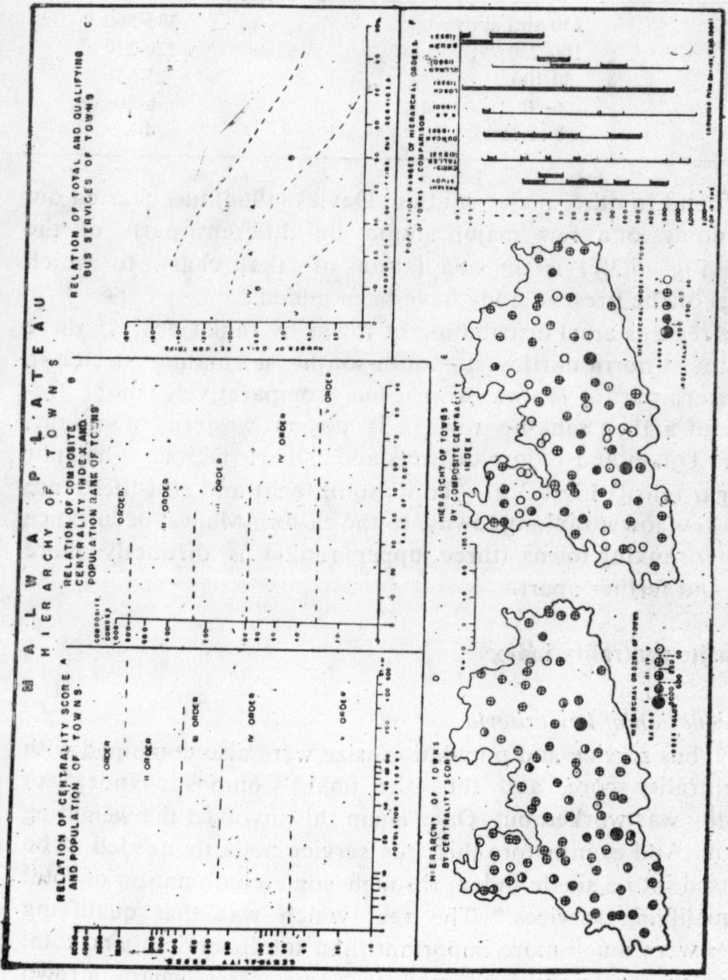

FIG. 6.3 (a)(b)(c)(d)(e)(f)(g): *Malwa Plateau—Hierarchy of towns*

TABLE 6.3 : **Malwa—Population ranges corresponding to hierarchical classes**

Class	Population range (Continuous) (in '000)	Population range (Discrete) (in '000)
I	250 and above	385-560
II	100-250	120-210
III	30-100	25-65
IV	6-30	6-20
V	8 or less	4-8

those found in other major studies. Davies (1964) has charted out such findings of a few major studies in different parts of the world. Fig. 6.3(f) is an adaptation of that chart, to which findings of the present study have been added.

As regards areal distribution of towns by rank orders, there is an almost north-northwest—south-southeast running stretch in the western part of Malwa which has comparatively more frequency of higher ranking towns. It covers western Mandsaur, Ratlam, Ujjain and Indore districts and Dhar, Dewas, Shajapur and Agar tahsils Fig 6.3(g). To its south-west and east there are quite a few lower ranking towns. In the eastern Malwa, occurrence of higher ranking towns (three upper ranks) is distinctly more spotty and farther apart.

Composite centrality index

A combination of key criteria

Finally, bus service and population size were also combined with the centrality score, and thus the final 'Composite Index' of centrality was worked out. Once again this involved the weighting problem. And even before this, bus service nodality needed to be converted into a single index through some combination of total and qualifying services.* The real which was that qualifying services were much more important than total services, and total services were seriously boomed in some cases where a town happened to be on a thoroughfare or very near a big city. Therefore, to combine them, with least ambiguity, the total and the qualifying bus services were multiplied and the square root of the

* The distinction between the 'total' and the 'qualifying' bus services is explained in the following section, 'Nodal Regions of Malwa'.

product was extracted. But in this, the towns with nil qualifying services and good many total services were drastically belittled as this gave them a zero value. In such cases, therefore, root of half the number of total services was taken. So derived, the bus service nodality index gives a very high direct correlation ($r = +0.97$) with centrality score and with population size of towns.

Now all the three variables were tabulated and bus service index, and centrality score were weighted proportionately by ratio of their respective totals to the total population size. The weighted values, were then combined with population size, which gave the overall or 'Composite Index' of centrality of each town. By plotting these 'Composite Index' values against population size ranks of towns Fig. 6.3(b) was obtained, on which again 5 hierarchical rank orders are identified. Here again the orders are quite distinct and discrete at top, and become progressively less so down the hierarchy. Upper three rank orders are almost self-evident. Thence downwards, there is more or less continuous scatter of points, so that the class limit between IV and V class is weak with only narrow gaps at 30 and 35 on the scale of composite Index. Here 30 has been taken as the limit, though Sonkatch town is almost on it (29.8). The upper three classes here again have much the same members as they do in the corresponding classes of centrality score, with only one notable change—Rajgarh from its high position in class III has now fallen to class IV, because not only it is very small (11.5 thousand population) in size, but in bus service nodality also it is quite poor. It is only in services that this town is rather unusually high. Two rather large towns, Bina and Nagda, could not improve their positions here also, because both are poor in bus-service nodality. They are simply special purpose, non-central towns, extremely specialised in single function ; but the case of Bina badly exposes a glaring weakness or inadequacy of data-base, as only road passenger traffic was considered and railway service excluded. That is why this solely railway junction town is though extremely specialised in transport, it appears so poor in passenger transport nodality.

Two lower classes are, however, not comparable. On the Centrality Score, IV class has 62 towns, while the V class has only 6, whereas in the Composite Index they have 40 and 30 towns, respectively.

Difference between the results of the two analyses

The overall difference in the results of Centrality Score and Composite Index is that quite a few towns, particularly the smaller ones, have moved a little downwards. This is because many of criteria or central functions are somewhat administration-biased. Not only is administration incorporated directly, but certain services like post offices, colleges, banks, etc., also are planned to locate conformally with administrative hierarchy. Thus, many of the small towns have some substantial central functions largely because they are headquarters of a tahsil, or sometimes even of a district. Raisen and Rajgarh are good examples of this situation. It shows that towns below about 20-25 thousand level are mostly incipient and indistinguishable from one another. What matters them most is : (1) whether they are headquarters of at least a tahsil or not, and (2) whether they stand on an important route or not, or at the junction of a few routes, at least one of them being an important route. An under-current, ubiquitous factor is, of course, the density of rural population.

Thus, there is but a mild change in results of ranking first by Centrality Score and subsequently by Composite Index. As such there is little difference in the distributional pattern of towns resulting from the two indices. Western Malwa, particularly the same tract covering districts of Mandsaur, Ratlam, Ujjain and Indore, and the adjacent tahsils of Dhar and Dewas continues to have a dominant share in towns of upper three classes, while in eastern Malwa they are fewer and farther apart Fig. 6.3(e). This difference between eastern and western part of Malwa has become slightly accentuated from Centrality Score to Composite Index result. This is because in the two indices, bus service nodality is the major differentiating factor, which is usually better developed in the towns of western Malwa than in those of eastern Malwa [Fig. 6.3(a) & 6.3(b)].

Nodal regions of malwa

Bus service hinterland definition

In order to avoid the tentalising problem of adjustment of boundaries, noted before, to workout composite hinterlands, the latter were delimited on the basis of the predominant orientation of passenger road transport services only. To a large extent, the method derives from the use of number of public road transport services between town and country and amongst the towns, as applied by Green (1950) and later further accomplished by Carruthers (1957). In such studies the passenger road transport links are employed as means defining areas looking to certain places which act as service centres, the assumption here made is that the count of the amount and type of public road transport into any centre, reflecting physical accessibility and the existence of some sort of town-country association, will give a fair indication of status (of towns) (Carruthers 1957, p. 372). The relevance and significance of bus service nodality may be assessed by the fact that it has a very high positive co-efficient of correlation with Centrality Score ($r=0.97$) and with the population size of towns ($r=0.97$), while a high value ($r=0.70$) obtains between these two latter elements.

To delimit hinterlands of towns at various orders of hierarchy it was inherently imperative to work out a hierarchical ranking of towns also by this criterion solely. Now out of the total number of return bus services issuing from or passing through a town such services were dintinguished and counted separately as served no place larger than itself. Thus there were two sets of data—the number of total daily return trips from or through each town, and from amongst them the number of daily return trips serving no place larger than the origin town itself. This is a fundamental distinction recognised by both Green and Carruthers (Carruthers 1957, p. 373). Following the logic that a bus service linking a number of towns should be regarded as belonging to the largest of them,* they contend, that services issuing from a town serving only smaller places should accrue to the bus service centrality of nodality of the town,** and remaining, through services, while strengthening its linkages to some other larger town/s, do not add to the centrality of the town in question. Thus while the total number of services indicates the strength of functional relationship of a town with both larger and the smaller towns as well as the villages, the number of services to only smaller places

* Here the larger or smaller towns should refer to their centrality status ; however, the population size is also almost as good as measure.

**The terms 'nodes and centres' as well as 'nodality and centrality' are regarded here as having the same meaning and are thus used interchangeably here.

signifies the extent to which a town is functioning as an independent centre for other smaller places around. The latter are thus regarded as 'qualifying' services, i.e., services the presence of which qualifies a town to be deemed as a functional centre of an area. To express these latter services relative to the former they are converted as percentage of the former.

Plotting these total daily return bus services on *Y*-axis against qualifying services expressed as percentage of the former on the *X*-axis, Fig. 6.3(c) was obtained. On this scatter plot 5 more or less discrete orders are easily discernible. It should be noted that both the class I towns—Indore and Bhopal—fall outside the graph, so that boundary between I and II classes does not appear on the graph.

Though a sub-class each has been recognised the II, III and IV classes, separate hinterlands for rank orders of these sub-classes has not been attempted. Also, hinterland boundaries have been drawn actually for only upper three rank orders. Grouping or nesting of towns into classes involved an intrinsic combination, with the numerical method indicated, of personal judgement and a knowledge of local conditions in some cases. Now, towns were again grouped into five orders of bus service nodality (which was worked out by multiplying the total and the qualifying services and extracting the root of the product, as explained in the preceding pages).

To delimit the hinterlands, also called nodal regions, the number of daily return bus services from each town to all other towns of the region were noted in the form of a matrix, on the basis of which a linkages map was prepared in the form of a topological graph, showing bus linkages as direct radial lines from each town to all those towns with which it has bus connections and to the country-side. These radial lines were grouped, or quantified, according to the number of daily return bus trips they represented. This map portrays the relative nodal status as well as the orientation of towns (i.e , the volume, range, and direction of nodality). On the basis of this linkage (Fig. 6.4), hinterland boundaries were drawn as noted before, also keeping in view, where necessary, terrain conditions, route orientation, administrative boundaries, and physical accessibility of local areas. Thus, nodal regions were obtained showing boundaries of hinterlands of upper three rank orders only, to which the towns classified by

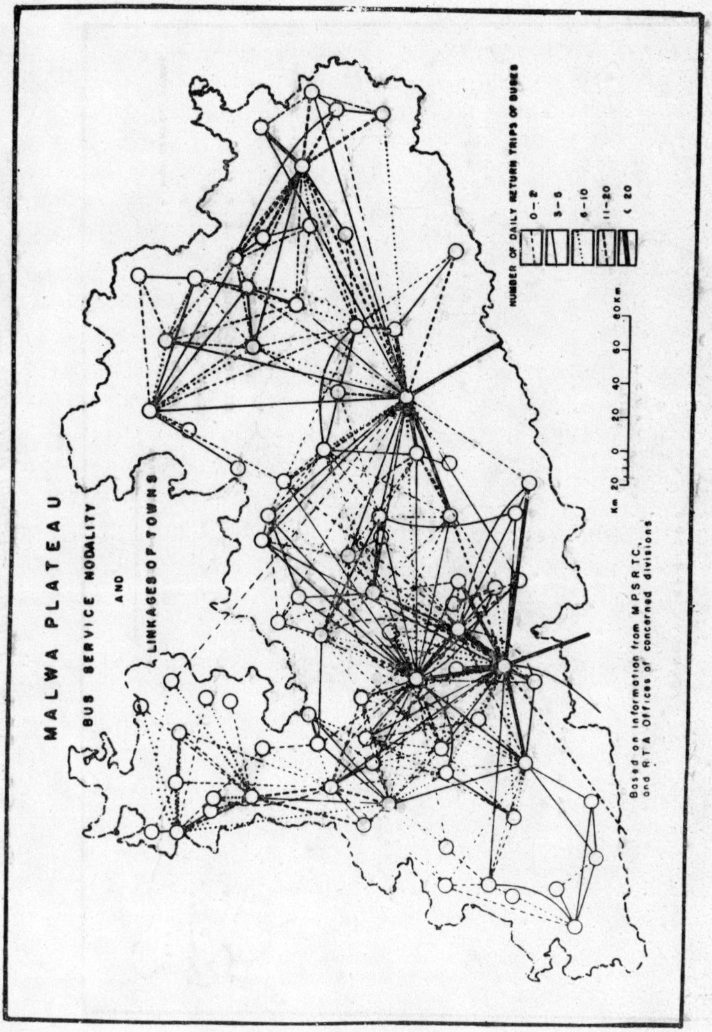

FIG. 6.4 : *Malwa Plateau—Bus service modality and linkages of towns*

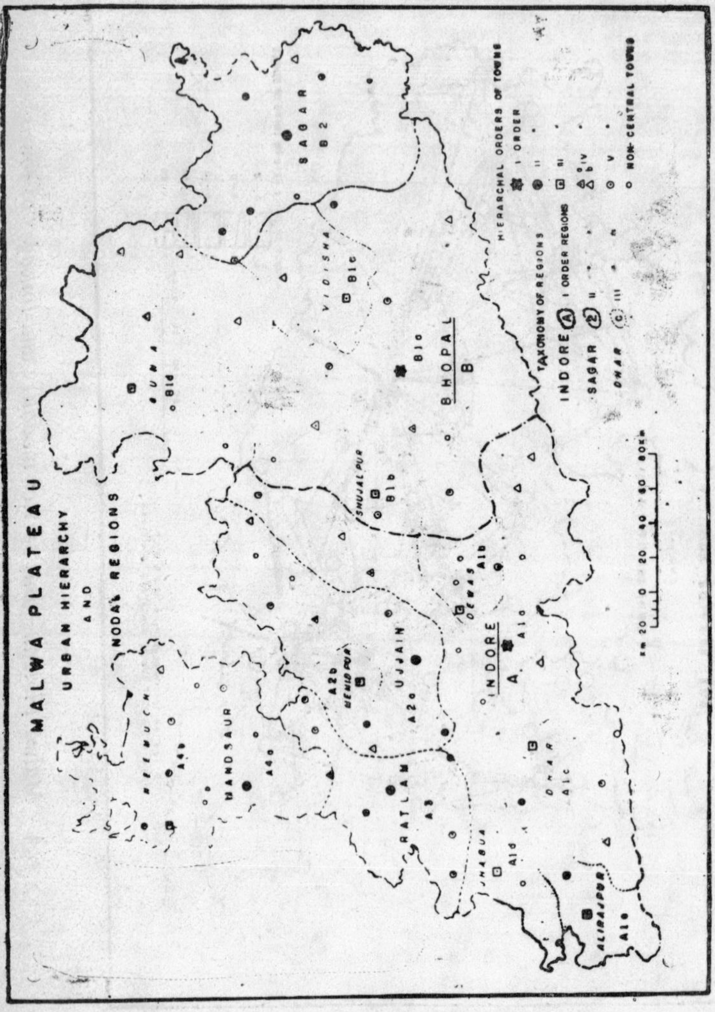

FIG. 6.5 : *Malwa Plateau—Urban hierarchy and modal regions*

ranks of bus service nodality were also added, so that the map provides a complete picture of bus service hierarchy and nodal regions. This map has also facilitated the association or nesting of lower order towns to the appropriate higher order towns.

Regional taxonomy and nested urban hierarchy of Malwa

On the basis of bus service linkages amongst towns and from towns to the country-side, Malwa is divided into 2 I-order regions—western and eastern Malwa, commanded respectively by Indore and Bhopal cities. Western Malwa is further sub-divided into 4 II-order and 10 III-order regions, while the eastern Malwa is sub-divided into 2 II-order and 5 III-order regions. Thus there are 2 I-order, 6 II-order, and 15 III-order regions, each commanded by an urban centre of corresponding order of hierarchy.

TABLE 6.4 : **Malwa—Taxonomy of nodal regions**

MALWA

I Order
- A Western Malwa (Indore)
- B Eastern Malwa (Bhopal)

II Order / III Order (Eastern Malwa)
- B1 Bhopal
  - B 1a Bhopal
  - B 1b Shujalpur
  - B 1c Vidisha
  - B 1d Guna
- B2 Sagar
  - B 2a Sagar

(Western Malwa)
- A1 Indore
  - A 1a Indore
  - A 1b Dewas
  - A 1c Dhar
  - A 1d Jhabua
  - A 1e Alirajpur
- A2 Ujjain
  - A 2a Ujjain
  - A 2b Mehidpur
- A3 Ratlam
  - A 3a Ratlam
- A4 Mandsaur
  - A 4a Mandsaur
  - A 4b Neemuch

Besides the centres of the upper echelons of nodal regions, other humbler places—of IV and the V order—are nested with appropriate III-order centres on the basis of relative distance, connectivity, route orientation and other local geographical conditions.

TABLE 6.5 : **Malwa—Nested hierarchy of smaller towns**

III Order Centres	Nested IV order towns	Nested V order and other non-central towns
A 1a Indore	A 1ai Indore	Susner*, Depalpur*, Bagli*
	A 1aii Mhow	Mhowgaon*
	A 1aiii Kannod	—
	A 1aiv Khategaon	—
	A 1av Shajapur	—
	A 1avi Sarangpur	Biora
A 1b Dewas	A 1bi Dewas	Hatpipalya, Sonkatch,* Bhaurasa*
A 1c Dhar	A 1ci Dhar	Sardarpur, Manawar, Dharampuri*
	A 1cii Kukshi	—
A 1d Jhabua	A 1di Jhabua	Ranapur,* Thandla
A 1e Alirajpur	A 1ei Alirajpur	Jobat
A 2a Ujjain	A 2ai Ujjain	Badnagar, Tarana
	A 2aii Rajgarh	Khilchipur*
	A 2aiii Agar	Susner, Nalkhera*
	A 2aiv Khachrod	Nagda
A 2b Mehidpur	A 2bi Mehidpur	—
A 3a Ratlam	A 3ai Ratlam	Sailana, Badnawar, Petlawad
	A 3aii Jaora	Tal, Alot
A 4a Mandsaur	A 4ai Mandsaur	Sitamau,* Narayangarh,* Malhargarh*
	A 4aii Bhanpura	Garotch,* Shamgarh
A 4b Neemuch	A 4bi Neemuch	Jawad, Manasa, Rampura, Gandhisagar*
B 1a Bhopal	B 1ai Bhopal	Berasia, Raisen, Begumganj
	B 1aii Sehore	Ashta, Ichhawar*
	B 1aiii Baraily	—
	B 1aiv Narsingarh	—
B 1b Shujalpur	B 1bi Shujalpur	Akodia
B 1c Vidisha	B 1ci Vidisha	—
	B 1cii Basoda	—
B 1d Guna	B 1di Guna	Ragogarh,* Chachaura*
	B 1dii Mungaoli	—
	B 1diii Sironj	—
	B 1div Ashoknagar	Chanderi
B 2a Sagar	B 2ai Sagar	Rahatgarh,* Bina, Khurai, Kurwai, Banda, Deori*
	B 2aii Garhakota	Rehli

Note : Towns marked with '*' are non-central towns, i.e., devoid of any qualifying bus service.

It is worth noting that an important class IV order town—Jaora in Ratlam district is extremely marginal between the hinterlands of Ratlam and Mandsaur. Class IV towns of Alot and Tal of the same district are also nested with it. Thus through its orientation with other towns, Jaora should nest with Ratlam even though it has a comparable number of bus connections with Mandsaur also. Badnawar town in western Malwa is again situated on the very margin between Indore and Ratlam hinterlands, whereas in the eastern Malwa, Kurwai town stands on the junction of Sagar, Vidisha and Guna hinterlands.

A geographical interpretation of spatial organisation

This study bears ample testimony to the fact that almost all towns of Malwa are essentially only central places, which in their entirety make an urban system in close harmony with the central place theory. Notwithstanding this close harmony between the actual urban system of Malwa and the theoretical central place system, the region furnishes an excellent example of the static, and, therefore inadequate, nature of the Christaller-Losch model of central place system, as it does not incorporate dynamic factors like the differential growth of towns. Thus, due to the very fast growth of Bhopal into a major city recently, the whole regional urban system has come to be structured about two cities—Indore and Bhopal—rather than around a single first o rder centre. These two cities command the western and the eastern parts of Malwa, respectively.

In the operational structural organisation of spatial system, the western and the eastern parts show some notable differences, with a much greater degree of overlapping or intermixing and competition among hinterlands in the western part. This is, to a great extent, the legacy of the peculiar recent history of that part, resulting in a highly intricate and intertwined territorial organisation of the numerous petty states in that part of the region. The same part also displays a larger degree of attenuating effects of major route orientations upon the size and shape of hinterlands, exemplified by the second and third order hinterlands of Indore.

The development of this urban system of Malwa in close consonance with the parameters of the central place theory was augmented and facilitated in a large measure by the fact that

(1) Malwa has a notably hospitable geographical background, highly congenial to the flourishment of agriculture, trade and related central services ; and (2) that the towns are located essentially on the most accessible, central locations, rather than at strategic locations with restricted approach, which was made feasible through peculiar historic processes and situations obtaining in Malwa over the last two centuries. (Jain 1979, Chapter 2—History and Its Imprints on Evolution of 'Towns' and Chapter 5—'Locational Analysis of Towns' and Singh 1968, pp. 204-9).

This system was remarkably saved from the distorting impacts of industrialization because of the conspicuous feature of Malwa that it has a virtual lack of all major localised industrial raw materials and inanimate power resources whose inherently fortuitous occurrence bears heavy constraints upon a central place system, and renders the growth and distributional pattern of towns notably erratic.

REFERENCES

Aboidun, J.O., "The Urban Hierarchy of a Developing Country 'Nigeria' ", *Eco. Geo.*, Vol. 43, 1967, pp. 347-67.

Carruthers, I., 'A Classification of Service Centres in England and Wales', *Geog. Jour.*, Vol. 123, 1957, pp. 371-385.

Carter, H., *The Study of Urban Geography*, London, 1972.

Christaller, W., *Die zantralen Orde in Suddentschland*, Jena, Fischer, E. Germany, translated by Baskin, C.W. as *Central Places in Southern Germany*, 1966, Englewood Cliff, New Jersey, 1933.

Davies, W.K.D., *The Hierarchy of Commercial Centres : A case study in South Wales*, Unpub. Ph.D. thesis, Univ. of Wales, 1964.

Davies, W.K.D., 'Centrality and the Central Place Hierarchy', *Urban Studies*, Vol. 4, 1967, pp. 61-79.

Galpin, G.J., 'The Social Anatomy of an Agricultural Community', Univ. of Wisconsin, *Ag. Exp. Stn. Res. Bull.*, 34, 1915.

Green, F.H.W., 'Urban Hinterlands in England and Wales : An Analysis of Bus Services', *Geog. Jour.*, Vol. 116, pp. 64-81, adapted in Gibbs, J.P. (1961), *Urban Research Methods*, pp. 263-285, New Delhi, 1960.

Jain, J.L., 'The Growth and Distribution of Towns in the Malwa Plateau M.P.', Unpub. doctoral dissertation, University of Saugar, Sagar, 1979.

Jain, J.L., 'Spatial Structure of Urban Settlement System of Malwa Plateau, M.P. : Distribution and Connectivity of Towns', Paper read at the National Seminar on 'Settlement Systems of India', Hyderabad, 1980.

Kolb, H.J., 'Service Relations of Town and Country', Univ. Wis., *Ag. Exp. Stn. Res. Bull.*, 34, 1923.

Lalaune, Leon, 'An Essay on the Theory of the Railway Systems, Based on Observation of Facts and Basic Law Governing Population Distribution' as reported in Berry, B.J.L., (1967), *Geography of Market Centres and Retail Distribution*, Prentice Hall, Englewood Cliff, N.J., p. 59, 1953.

Richardson, H.W., 'The Theory of the Distribution of City-sizes : Review and Prospects', *Regional Studies*, Vol. 7, 1973, pp. 239-251.

Singh, K.N., 'The Territorial Basis of Medieval Town and Village Settlement in Eastern Uttar Pradesh, India', *Annals, Assoc. of Amn. Geogrs.*, Vol. 58, 1968, pp 203-20.

SEVEN

JOE U. UMO

BASIC NEEDS GRADIENTS IN A PRIMATE CITY-STATE
The Case of Lagos

INTRODUCTION

THE apparent failure of high GDP growth rates to equitably spread the fruits of economic progress in LDCs has, in recent years, led the development community to turn to an alternative strategy viz., the Basic Needs Approach (BNA). This approach essentially seeks to deal with absolute and relative poverty by synthesising strategies of growth, employment and poverty eradication (List, 1977).

Although BNA has been widely embraced, its discussions and implementation strategies tend to abstract from spatial considerations. There seems to be an implicit assumption that the moment basic needs are provided they will automatically be accessible to the target group (i.e., the poor) at the given quantitative levels. This assumption can be seriously undermined by existence of some spatial frictions which policy makers often ignore.

Besides, the studies of both intra-city and inter-regional income inequality as they relate to city sizes in developed countries (DCs) can hardly be generalisable to contemporary LDCs for at least two reasons : (i) the single instrument used as a measure of inequality, i.e., income, fails to capture the key concerns of poverty eradication in LDCs, and (ii) the impact of primate city phenomenon can make a difference to the accessibility to basic needs.

The paper therefore seeks to develop an inter-regional/intra-urban distributional hypothesis based on basic needs concept.

This will then be tested against the background of city-primacy, in an LDC—Nigeria. More specifically, the paper will advance a basic needs gradient hypothesis and use a primate city-state, Lagos for empirical verification.

The first section of the paper reviews the theoretical background and develops the basic needs gradient hypothesis (BNGH). The second section examines the empirical materials relating to BNGH. The third concludes with possible explanations of BNGH and an analysis of policy implicatons.

SECTION I

RELATIONSHIP BETWEEN CITY SIZE AND INCOME DISTRIBUTION

The relationship between city size and income distribution has been a subject of unresolved debate among urban scholars. Richardson (1973) for instance, using average high/low income ratio as a crude measure of inequality concluded that income distribution becomes more equal as city size increases. If Richardson's finding is plausible, especially in terms of having a cross-cultural applicability, the policy implications would be straightforward but disturbing. It would imply that the overgrown cities of most LDCs should be encouraged to grow if further distributional inequality is to be reduced. Interest in this option has, however, been dampened by emerging evidences to the contrary.

Farbman (1975) has shown that income inequality is a positive function of city size. He anchores his finding on the argument that large cities attract highly talented migrants who correspondingly earn high incomes. By analogous reasoning, it would follow that if low-skilled or unskilled migrants predominate, the relationship between city size and inequality would be negative. Such a 'differential migration hypothesis' would intuitively predict a negative income-size relationship for most cities in LDC's since their migrants tend to be low-skilled. In Nigeria, for instance, school leavers form the majority (over 60%) of urban unemployed migrants. Harthworth *et al.* (1978) has used the notion of 'monopoly hypothesis' to explain their empirically validated positive relationship between city size and inequality.

According to Harthworth and his associates, growth in any urban context generates quasi-rents on owners of both human and non-human capital assests. And since such asset owners often locate in cities, a pattern of inequality is often set and maintained as the city grows.

Two observations can be made in respect of the studies reviewed above. First, they all use income as a measure of inequality either in a regression analysis context (Harthworth *et al.* for instance) or as a measure of Gini concentration coefficient (Farbman). The shortcomings of these measuring instruments are very well known to require elaboration here. Income measure although serving a composite proxy, seems too narrow to capture the multidimensional concerns of poverty-reduction strategy in an LDC. The Gini concentration ratio is very well known for its insensitivity to changes near the centre of distribution.[1] Obviously a more meaningful instrument that avoids these problems would be preferrable.

Second, the explantions for results obtained are devoid of spatial content. This means that the introduction of spatial considerations may either change the results of the models or account differently for the observed behaviour. Eitherway, their cross-cultural generalisation is limited.

In what follows therefore an attempt will be made to develop an hypothesis which takes space explicitly into account and efforts will be made to use BNA which we consider has more suitable instrumental elements for examining the validity of the hypothesis advanced.

THE NEGATIVE BASIC NEEDS GRADIENT HYPOTHESIS

Using basic needs provision as an indicator of income (welfare) distribution, we posit that a typical primate city distributes its basic needs services regressively with distance from the city's central core. More formally, there is a negative gradient of basic needs provision with distance from the primate city's core. This proposition and its analytical implications are explored in Fig. 7.1.

Fig. 7.1 shows distance away from the city's core on the horizontal while basic needs supply $(BN)^2$ is shown on the vertical. Basic needs supply as a negative function of radial

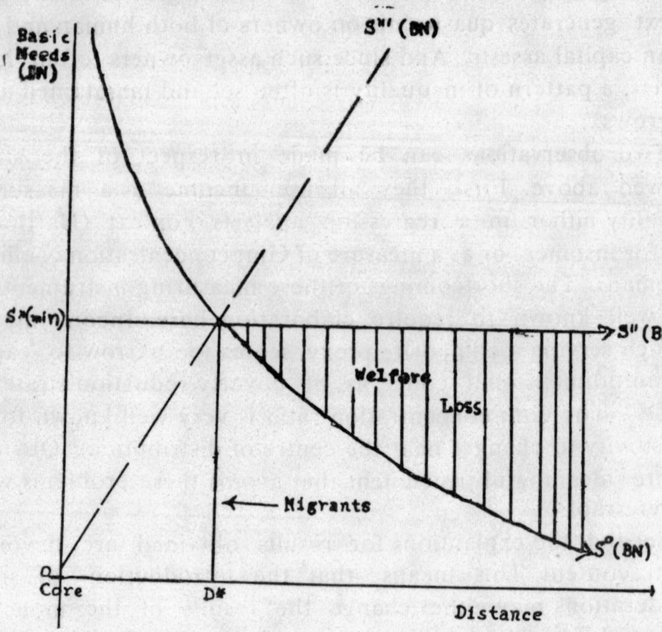

FIG. 7.1 : *Basic needs supply gradients*

distance from the core is shown as S° (BN). Given the friction of distance and the administrative bottlenecks characterising the provision of basic needs in a typical LDC primate city, this relationship is expected.

Suppose, for instance, that people living OD^* distance from the city centre can get OS^* (min)S'' minimum level of basic needs, the implication is that the farther away one locates the greater one's welfare loss in terms of the deviation from the minimum (see shaded area).

If, it is hypothetically assumed that all the technical, frictional and administrative impediments giving rise to a distance-decay (basic needs) function, are overcome, $S''(SB)$ functional form would imply greater welfare for citizens as they locate away from the core. This would represent the spread effects of the city's impact.[3] Such 'spread' impact can be more assured in a classical monocentric city where the rich live in the periphery, not in a primate city structure where the poor are 'driven' as it were, to the pheripheries.

Another implication of location at D^* that needs stressing is as follows. Since people locating away from this minimum welfare zone are suffering welfare losses, this generates long-term incentives to migrate towards the core (see arrow). The effect of this is to cause a deterioration in the quality of needs provision. But more importantly, efforts to decentralise basic need facilities have very limited success.

In the next section, we seek some empirical verification of the above propositions using Lagos in Nigeria as a test case.

SECTION II

EMPIRICAL ANALYSIS

Methodology

Any rigorous test of a gradient hypothesis such as posited above should normally find data to calibrate the standard formula, viz.,

(1) $$N = AD^{-BeU}$$

where N, A, D, B and U stand for basic needs vector, shift parameter distance, constant parameter and stochastic error term respectively.

On livearising (1) for estimation purposes, we have (2) $\log N = \log A - B \log D + U$.

Three problems in our context arise from using (2) : first, the use of income as a composite measure of N is inconvenient given the multidimensional nature of basic needs as had already been elaborated (see Section I), second (2) assumes continuous linearity which, although mathematically convenient, does not reflect possible spatial 'bumps' (frictions) and third but perhaps more important, data on income were not available.

The next, hopefully 'best' thing to do was to use a tabular/percentile analysis derived from a statistical survey data carried out in Lagos State in 1976, to explore the concerns of the hypothesis advanced. Pertinent data from other sources were also used as supplements.

Although this 'traditional' percentile approach to the issue is less statistically elegant, it has the advantage that it permits us to explore even if tentatively, the concerns of the hypothesis with some reasonable depth. Before, we do this, a background description of Lagos will put matters in perspective.

Lagos city-state : A profile

Up till this time of writing, Lagos still remains the capital of Nigeria[4] just as it had been since 1914 when the British colonial authority amalgamated Northern and Southern Nigeria into one.

In 1967, the metropolitan area (Lagos mainland and Ikeja) with its immediate environs was created into a state. And since Lagos has served the dual role of national capital and the headquarters of the Lagos state government. With a size of 3,577 square kilometres, representing approximately 0.4 per cent of the country's area, Lagos is the smallest of the present 19 states into which the country was divided in 1976. Yet it harbours about 4.6 million (1980 estimate) people out of the country's estimated population of 80 million. It therefore has the highest population density in the country—about 20,000 per square kilometre. The rate of new migrants into Lagos is estimated at 25,000 people per month; and this works out to new arrivals of about 34 persons per hour (Lagos State, 1981, p. 1).

The extent that about 90 per cent of the population is located in the metropolis, Lagos can reasonably be designated a city-state.

Perhaps, the first major seed of its primacy was sown during the country's First National Development Plan (1962-68) when (unmindful of the spatial implications) 61 per cent of the total planned expenditure was devoted to Lagos[5] whose population was then about .6 million (1963 census). Not surprisingly, therefore, by 1967, Lagos alone accounted for 70 per cent Nigeria's foreign trade, and this rose to 90 per cent during the civil war years (1967-70). Lagos port then handled over 80 per cent of the nation's value of imports. The metropolis accounts for about 50 per cent of industrial establishments and about 57 per cent of total value added in the manufacturing sector. It contains over 40 per cent of Nigeria's highly skilled manpower.

Given the above background, and the forecast that by the year 2,000, Lagos population will range between 12-20 million people[6] (depending on forecasting assumptions used) it becomes very pertinent to ask the question: How does an ordinary man fare in terms of the city-states ability to provide him with his basic needs ? Let us now explore the answer to this question using the data avilable to us.

Basic needs distribution

Five basic need instruments will be used to verify our hypothesis. These are education, employment, revenue generation, housing and health. Although these are rather few, they do encompass the two standard categories of basic needs—instrumental or infrastructural as well as personal consumption needs.[7] Each will be examined in turn.

EDUCATION

This is an instrumental basic need since it facilitates access not only to other basic needs as we shall see, but 'higher' human needs (which does not concern us here).

Table 7.1 shows the data on relevant aspects of the distribution of primary and secondary education in the five local government areas (LGAs) into which Lagos State had been divided (since 1979).

The main features of Table 7.1 can now be summarised as follows :

(1) The primary school-population ratio in 1972 declined from 60.22 for Lagos division (mainland) to 5.51 per cent for Epe. This same pattern repeated itself in 1979/80 (see Column 6).

(2) The primary school enrolment rate was a declining function of distance from the core in 1972 but stabilised at a plateau of 105 per cent in 1979/80 reflecting the impact of free universal primary education which was launched in 1976.

(3) Secondary school educational services are also characterised by distance decay from the core in respect of school—population ratio and enrolment ratio (see figures in parentheses in columns 3, 4, 6 and 7).

(4) More interesting perhaps, is the observation that when trends of all the relevant data in columns 3, 4, 6 and 7 are observed from the viewpoint of Lagos as a metropolitan area (i.e., a combination of Lagos Mainland and Ikeja LGAs) the decline in services become very sharp. Examples : The primary school-population ratio were 206.19 for Metropolitan Lagos, 98.59 (for Badagry), 58 (for Epe) and 30 for Ikorodu. In the same vein, the secondary school-population ratio in 1979/80 were 35 for

TABLE 7.1 : **Distribution of primary & secondary education in divisions of Lagos state (1972-79)**

Divisions of Local Government Area (LGAs)	1972			1979–80		
	School Age Population	School Population Ratio (%)	Enrolment Rate (%)	School Age Population	School Population Ratio (%)	Enrolment Rate (%)
Lagos	129.761	60.22	125.55	165.638	46.09	105.5
	(87.895)	(11.19)	(24.28)	(10.425)	(29.04)	—
Ikeja	75.891	22.62	80.64	968.73	26.95	105.6
	(5.140)	(5.17)	(19.20)	(64.585)	(6.33)	(61)
Badagry	23.823	8.68	98.59	304.16	8.46	105.6
	(16.137)	(0.34)	(9.95)	(20.274)	(4.62)	(55)
Epe	25.423	5.51	58.65	32.459	9.03	105.6
	(17.225)	(1.38)	(15.25)	(21.639)	(2.91)	(32)
Ikorodu	26.688	22.96	30.07	34.041	9.47	102.7
	(18.026)	(0.70)	(7.42)	(22.691)	(2.31)	(24)
Total State Average	281.600	99.99	96.07	359.458	105.19	105.6
	(190.698)	(19.29)	(21.05)	(239.614)	(55.22)	(55)

Note : Figures in parenthesis are Secondary School data.

Source : Compiled from, Lagos State, *Third National Development Plan*, 1975-80.

metropolitan Lagos, 4 6 for Badagry, 2.91 for Epe and 2.31 for Ikorodu. It is therefore clear that in general something like a step declining function like *S*(*BN*) in Fig 7.2 is observed.

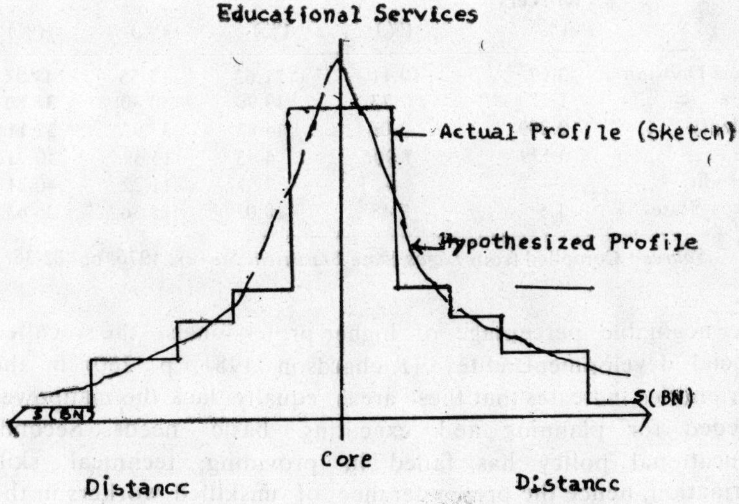

FIG. 7.2 : *Sketch of step-function profile of educational services in a primate city-state*

Impact of previous education on skill formation

It will also be enlightening to examine the imp:ct of previous education on skill formation in Lagos city state. The data on Table 7.2 show the relevant trend for each division of the state and major skill categories.

The patterns of education-induced occupational categories on Table 7.2 can be summarised as follows :

(1) There was a clear sharp educational gradient as shown by the decline in the combined percentage of higher administrative and professional workers as one moves away from metropolitan Lagos as well as down the skill levels.

(2) Although unskilled workers predominate in general the proportion of clerical and skilled workers are quite substantial in the metropolis.

Two implications can be noted from the above trends, first,

TABLE 7.2 : **Selected occupational categories in divisions of Lagos state (1976)**

Division/State	Higher Admin. Workers (%)	Professional (%)	Clerical Workers (%)	Skilled Workers (%)	Unskilled Workers (%)
Lagos Division	3.17	10.11	21.62	15.55	43.07
Ikeja ,,	1.12	7.73	19.90	30.30	32.80
Badagry ,,	0.299	3.06	14.83	37.92	32.11
Epe ,,	0.139	7.906	4.43	13.59	40.91
Ikorodu ,,	—	—	7.57	11.22	40.21
Lagos State	1.5	7.48	18.02	25.36	36.63

Source : Compiled from *Lagos State Statistical Survey*, 1976, pp. 32-36.

the negligible percentage of higher professionals—the so-called 'social development elites' (Richardson 1981, p. 280) in the peripheries indicates that these areas equally lack the manpower needed for planning and executing basic needs. Second, educational policy has failed in providing technical skill formation, hence the preponderance of unskilled workers in the area. This has implication for employment which we examine next.

EMPLOYMENT

Employment as an instrumental basic need hardly needs any stress since it confers a generalised ability for the fulfilment of other rudimentary needs like food, water, etc. Two data sets will be used to study both the actual and potential distribution of employment in Lagos City-State. Table 7.3 displays the data on unemployment situation in 1976.

As Table 7.3 clearly demonstrates, although the percentage of labour force population is an increasing function of distance from the core [column (2)] employment varies inversely with distance from the core in accordance with our negative gradient hypothesis. This is inferred from the observation that unemployment (column 3) is a positive function of distance from the core : varying from 3.55 per cent for Ikeja division to 10.55 per cent for Ikorodu LGA.

TABLE 7.3 : **Unemployment in Lagos state local government divisions (1976)**

Division/State	% of Population in Labour Force	% of Unemployed	Unemployed as % of Labour Force
Ikeja Division	63.46	3.55	5.59
Lagos ,,	61.54	4.01	6.52
Badagry ,,	69.59	9.76	14.04
Epe ,,	64.45	3.87	6.00
Ikorodu ,,	76.82	10.55	13.74
Lagos State	65.40	5.16	7.89

Source : Compiled from *Lagos State Statistical Survey*, op. cit., pp. 62-64.

If unemployment-labour force ratio is used as a proxy for unemployment burden, it will be seen that such burden weighs more heavily on the peripheries of Lagos metropolis like Badagry (14.04%) and Ikorodu (13.74%) than in the metropolis itself (see column 4).

Table 7.4 depicts the employment potentials in the region.

Using employee-employer ratio (EER) or its reciprocal (1/EER) as a crude measure of employment potential, Table 7.4 shows that this ratio declines from 5 per cent for Lagos division to 3 per cent for Epe division. Consequently as one moves away from the core, the probability of getting a job is on the decline.

Conversely, the percentage of own account workers is an

TABLE 7.4 : **Employment potentials in Lagos state (%)**

Division/State	Employers	Employees	Own Account Workers	Employee/ Employer Ratio (EER)	1 (EER)
Lagos Division	3.052	59.396	37.552	19.46	0.051
Ikeja ,,	2.134	64.517	33.349	30.23	0.033
Badagry ,,	1.343	45.94	52.71	34.20	0.029
Epe ,,	0.693	20.388	78.918	29.00	0.03
Ikorodu ,,	—	28.497	71.503	—	—
Lagos State	2.099	55.256	42.644	100	

Source : Calculated from *Lagos State Statistical Survey*, op. cit. pp. 44-49.

increasing function of distance from the core: varying from 5 Lagos (37.5%) to Epe (78%). This reflects an increasing reliance of periphery dwellers on informal sector for economic survival. And given the general official neglect of this group of workers, survival can only be expected to be at a subsistence margin.

REVENUE GENERATION

The quantum and quality of urban basic needs any metropolis can offer its dwellers depend to a very large extent on its revenue base. The main sources of revenue to states and local government include government (statutory) allocation, sales and property taxes and other forms of miscellaneous levies and fines. The data for each source were not available for our study area. The available aggregate revenue trends for each local government area of the state will, however, give a clue as to the ability of each Local Government Area to finance its basic service. These are shown on Table 7.5.

As this table clearly brings out there is a negative revenue gradient with respect to radial distance from Lagos Local Government Area and the metropolis defined to include Lagos Island Local Government (LILG), Lagos Mainland Local Government (LMLG), Ikeja, Mushin and Shomolu Local Government Area,[8] generally. Annual total revenue varied from 26.67 per cent for LILG to 0.39 per cent for Epe during the 1980 growth fiscal year, shown on Table 7.5.

In particular it is interesting to note again the step function phenomenon in revenue gradient. The sharp drop starts from 84 per cent for Lagos metropolis as defined above to 7.84, 5.52 and 3.9 per cent for Badagry, Ikorodu and Epe respectively. This same pattern holds for each of the nine months.

The negative revenue gradient is basically explained by absence or limited revenue generating economic activities within these sub-regions. It is also symptomatic of the failure of recent official policies to decentralise industrial location in the metropolis.[9]

HOUSING

Housing is a basic consumption need. Its stock and quality cons-

TABLE 7.5 : **Revenue trends/distribution within Lagos state 1980 in Naira**

(*Percentages in Parenthesis*)

Month	L.I.L.G.	L.M.L.G.	Ikeja	Mushin	Shomolu	Badagry	Ikorodu	Epe	Lagos total
April	271928.07	192444.30	121096.17	126798.31	149346.46	84889.53	50919.75	4371.06	1001793.65
	(27.14)	(19.20)	(12.08)	(12.65)	(14.90)	(8.47)	(5.08)	(0.43)	(100.00)
May	282975.84	191938.60	153776.62	128117.52	127568.34	97430.58	65054.80	5727.55	1052589.85
	(26.88)	(18.23)	(14.61)	(12.17)	(12.12)	(9.25)	(6.8))	(0.54)	(100.00)
June	281146.67	204737.40	156657.43	134042.10	118625.17	71811.63	59883.70	2990.30	1029894.40
	(27.27)	(19.86)	(15.19)	(13.00)	(11.50)	(6.96)	(5.81)	(0.29)	(100.00)
July	362397.91	218283.20	198330.25	184948.77	148536.91	88015.50	90948.57	4327.11	1295788.22
	(27.94)	(16.83)	(15.29)	(14.26)	(11.45)	(6.79)	(7.01)	(0.33)	(100.00)
August	252233.37	183792.60	152884.83	142030.58	146767.79	79081.98	46637.00	4000.00	1007428.15
	(25.02)	(18.23)	(15.16)	(14.09)	(14.56)	(7.84)	(4.62)	(0.40)	(100.00)
September	260253.67	188948.80	148154.66	145865.80	169118.84	83029.58	51032.88	3000.00	1049404.23
	(24.77)	(17.99)	(14.10)	(13.88)	(16.10)	(7.90)	(4.84)	(0.28)	(100.00)
October	309264.62	197302.00	134665.15	152676.99	170668.74	61802.37	54474.30	3448.58	1024302.75
	(30.18)	(13.40)	(13.14)	(14.90)	(16.66)	(6.03)	(5.32)	(0.33)	(100.00)
November	301261.00	198273.80	116623.21	144966.15	160145.53	88264.17	57530.80	3054.19	1070118.92
	(28.14)	(18.52)	(10.89)	(13.54)	(14.96)	(8.24)	(5.37)	(0.28)	(100.00)
December	319645.26	114687.90	142787.38	240920.50	196909.10	86215.86	70209.30	7776.00	1179151.30
	(27.10)	(9.72)	(12.11)	(20.43)	(16.70)	(7.31)	(5.95)	(0.66)	(100.00)
'Annual total'	2641106.41	1630408.60	1324975.70	1400366.72	1387686.88	740541.17	546691.10	38694.09	9813471.41
	(26.67)	(16.47)	(13.38)	(14.14)	(14.01)	(7.48)	(5.52)	(0.39)	(100.00)

Source : Computed from *Lagos State Government* : *Annual Activity Reports of Ministries/Extra Ministerial Department*, Jan.—Dec., 1980, p. 158, Annexure 9.

titute an important indicator of welfare in a particular urban environment. However, a measure of adequacy of housing calls for an examination of housing attributes which basically constitute the housing demand vector.

Table 7.6 shows the state of the housing attributes where data were available.

The following facts are highlighted by Table 7.6.

(i) Extreme overcrowding characterise all the houses in Lagos metropolis and its environs. Logos Local Government Area in particular registers 4.2 persons per room which is second only to Epe with 5.6 persons per room.

(ii) The percentages of buidlings in poor condition, poor access road and poor drainage[10] shows a clear pattern of deterioration as one moves away from Lagos metropolitan core [see columns (3) to (5)].

(iii) Similarly the percentage of households with electricity and pipe-borne water (column 6) as well as households with toilets (column 7) declined sharply with distance from the core in conformity with our hypothesis.

HEALTH

The importance of good health as a basic need rests on its necessity for effective functioning of a human being as an economic and social agent.

According to health statistics of Lagos State shown on Table 7.7, the spatial distribution of all health indices were highly skewed in favour of Lagos mainland.

Indeed a step function phenomenon in the distribution of health facilities is very glaring on Table 7.7. In 1969, Lagos alone had between 86 and 94 per cent of daily attendance, annual inpatient admissions, bed compliments, number of nursing staff, and number of doctors ; while all other Local Government Areas had to share the remaining proportion almost in proportion to their distance from Lagos. Badagry and Epe for instance, had only 1 doctor each while Ikorodu had none.

TABLE 7.6 : **Housing conditions and attributes in Lagos state (1976)**

Division/State	Average No. of Persons Per Household	% of Buildings in Poor Condition	% of Access Road in Poor Condition	% of Drainage in Poor Condition	% of House- with Electricity and Pipe Borne water	% of House- with No Toilet
Epe	5.635	21.010	35.786	54.181	0.669	69.899
Ikorodu	3.587	69.014	68.075	92.488	1.869	36.448
Badagry	3.539	38.584	62.329	70.396	10.883	25.494
Ikeja	3.482	51.852	66.888	80.216	33.717	11.064
Lagos	4.231	32.584	41.671	56.571	61.584	14.215
Lagos State	3.819	37.468	56.997	70.352	35.248	18.023

Source : Compiled from *Lagos State* : *Statistical Survey*, op. cit., pp. 68-71.

TABLE 7.7 : **Health statistics, Lagos state 1969**

(Percentages in Parenthesis)

Division of Lagos state	OPD/Casualty Daily Attendance	Annual Inpatient Admissions	Bed Complement	Number of Nursing Staff	No. of Doctors
Lagos	6250	45,554	1922	865	168
	(89.1)	(86.1)	(89.3)	(88.3)	(93.8)
Ikeja	518	4035	95	55	9
	(7.4)	(7.6)	(4.4)	(5.6)	(5.0)
Ikorodu	24	382	8	9	—
	(0.3)	(0.7)	(0.4)	(0.9)	(0.0)
Badagry	69	1,449	48	21	1
	(1.0)	(2.7)	(2.2)	(2.2)	(0.6)
Epe	153	1,463	80	29	1
	(2.2)	(2.9)	(3.7)	(3.0)	(0.6)
Lagos State Total	7014	52,883	2,153	9.79	179
	(100)	(100)	(100)	(100)	(10)

Source : Compiled from Lagos State Government Four Year Development Plan, 1970-1974.

SECTION III

SUMMARY AND POLICY IMPLICATIONS

The paper develops the view that basic needs provision (distribution) in a primate city is a negative function of radial distance from the core. Cross sectional data on five basic need variables viz., education, employment, revenue generation, housing and health have been used to verify this hypothesis in respect of Lagos city-state. Each of the variables has shown a distance decay trend from the core to the periphery thereby confirming the general hypothesis. The negative basic need profiles have in particular been characterised by a step function which suggests extreme regressivity in the distribution of basic needs beyond immediate Lagos metropolis.

Reasons for this phenomenon though not formally probed in the study can be attributed to at least four causes.

First, the friction of distance must have created the skew in the observed pattern of basic need distribution. Lagos state has some topographical problems like water logged areas, lagooms, etc. This might create transportation problems that effectively reduce the accessibility of its inhabitants to basic needs. The problem with this explanation, however, is that a rational policy of basic needs provision should have included the removal of such distance frictions as part of its basic needs package. That this was not done would appear to suggest policy neglect.

Second, thirteen years of military administration in the country (1967-1979/80) has meant that the issue of basic need provision was not only given scant attention ; but its pattern of distribution was out of the question. Indeed most facilities in the city completely broke down under the pressure of increased migration during the period. Available resources were probably devoted to maintaining facilities at the core.

Third, the phenomenon of basic needs gradient is reflective of the primate city's overwhelming concern with growth rather than distribution. In this connection it is significant to note that there has been a high correlation between the growth of the Nigerian economy and the growth of Lagos especially after the war. The proceeds of Nigeria's oil-induced wealth were massively spent in developing super highways, and fly-over bridges within the Lagos metropolis. Such expenditure programmes obviously benefited the rich who own cars for plying these highways. Building access roads for peripheral dwellers was not part of this programme.

And fourth, the poor residents hardly had any say or control over the dynamics of the changing urban scene in Lagos. Thus without the political control of the urban resources, it is difficult to see how the regressive pattern of basic needs provision could have been reversed.

Although both our empirical evidence and suggested explanation can be regarded as tentative, three policy issues have been raised by the study. First, there is need to undertake a comprehensive threshold analysis of Lagos City-State. Such a study is necessitated by overwhelming evidence pointing to the 'back wash' impact of Lagos growth on its immediate environs and the nation which have been analysed here and elsewhere (Umo, 1975 & 1979). This will permit a formal identification of the real limits to its growth and what opportunities (if any) may still exist for 'frontier' development.

Second, the potentials for developing small urban centres as migrant interceptors within its peripheries also need exploration. Such centres must have high employment potentials in order to succeed in intercepting Lagos bound migrants within the state and the nation.

And last, the masses must be organised for loc alparticipation in their development concerns. The absence of 'social development elites' at the peripheries as was pointed out probably accounts most for the political neglect which they have been suffering. As Kotler (1969, p. 71) rightly puts it, "the poor need neighbourhood government to secure the liberty to achieve prosperity." The newly created local governments areas can form a basis for organising such 'neighbourhood' governments.

FOOTNOTES

1. See proof of this in Frank and Webbs (1977, 504-505).
2. The supply functions are shown with arrow heads since basic needs are regarded geometrically as vectors with well defined elements.
3. See elaboration in Hirschman (1957, pp. 183-201).
4. Plans to build new capital city at Abuja are being vigorously pursued at present.
5. See First National Development Plan (1969-68, p. 41).
6. See Lagos State Regional Plan (1980-200, p. 1).
7. See categorisations in Green (1970) and Seer (1981).
8. The LGA's are created newly by the civilian state administration which started operation in 1980.
9. See Lagos State, National Development Plan (1981-85, p. 25).
10. The use of the designation 'poor' to describe the attributes of housing is in conformity with the usage by authors of Lagos Statistical Survey Project (1976) who infact had devised consistent criteria for the measuring of the different attributes. This has reduced the seeming subjectivity.

REFERENCES

1. Farbman, M., The Size Distribution of Income in US SMAS, 1959, *The Review of Income and Wealth*, Vol. 2, 1975, pp. 217-37.
2. Frank, C.R. and Webb, R.C. eds., *Income Distribution and Growth in LDCs*, Washington DC : Brookings Institute, 1977, pp. 491-517.
3. Green, Reginald H., *Employment Growth and Basic Needs Development Dialogue*, Vol. I, 1970, pp. 53-58.
4. Harworth, C.T. ; James Ebong ; and David Rasmussen, 'Income Distribution, City Size and Urban Growth'. *Urban Studies*, February,

1978.

5. Hirschman, A.O., *The Strategy of Economic Development*, New Haven, Connecticut : Yale University Press, 1957.
6. Kotler, M., *Neighbourhood Government : The Local Foundations of Political Life*, Indianapolis, 1969.
7. Lagos State, *Statistical Survey of Lagos State*, November/December, 1976, Lagos : Ministry of Economic Development and Establishment, 1980.
8. Lagos State, *4th National Development Plan 1981-85*, Ministry of Economic Development and Establishment, 1980.
9. Lagos State, *Lagos State Regional Plan 1980-2000*, Ikeja : Ministry of Economic Planning and Land Matters, 1981.
10. List, Franklyn, "Conventional Development Strategies and Basic Needs Fulfilment : A Reassessment of Objectives and Policies", *International Labour Review*, March-April 1977, Vol. 155, No. 2.
11. Nigeria, *First National Development Plan (1962-68)*, Lagos : Federal Ministry of Economic Development.
12. Richardson , *The Economies of Urban Size*, Westmead, Saxon House, 1973.
13. Richardson, National Ubran Development Strategies in Developing Countries, *Urban Studies*, Vol. 18, 267-283.
14. Seers, Dudley "What Needs are Really Basic in Nigeria ?" *International Labour Review*, EHR No. 6, November-December, 1981.
15. Umo, J.U., "Some Aspects of Urbanisation and Implications for Development in Nigeria", *African Urban Notes*, Michigan State University Ser B., Vol. I, No. 3 , 1975.
16. Umo, J.U., "Urban and Regional Development in Nigeria : Some Considerations for a Planned Disequilibrium Strategy", *Geographical Review of India*, Vol. 41, March, 1979.

EIGHT

BARRY LENTNEK

PRIMACY'S PEAK
20th Century Mexican Urbanization

THE foci of this paper are upon the manner in which the evolution of city distributions may be statistically characterized and upon the substantive conclusions which can be gleaned from an examination of these stylized facts. An application is made to the twentieth century experience of urbanization in Mexico. The paper is organized as follows :

(1) A re-examination of the rank-size rule as one of a number of alternative ways to stylize facts concerning national urban systems. In particular, the use of the Lorenz Curve and Gini-coefficient are proposed as alternative characterizations and the mathematical relationship of the Rank Size Rule to the Gini-Coefficient is demonstrated.

(2) A presentation of alternative Mexican data bases and analysis of these statistics is made for the 1900-1970 period ; and

(3) A critique of the methodology and suggestions for improvement in our ability to conduct time series and cross-national studies of urban population size distributions is offered.

Rank-size distributions and economic development : An hypothesis

Zipf's rule related the population of the nth ranked city (P_n) to the population of the largest city (P_1) where urban populations are ordered or "ranked" by descending size from 1 to N ; that is $P_n = P_1/n$ so that the population of the second city is half that of the first, the population of the third city is a third that of the first and so forth. Actually, the rule is a limiting case of a Pareto distribution : $P_N=(M/N)\ P_M K$ where P_N is an item (city) of rank, N, P_M is the rank of an item (city) of rank M and K is some proper fraction (much of the basis for this brief review is an excellent review article by H.W. Richardson).[1] The Pareto distribution requires a minimum size threshold as does Zipf's rule in practice. The rule can be generalized, denoting by R the rank measurement ; $R=KP^{-q}$ or $LnR=LnK_{-q}\ LnP$ and so one attractive feature of the rule is that it requires a simple bivariate regression where the data source is a simple, ordered list of population counts. Given the extreme simplicity of the "rule" it was amazing to early investigators to discover that city population size distributions were in fact highly linearized (the function can be either convex or concave to the origins in logarithmic units but, in fact, rarely is). The most common exceptions are found in the fact that the largest or the two or three largest cities are much bigger than one would "expect" given the rule. This disproportionate size of the largest city (cities) was promptly labelled "primacy" following a separate but parallel line of thought. A review of previous empirical studies lies outside the scope of this paper.

The discovery that city size distributions often are log linear elicited a great variety of speculative theories over the past thirty years. Tinbergen pointed out, a decade ago, that "No scientific explanation worthy of that name has been advanced so far".[2] His comment may still stand. Disagreeing with Tinbergen's judgement as being too harsh, Richardson pointed out in 1973 that explanations of city size distributions suffer from at least two disabilities. First, the forces which produce a distribution of city sizes are so varied and complex that the existing explanations are either too simple or too complex (Richardson quoting Champernowne on the relationship of income to city size distributions). Second, " . . . any one of the observed statistical relationships is compatible with several theories while many of the individual theories are consistent with more than one of the standard empirical distributions."[3]

Since Richardson provided an excellent literature review, there is no need to repeat portions of the review in this space. Hence, we shall focus our discussion upon aspects of the literature dealing with explanations of the *evolution* over time of rank size distributions. In an unpublished paper, presented at an I. G.U.

conference and not reviewed by Richardson, Berry returned to a theme which he published in 1961 in which he postulated an evolution of city size distributions from primate to log linear to "degenerate" log linear (i.e., the lower tail of the distributions below about 250,000 in the U.S.A. show a sharped increased negative slope).[4] Berry argues that primacy results from the transmission of growth impulses from a heartland economy to the capital city of a dependent economy which are articulated and directed from the dependent or colonial capital. This gives use to a core-periphery or hinterlands model of spatial interaction within the dependent economy (an argument strikingly similar to John Friedmann's theory of growth centres).[5] Asserting that citics constitute the instruments by which regions are articulated with one another, Berry goes on to argue that "Impulses of economic change are transmitted in such a system simultaneously along three planes :

(a) Outwards from heartland metropoli to those of the regional hinterlands ;
(b) From centres of higher to centres of lower level in the hierarchy, in a pattern of "hierarchy diffusion" ; and
(c) Outwards from urban centres into their surrounding urban fields" (p. 10).

Again, these postulates are strikingly similar to those argued by Friedmann. He relates these processes to Gibrat's Law of Proportionate Effect in which the growth of cities is proportionate to their size (although there may be random variations from the expectation).[6] Of course, this leads to a distribution of city sizes which is log normal or a rank-size distribution (p. 12). After explaining various mathematical aspects of this thesis, Berry then goes on to a discussion of primacy the conclusion of which is the following hypothesis which follows from the work of Linsky and El Shaks,

> " . . . the greater the size of the country, the longer its history of urbanism, the greater the complexity and interdependence of its economic, administrative and political structures, and the greater its degree of modernization, the greater the probability that it will have a rank-size distribution

of city populations".[7]

Implied in this complex statement is the dynamic hypothesis that primacy should begin at a low level, rise and then fall as economic development increases. It should be noted that the same dynamic hypothesis concerning the relationship of the city size distributions to economize development can be extracted from the growth centre theory literature.

The rank-size rule and Gini's coefficient of dispersion

The rank-size rule itself completely directs attention towards only one aspect of the distribution of urban populations : namely, the ratio of the nth city to the $n^{th}+1$ city in an ordered list of urban populations $n=1, 2, \ldots, N$. Gini's coefficient of dispersion, on the other hand, provides a well known measure of the level of dispersion or disparity in the domain of observation. Together, the rank-size rule and Gini's coefficient come close to a complete characterization or "stylization" of city size distributions. Finally, both the slope (or "q") and the Gini coefficient (or "G") can be made functions of time and thus permit a comparative statics analysis of the evolution of city size distributions. This possibility has long been recognized in the literature. The problem is to demonstrate mathematically how "q" is related to "G". The purpose of this section is to provide that proof and present some sample tabled values of conversion.

Under the assumption that a variate, X, grows according to Gilbrat's law of proportionate effect, it has been shown that :

(1) The variate, X, will ultimately develop a log normal distribution (see Aitchison and Brown and Berry).[8]
(2) A rank-size distribution of the variate will also arise as a by-product.

These two results have "important" implications in describing urban population systems. Let the variate X denote city urban population. The direct result implies that $y=ln\ X \sim N(\mu_y, \sigma^2_y)$.[9] Let R denote the rank variable. The second result implies that X and R will be related according to the following expression.

$$ln\ X = K_{-q}\ lnR, \qquad \ldots(1)$$

where K and q are constants. The slope coefficient, q can be expressed in terms of the moments of the distributions of $lnX(=y)$ and $lnR(=t)$ as follows

$$q=\rho\ \sigma_y/\sigma_t, \qquad \ldots(2)$$

where ρ denotes the correlation coefficient between y and t. This correlation coefficient will approach one when relationship (1) holds perfectly. Notice that q depends merely on the measures of dispersion of both distributions. The value of this coefficient (q) is commonly used to describe urban systems. When $q=0$, all the cities of the system have the same urban population size. If $q>1$, primacy is present, and $q=1$ implies the rank-size rule.

A statistic commonly employed to describe income distributions is the Gini concentration coefficient. Aitchison and Brown show that under the assumption that income, I, is lognormally distributed, i.e., $ln\ I \sim N\ (\mu_I,\ \sigma^2_I)$, this coefficient is a function of σ^2_I.[10] They show that

$$G=2\ Pr\left\{\frac{Z\leqslant\sigma_y}{\sqrt{2}}\right\}-1,$$

where G denotes the coefficient and $Z\sim N\ (0,\ 1)$. Berry suggests the use of G for describing urban population distributions.[11] Thus, under the assumption that city urban population, X, grows according to Gilbrat's law of proportionate effect, one has that $y=lnX\sim N(\mu_y,\ \sigma^2_y)$ and so,

$$G=2\ Pr\left\{\frac{Z\leqslant\sigma_y}{\sqrt{2}}\right\}-1. \qquad \ldots(3)$$

When the value of $G=0$, all the cities have the same population size.[12] If $G=1$, one will have one single city containing all the urban population.

Both statistics, G and q, are functions of the measures of dispersion, σ^2_y and σ^2_t. Assuming that these variations and the correlation coefficient are known, G and q are related by the expression

$$G=2\ Pr\left\{\frac{Z\leqslant q\sigma_t}{p\sqrt{2}}\right\}-1. \qquad \ldots(4)$$

Notice that even if one maintains the value of q fixed (for a given ρ value), the value of G will vary with the value of σ_t. As σ_t increases, G will also increase in value, and *vice versa*. Also, see that keeping σ_t constant, the value of G depends upon the value of the relation q/ρ. A special case of interest of this relationship is that in which $q/\rho=1$, $q=1$ and $\rho=1$. For this case, one has that (1) is perfectly held, and that it actually describes the rank-size rule. Finally, notice that even if $q/\rho=1$, the value of G will still depend upon the value of σ_t.

Effects of growing population on q and Gini indices

In a recent paper, Petersen shows that if income grows at a fixed rate, say l per cent, it may lead to shifts of the Lorenz curve, and so to changes in the values of the Gini coefficient.[13] He points out that this effect must be taken into consideration whenever intertemporal comparisons of these two characteristics are made. This section is aimed to show what would be the effect of a constant growth of l per cent in population (or income) when it is lognormally distributed.

Suppose that urban population, X, is such that $y=ln\ X \sim N(\mu_y, \sigma^2_y)$. In this variate ($X$) grows at a fixed rate, l, one will have a new variate X^1 such that

$$X^1=(1+l)X.$$

In logarithmic terms, this implies that

$$ln\ X^1=(1+l)+ln\ X$$

or

$$y^1=K(l)+y,$$

where $K(l)$ is a constant that depends on the value of l. Thus, varying the population at constant rates of l per cent will result in an upward shift of the rank-size distributions (K will increase), and that a new variate $y^1 \sim N(\mu_y+K(l), \sigma^2_y)$ will result. This implies that since the Gini coefficient value depends on the value of σ_y^2, there will not be any effect in this value with the constant growth of population.

Estimation of G and q

Under the assumption that the values of all the parameters, σ_y, σ_t and ρ are known, the values of G and q may be computed from Tables 8.1 and 8.2.

A particular situation is that in which one would like to estimate the values of G and q from a given sample.[14] The estimation of q may be obtained via least squares. The estimator for q would be given as follows :

$$\hat{q}=\frac{r\ s_y}{s_t} \qquad \ldots(5)$$

where r, s_y, and s_t denote the sample correlation between y and t, the sample standard deviations of y and t respectively. This estimator will be the best linear unbiased estimator for q.

TABLE 8.1 : **Values of q and G for various values of σ_y and ρ/σ_t***

σ_y	ρ/σ_t											
	0.20	0.30	0.40	0.50	0.60	0.70	0.80	0.90	1.00	1.25	1.50	G
0.00	0.000	0.000	0.000	0.000	0.000	0.000	0.000	0.000	0.000	0.000	0.000	0.000
0.25	0.050	0.075	0.100	0.125	0.150	0.175	0.200	0.225	0.250	0.313	0.375	0.1405
0.50	0.100	0.150	0.200	0.250	0.300	0.350	0.400	0.450	0.500	0.625	0.750	0.2767
0.75	0.150	0.225	0.300	0.375	0.450	0.525	0.600	0.675	0.750	0.938	1.125	0.4039
1.00	0.200	0.300	0.400	0.500	0.600	0.700	0.800	0.900	1.000	1.250	1.500	0.5204
1.50	0.300	0.450	0.600	0.750	0.900	1.050	1.200	1.350	1.500	1.875	2.250	0.7108
2.00	0.400	0.600	0.800	1.000	1.200	1.400	1.600	1.800	2.000	2 500	3.000	0.8415
2.50	0.500	0.750	1.000	1.250	1.500	1.750	2.000	2.250	2.500	3.125	3.750	0.9233
3.00	0.600	0.900	1.200	1.500	1.800	2.100	2.400	2.700	3.000	3.750	4.500	0.9660

* Note that this table can also be used to obtain the values of $\overset{\frown}{q}$ and $\overset{\frown}{G}$ for various values of $\overset{\frown}{\sigma^2_y}$ and r/R_t

TABLE 8.2 : **Values of G for several values of σ_t and $q/\rho=1$***

σ_t	G
0.00	0.0000
0.25	0.1405
0.50	0.2767
0.75	0.4039
1.00	0.5204
1.50	0.7108
2.00	0.8415
2.50	0.9233
3.00	0.9660
3.50	0.9869
4.00	0.9953

*($\breve{q}/r=1$)

Another estimator for q would be given by

$$\breve{q}=\frac{(N-1)\,\hat{q}}{N}=\frac{r\,\breve{\sigma}_y}{s_y},$$

where $\breve{\sigma}_y=\frac{(N-1)s_y}{N}$. This is a maximum likelihood for σ_y which is also sufficient, and tends to unbiasedness as the sample size, N, increases. Since G is a function of σ_y a maximum likelihood estimator for it is the following.

$$\breve{G}=2\,Pr\left[\frac{Z\leqslant\breve{\sigma}_y}{\sqrt{2}}\right]-1$$

or

$$\breve{G}=Pr\left\{\frac{Z\leqslant(N-1)s_y}{N\sqrt{2}}\right\}-1\,.$$

Tables 8.1 and 8.2 show the values for $\breve{q}$ and $\breve{G}$ for several values of $\breve{\sigma}_y$, r, and r_t.

An application : The Mexican case

Substantially urbanized by the beginning of the last quarter of the twentieth century, Mexico's new found oil riches seem destined to complete an urbanization process which had its modern roots in the era of Porfirio Diaz a century ago. The purpose of this section of the paper is to examine one facet of the urbanization process during the twentieth century ; the evolution over time of the rank-size distributions of Mexico's cities. It should be emphasized from the beginning that the author does not regard the rank-size rule as popularized by Zipf (but first stated by Auerbach) as anything more than a "stylized fact" which can and should be used along with other (and explicitly spatial) characterizations to describe and analyze the pattern of urbanization.[15] Nonetheless a perfect rank-size rule distribution of urban population states a constant proportional relationship between the population sizes of different urban areas. Like the lognormal distribution of family incomes, Zipf's rank-size rule has occasioned considerable speculation for it may be yet another example of the law of proportionate effect.

Before describing the case study in detail, however, it should be noted that Mexican economic history during this century closely approximates the conditions set by Berry for countries possessing a rank-size distribution of city sizes ; namely,

(1) Mexico is one of the largest countries in the world (area is approximately one million square kilometres) ;
(2) Its history of urbanism extends for more than two centuries (with major growth in urbanization for more than the past half-century) ;
(3) Its degree of complexity and interdependence of economic, administrative and political structures has grown steadily since the close of the Mexican Revolution (circa 1918-1920) ; and
(4) The degree of modernization of the Mexican economy by virtually all measures has grown through the Twentieth Century to date.

For these reasons, it is believed that Mexico represents a fair "test" of the Berry thesis.

The evolution of city size distributions in twentieth century Mexico

Like almost all of Latin America, Mexico has been urbanizing at a very rapid pace while simultaneously experiencing the pains of the demographic transition. As seen in Table 8.3, national population increased from 14 to 50 millions (357%) while urban

TABLE 8.3 : **Mexican urbanization : Panel and national totals**

Date	Urbanized Areas			County Areas		
	(A) National*	(B) Panel	A/B	(A) National**	(B) Panel	A/B
1900	2,640,000	1,706,558	0.65	13,681,000	2,878,609	0.21
1910	3,669,000	2,051,281	0.56	***	***	***
1921	4,466,000	2,341,123	0.52	14,450,000	4,125,269	0.29
1930	5,541,000	3,055,431	0.55	16,696,000	4,530,725	0.27
1940	6,896,000	3,956,614	0.57	19,923,000	5,725,628	0.29
1950	10,983,000	6,712,421	0.61	26,185,000	8,870,976	0.34
1960	17,705,000	11,321,941	0.64	35,584,000	13,542,970	0.38
1970	28,710,000	18,929,866	0.66	49,838,000	22,065,914	0.44

* Total urbanized population in Mexico (see Unikel [16]).

**Total national population in Mexico (from census).

***1910 Census figures are unreliable.

population increased from 2.6 to 28.7 millions (1,140%) from 1900 to 1970. So, the proportion of Mexico's population living in urban areas increased from 19 per cent to about 58 per cent (for an excellent presentation and analysis of census data on Mexico's cities, see Unikel).[16] There seems little doubt that the 1980 Mexican census will find nearly two-thirds of the population living in urban areas.

Given that definitions of "urban" areas are always somewhat arbitrary, this section presents two parallel sets of data. The first refers only to "urbanized areas" and is based on an enormously detailed tract-by-tract study directed by Sr. Unikel (see citation above). Unikel's definitions essentially boil down to built up areas which, in the Mexican case, are easily identifiable because their cities are constructed at very high densities of dwelling units per hectare. The "urbanized area" definition is quite conservative because many nearby townspeople and villagers work in the cities while dwelling outside of them. The alternative definitions are the *municipios* or counties. These tend to include almost all of the commuting population because Mexican counties are often much larger spatial units than the built-up areas. Unfortunately, for the same reason, county populations tend to over-estimate the population living in and/or working in urban areas. Our purpose in presenting both data sets is to test the sensitivity of the conclusions to definitional variation. The "ideal" data set would be based on flow studies of journey-to-work patterns; unfortunately, such studies on a national basis are unobtainable.

The other definitional problems which must be resolved relate to either bound on the list of "cities" included in the rank size analysis. On the upper bound, the problem is metropolitan definitions for the largest cities. We have chosen to follow Unikel's lead in defining these areas because he is very closely acquainted with the original tract data set (see Part B of Table 8.4). On the lower bound, there is a problem of distinguishing between "towns" (defined as small urban settlements with a purely local economic significance rarely extending over more than its own county and one or two adjacent counties) and "cities" which have regional or national economic significance. Our choices of the latter are listed in Part A in their rank order as of the mid-point of the study period, that is, 1940.

Part A of Table 8.5 presents two sets of bivariate regression

TABLE 8.4 : **Panel cities and metropolitan areas**

A. *Rank ordered in 1940 by municipio population*

Rank	Name
1.	Mexico
2.	Guadalajara
3.	Monterrey
4.	Puebla
5.	Torron
6.	Leon
7.	Merida
8.	Tampico
9.	San-Luis Potosi
10.	Aguascalientes
11.	Orizaba
12.	Toluca
13.	Culiacan
14.	Chihuahua
15.	Morelia
16.	Vera Cruz
17.	Saltillo
18.	Queretaro
19.	Mazatlan
20.	Villahermosa
21.	Irapuato
22.	Fresnillo
23.	Pachuca
24.	Cd. Juarez
25.	Penjamo
26.	Matamoros
27.	Jalapa
28.	San Pedro
29.	Celaya
30.	Guanajuato
31.	Acambaro
32.	Mexicali
33.	Teloloapan
34.	Vide Santiago
35.	Tapachula
36.	Puruandiparo
37.	Tepatitlan
38.	Ahome
39.	Salvatierra
40.	San Felipe
41.	Salamanca
42.	Minatitlan
43.	Lagos de Moreno

44. Guasave
45. Mocorito
46. Zitacuaro
47. San Juan del Rio
48. Sinaloa
49. Allende
50. Huejutla
51. Cd. Dr. Hdez. Alvarez
52. Santiago Ixcuintla
53. Atlixco
54. Papantla
55. Matehuala
56. Hidalgo
57. Tamazunchale

B. *Metropolitan area definitions**

1. *Mexico* (Distrito Federal)
2. *Guadalajara*, Tiaquepaque, Zapopan and Tonala
3. *Monterrey*, cd. Guadalupe, Sni Nicolas de los Garra, San Pedro Garcia and Santa Catarina
4. *Torreon*, Gomez Palacio and Lerdo
5. *Puebla*, San Felipe, San Geronimo, Cuautiancingo Amozoc, San Pedro De Caolula, San Pablo (Tlaxcala), Xicotencantl (Tlaxcala) and Tenancingo (Tlaxlala).
6. *Vera Cruz* and Boca Del Rio
7. *Chihuahua* and Aquiles Serdan
8. *Leon* and San Francisco Del Rincon
9. *Merida* and Progreso
10. *San Luis Potosi* and Soledad
11. *Tampico*, Ciudad Madero and Pueblo Vieju
12. *Orizaba*, Tenango, Camarino, Nogales, Huiloapan, Fortin and Ixtaczuquitlan

* Each of these county groups were considered as single metropolitan areas throughout the twentieth century. We followed Guidelines set by Unikel in metropolitan definitions. In all cases except for the federal district (where we undercount somewhat by 1970), this results in overestimation of urbanized population.

analyses after the 56 cities (all panel cities except greater Mexico City) were "ranked" and both populations and rank were transformed into natural logarithms. The slope coefficients ("*q*" in the rank-size distribution) for both data sets are essentially stable during the first twenty years of the twentieth century, i.e., the last ten years of the Porfiriato and the subsequent decade of revolution. Thereafter, both data sets show a marked tendency to

TABLE 8.5 : **Rank size distribution estimates**

A. Cross Section Data (N=56)

Date	Urbanized Areas			Countries		
	Intercept	Slope ("'q')	R^2	Intercept	Slope	R^2
1900	12.50	—0.78	0.97	12.30	—0.51	0.97
1910	12.39	—0.80	0.97	—	—	—
1921	12.59	—0.80	0.97	12.47	—0.51	0.98
1930	12.96	—0.87	0.98	12.86	—0.65	0.99
1940	13.20	—0.90	0.99	13.36	—0.76	0.94
1950	13.64	—0.89	0.99	13.54	—0.71	0.99
1960	14.22	—0.93	0.98	14.11	—0.77	0.98
1970	14.79	—0.94	0.94	14.75	—0.84	0.98

B. Time Series Data ($q=a-bt$ Where t=Time in Years)

Date	Intercept	Slope	R^2	pw	t^*	n	Intercept	Slope	R^2	pw	t^*	n
1900-1970	0.71	+0.00244	0.90	2.13	7.68	8	0.34	+0.00487	0.86	2.53	5.62	7
1921-1970	0.70	+0.00247	0.80	1.78	4.09	6	0.29	−0.00552	0.82	1.87	4.23	6

* Slope coefficients are significant at 95% confidence.

decline with time. Over the half century 1920-1970, "*q*" declined from −0.80 to −0.94 for tightly defined urbanized areas and from −0.51 to −0.84 for the county or municipio data. In the case of both data sets, the intercept values increased substantially. As Figure 8.1A and B shows, the rank size distribution of urban population rotated clockwise over the half century. Part B of Table 8.5 presents regressions of time (where 1900=0) against the "*q*" values in order to determine the degree of consistency in the rotation and its rate over time. Since there was virtually no change in the distribution of urban populations during the first twenty years, we regressed time against "*q*" for both the 1900-1970 and 1920-1970 periods in order to see whether or not it makes a difference. As the table demonstrates, the clockwise rotation of the rank-size equation is highly consistent regardless of definition of length of period of estimate. Based on the available evidence we estimate that the national urban system will reach −1 around the year 2005 based on a "tight" definition (or around 2004 based on the county-wide data).

One way to measure primacy is to calculate the *difference* between the slopes of rank-size equations where the first slope is that between the primate city (Mexico City) and the second largest place (Guadalajara) and the second slope is the ordinary least squares regression estimate for all cities in the panel except for the largest. Table 8.6 and Figure 8.2A and 8.2B present the measured primacy indices for urban and county based data. It is clear from the evidence that the primacy's peak occurred around 1935 in Mexico. Measured on a county level data base, primacy should reach its 1900 level sometime around 2000, or about the same time as the rest of Mexico's national urban system approaches Zipf's value of −1.

Table 8.7 presents an expanded set of statistics concerning city size distributions in Twentieth Century Mexico. Table 8.7 provides fairly conclusive evidence that inequality in urban sizes has increased steadily over the century within the panel of cities which were adapted. As Petersen argued in a 1979 *Econometrica* article, part of this increase in disparity is due to simple growth at the top of the system without adding new categories at the top.[17] Indubitably, urban population growth within a fixed sample number of cities also has a tendency to produce a clockwise rotation in rank-size estimating equations even though the

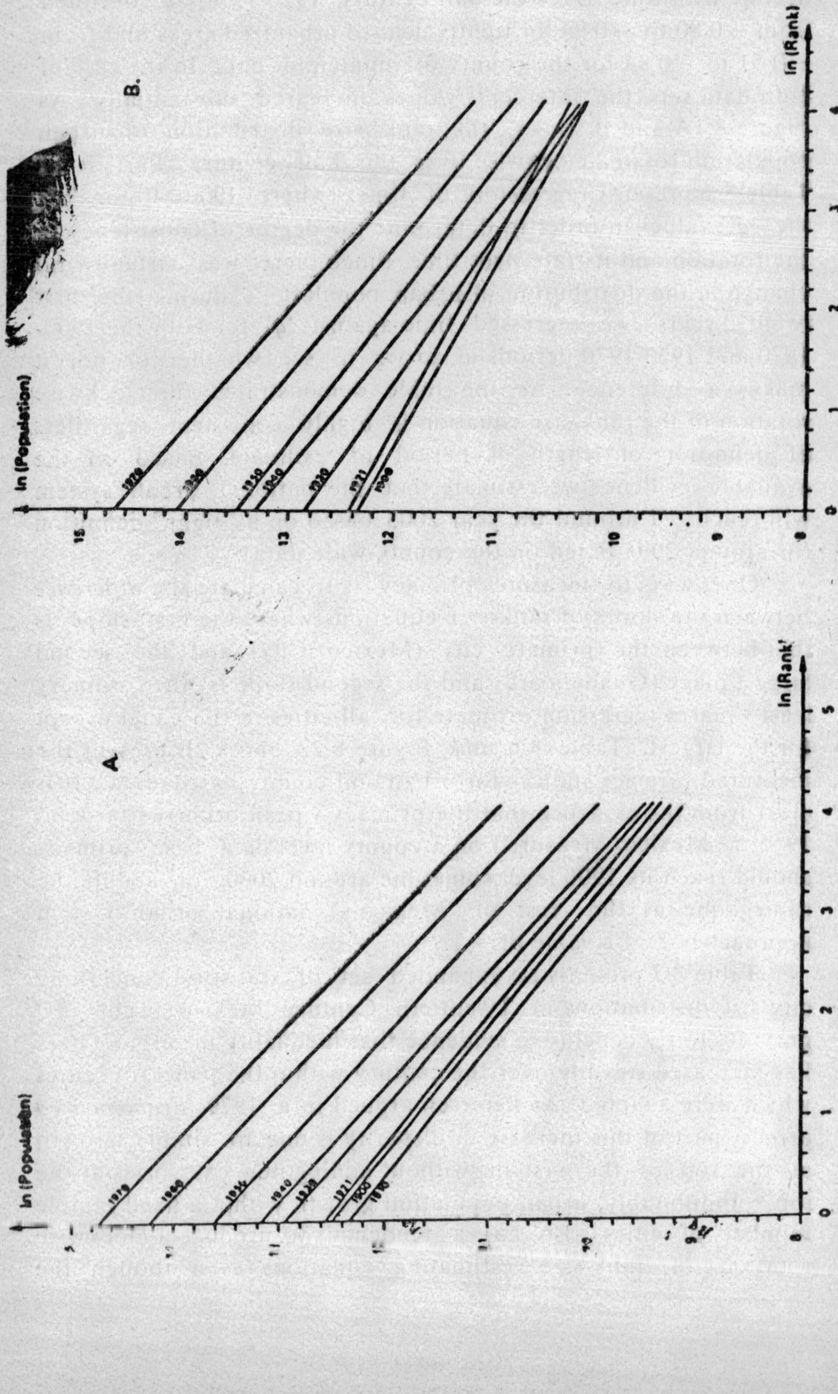
A.
ln (Population)
ln (Rank)
B.
ln (Population)
ln (Rank)

(*a*)

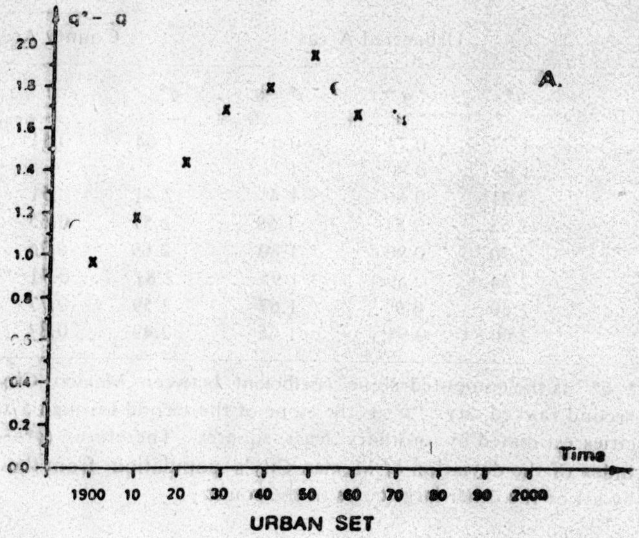

(*b*)

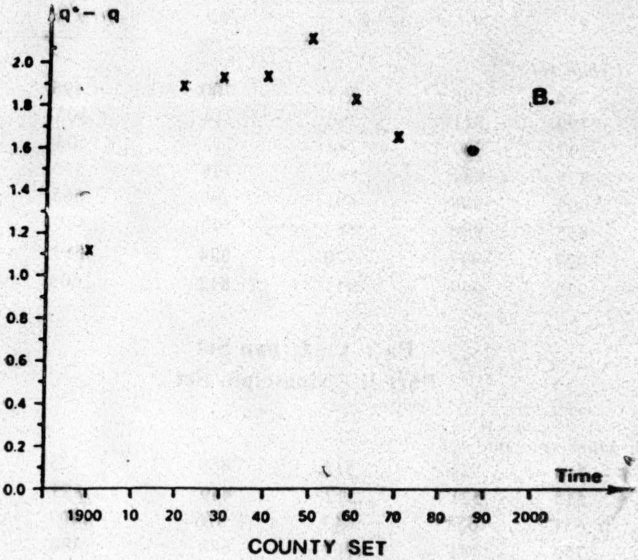

FIG. 8.2 : *Primacy indices*

q^*=Slope between Mexico City and second ranked city.
q=Estimated rank-size slope for 2nd through 57th cities.

TABLE 8.6 : Indexed primacy in Mexico

Date	Urbanized Areas			County Areas		
	q^*	q	$q^*—q$	q^*	q	$q^*—q$
1900	1.77	0.78	0.99	1.64	0.51	1.13
1910	1.98	0.80	1.18	—	—	—
1921	2.21	0.80	1.41	2.41	0.51	1.90
1930	2.55	0.87	1.68	2.57	0.65	1.92
1940	2.70	0.90	1.80	2.69	0.76	1.93
1950	2.84	0.89	1.95	2.81	0.71	2.10
1960	2.60	0.93	1.67	2.59	0.77	1.82
1970	2.60	0.94	1.66	2.49	0.84	1.65

*"q^*" is the computed slope coefficient between Mexico City and the second ranked city. "q" is the slope of the second through 57th ranked cities estimated by ordinary least squares. Therefore, ($q^*—q$) is an index of the deviation of Mexico City's population from the trend set by all of the other large cities in the country.

TABLE 8.7 : An expanded statistical view

	$\hat{q}$	$\hat{q}/r$	$\overset{\frown}{q}/r$	$s_t\overset{\frown}{q}/r$	$s_t\overset{\frown}{q}/r\sqrt{2}$	$\overset{\frown}{G}$
Part A. Urban set						
1900	.784	.796	.781	.700	.495	.3758
1910	.799	.811	.796	.714	.505	.3830
1921	.797	.809	.794	.712	.503	.3900
1930	.875	.884	.868	.778	.550	.4180
1940	.903	.908	.891	.799	.565	.4314
1950	.895	.900	.884	.792	.560	.4246
1960	.927	.937	.920	.824	.583	.4400
1970	.939	.969	.951	.852	.603	.4514

Part A—Urban Set
Part B—Municipio Set

	$\hat{q}$	$\hat{q}/r$	$\overset{\frown}{q}/r$	$s_t\overset{\frown}{q}/r$	$s_t\overset{\frown}{q}/r\sqrt{2}$	$\overset{\frown}{G}$
Part B. Municipio set						
1900	.514	.521	.512	.459	.325	.2560
1921	.515	.521	.512	.459	.325	.2560
1930	.651	.655	.643	.576	.407	.3182
1940	.757	.781	.767	.688	.486	.3720
1950	.705	.709	.696	.624	.441	.3400
1960	.771	.779	.765	.686	.485	.3700
1970	.837	.846	.831	.745	.527	.4040

rotation is not forced. Indeed, the application of Gibrat's Law of Proportionate Effect leads to an upwards, *parallel* shift in the rank-size distribution.

The results of the empirical analysis may be summarized as follows :

(1) Mexico began the century with a primate distribution of city at a low level of urbanization ;
(2) At mid-century, Primacy peaked and the rate of urbanization was very high ;
(3) At century's end, it appears that Mexico will have a rank-size distribution of all cities except the captial at levels of urbanization common to the rest of North America ;
(4) At century's end, it appears that the level of primacy (as indexed by $q^* - q$) will have returned to 1900 levels.

Evaluation

Berry and El Shaks' assertion that primacy should increase, maximize and then decrease toward log linearity as economic development increases is consistent with the Mexican experience. The urban focused theories of Friedmann *et al.* which argue that many forces cause great concentration in a national metropole followed by hierarchically organized diffusion of urban growth with the final product being a network of polarized spaces is not inconsistent with the evidence presented in this paper. The other major conclusion is that the capital city clearly follows a pattern of evolution different from the rest of an emerging national urban system. Prior speculations concerning the unique role of the primate city in headquarters, political and bureaucratic functions seem quite plausible in a national political system which has always been highly centralized. The major substantive question raised concerns the reasons for primacy's peak at mid-century.

Of course, the data used in this study is nearly the simplest imaginable, merely the numbers of people in each of a set of 57 cities at various times during this century. Still the pattern of urbanization is suggestive. Nay, it is intriguing.

There are many unanswered questions. Some are the obvious kinds found at the end of most graduate theses, i.e., others should replicate the author's work someplace else. Others may not be completely self evident. For example, given the proven relationship between the Gini Coefficient and Zipf's Rule provided here, can we relate the level of dispersion in urban population sizes to the level of per capita income to the level of inequality (injustice ?) in income distributions, to rate and level of rural-urban migration and to the political choice which nations make ? Do middle sized cities which are currently "straightening out" the kink in Mexico's rank-size distribution concentrate in great industrial belts ? What happens after "—1 ?" Do major cities continue to become less equal or does the system's slope reverse direction and move toward the "O" in both Zipf's and Gini's indices (as may be happening here in the U.S.A.) ? The Mexican data proved robust under changes in the length of list (not reported here), data transformations or measures of inequality. What happens when you group nations (such as the three in North America) ? Some have asserted that nations being artifices, the rule depends on the definition of territory. How sensitive are these measures to areal definition ? If they are consistently sensitive then that is an intriguing fact because we can then develop a scale rule. If not, we have created one international yardstick for the state of urbanization.

This being a pragmatic era one feels compelled to face up to the question "So what ?" Apart from the justifiable temptation to say "Well, it is interesting", it can be asserted that most regional development strategies depend upon a view that promoting regional urban growth is somehow a necessary and desirable task. What is the evidence from the pattern of urban development, i.e. : what is likely to occur *without* planning ? Are there universal sequences of temporal and spatial patterns of urbanization ? If there are, both science and practice would benefit greatly from knowledge of what they are.

FOOTNOTES

1. Richardson, H.W., "Theory of the Distribution of City Sizes : Review and Prospects," *Regional Siudies*, Vol. 7, 1973, pp. 239-51.
2. Tinbergen, J., "The hierarchy model of the size distribution of centres," *Papers and Proceedings of the Regional Science Association*, Vol. 20, 1968, pp. 65-68.
3. Richardson, *op. cit.*, p. 239.

time is, by definition, determined by speed and distance, both of which are adversely affected by the increase in population, we would expect travel time to increase. A third reason for the increase in travel time which follows an increase in population is that the rising price of land in the CBD makes the opportunity cost of land set aside for transportation (streets, parking, etc.) much higher. Thus, if less land is made available for commuting, even greater congestion is created which further reduces speed and thus travel time.

To sum up the predictions for the monocentric city, it is expected that travel time will be more strongly effected by changes in city size (because of increased congestion) than will travel distance. For the extreme cases in which $E_L = 0$, distance would be the same for all different city sizes while travel time would be expected to rise with city size. If $E_L > 0$, then it is expected that increases in city size will also have a positive effect on travel distance. The higher is E_L, the stronger this effect is expected to be.

Because the monocentric model is not always consistent with actual urban structures, the above discussion must be modified to account for the evolution of urban subcentres. In general, the creation of subcentres should make the effect of city size on travel time and travel distance much weaker than for the monocentric city.

It is possible that the creation of subcentres is subject to a threshold effect. As can be seen in Figure 9.1 a threshold effect results when a subcentre is spawned after the city reaches a certain size (P_1). The effect of added subcentres (1, 2, 3, etc.) is to reduce travel distance (Fig. 9.1A) as some commuters no longer travel to a CBD worksite. As Figure 9.1B indicates, we would also expect average travel time to fall since CBD congestion is reduced with the development of the subcentre and since average travel distance has been reduced. Figure 9.1A suggests that while a general positive relationship between city size (population) and distance (or time) would be expected to hold, the slope of the function may be very different depending upon the number of subcentres in the SMSA.

For travel distance, as the number of subcentres increases, we might expect that the slope of the population—travel distance relationship becomes flatter. This indicates that equal increments

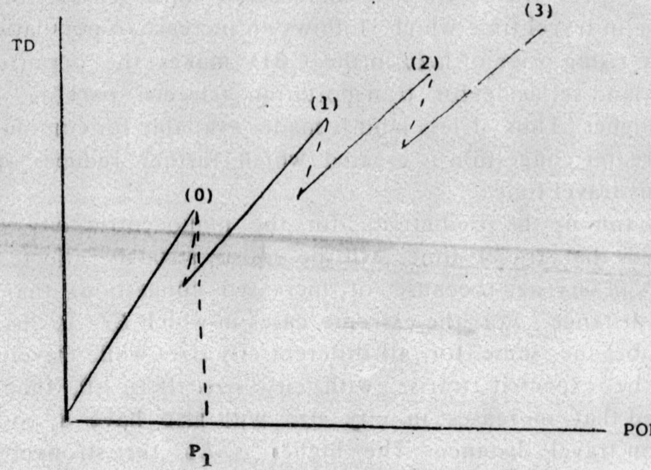

FIG. 9.1 *A* : *The relationship between population and mean travel distance*

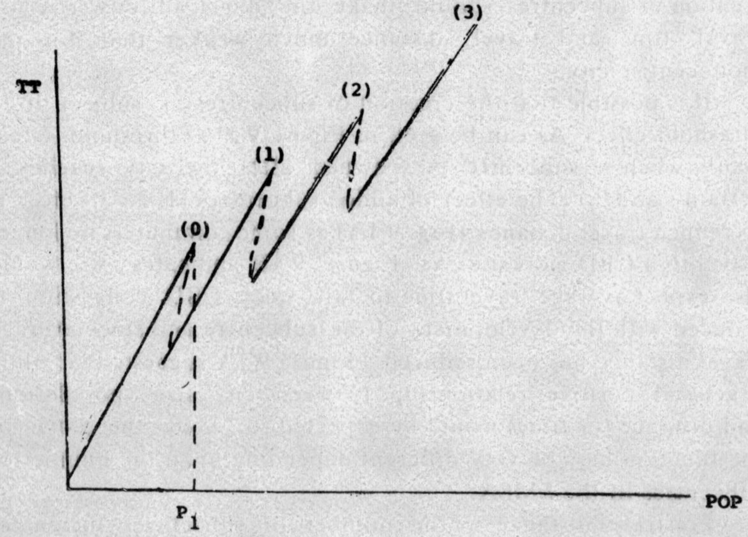

FIG. 9.1 *B* : *The relationship between population and mean travel time*

of population have relatively smaller effects on travel distance in cities which are decentralized (many subcentres) as compared to a monocentric city.

This result would contrast with the hypothesized relationship between population and travel time for varying numbers of subcentres as illustrated in Fig. 9.1B. With respect to travel time, Fig. 9.1B suggests that the rate of increase in travel time with respect to a change in city size is relatively less variant with respect to the number of subcentres in the city. The difference in the two hypothesized relationships stems from the fact that a city with a greater number of subcentres may be relatively more specialized in terms of the functions and interrelationships of the subcentres with the CBD. Households would thus orient themselves with the CBD or a particular subcentre which would lower the average J.T.W. distance. However, assuming that E_L is increasingly lower as physical constraints increasingly limit the potential area of the city, and assuming that the demand for land at the periphery begins to slacken due to an increased geographic isolation from the original CBD as the city grows, we would anticipate that congestion in the CBD and subcentres would increase relatively more and more as the city grows. As the population increases, these limits on the areal expansion of the city imply that the average travel time rises with the increased congestion, thus offsetting to some degree the reduction in travel time resulting from the emergence of subcentres and the consequent reductions in travel distance. Figure 9.1B illustrates this possibility by showing a relatively slower rate of decline in the slope of the travel time-population relationship as the number of subcentres increases when contrasted with the analogous travel distance relationship.

In summary then, the positive relationship between city size (population) and travel time and travel distance is expected to be weaker the greater the number of subcentres in the SMSA. This weakened relationship would be reflected by a generally flatter sloped function as city size increases. Further, the relative flattening in the function relating city size to travel distance should be greater than the flattening of the city size travel time function since greater congestion would offset some of the travel time gains resulting from the lower travel distances which follow the rise of subcentres.

Another dimension of J.T.W. behaviour involves the use of public transportation. Two lines of investigation are addressed here. First, what is the effect of the availability and use of mass transit on travel time and travel distance ? In other words, does the availability of mass transit have any effect on location decisions ? Second, what variables determine the "model split" ; that is, how do we explain the variance in the proportion of the commuting public which uses mass transit, carpooling, or public transit in general [which in this study is the sum of the proportion of mass trans (PMASS) and carpooling commuters (PCARP)].

As can be seen in Table 9.1, the relative importance of public transportation in American cities is small. Even with our broad definition of the proportion of the city's population using public transit (PPUB), less than one quarter of the population used public transit in 1975 and only one out of five travellers used public transit in 1977.[5]

TABLE 9.1 : **Means (%) and standard deviations (%) of**

Variable	Year		
	1975	1976	1977
PPUB	23.28 (4.16)	21.52 (7.07)	20.69 (5.43)
PMASS	6.62 (4.46)	5.52 (8.28)	5.18 (4.56)
PCARP	16.65 (2.83)	15.99 (2.88)	15.50 (2.04)

Source : Annual Housing Survey(s), 1975, 1976, 1977.

Mass transit requires high density areas if the large capital investments implied by rapid rail facilities is to be justified. Because of the positive relationship between city size and density (see Hoch[5]), it is expected that city size would have a positive effect on the relative use of mass transit. Carpooling is more flexible given low scale economies and would be equally suited to all density levels characteristic of cities. However, the increased congestion which is hypothesized to correspond to increases in population should imply a positive relationship between city size and carpooling behaviour.[6]

During 1973 and into 1974, the major interruption of oil and gas supplies not only drove up the price of gasoline substantially but introduced great uncertainty with respect to the availability and the future price of gasoline as well. These changes would be expected to encourage commuters to better utilize mass transit or carpooling as an alternative to the private car. Further, we would expect a gradual centralization of households as families adjust to the now higher transportation costs by locating closer to their job sites (or by employers moving closer to concentrations of labour). Taken together, the 1973 embargo would be expected to make mass transit and carpooling more attractive because of, one, a substitution effect and, two, the effect of higher density (higher residential concentration). Further, to the extent that real income fell as a result of the 1974-75 recession touched off in large part by the supply shock of the oil embargo, the demand for public transit should rise as public transit is generally viewed as an inconvenient mode of transport and thus an inferior good. Consequently, lower real incomes should encourage commuters to shift to public transit as they substitute inconvenience for transport cost savings.

The effect of public transportation facilities (especially mass transit) on household location is to increase density along the transit routes. To the extent that mass transit encourages centralization by concentrating people around transit lines, we would expect a negative relationship between the proportion of the population using public transportation (PPUB) and travel distance. Total travel time, on the other hand, might easily show a positive relationship with PPUB since actual travel time ["line haul" time for Mills (6, p. 145)] plus waiting time [suburban collection" and "downtown distribution" time ; (ibid.)] should be higher for mass transit commuters than for private car commuters. In other words, the greater the proportion of commuters using mass transit, the higher the average travel time. This prediction would be further reinforced through the density/congestion characteristic of any city with well developed public transit facilities ; that is, the more densely developed the c ty (such that mass transit is justified), the greater the congestion and thus the lower the speed of all forms of commuting.

Because total transportation costs are the sum of money costs and time costs, an analysis of the speed of travel is important to our examination of household location and J.T.W. behaviour. While it may be reasonable to assume that the monetary costs of a commute are proportional to travel distance, assuming the same relationship between distance and time costs would only be valid if the speed of travel were constant between cities as well as across a given city. However, the amount of time it takes to travel a given distance depends on several variables such as road conditions (e.g., expressway vs. side street travel, road width, relative curvature, and surface condition), weather conditions, public investments in traffic control, and the volume of traffic. Because of variations in speed, it is sometimes possible to substitute distance for time, for instance, by locating further from the work site but gaining direct rapid rail or high speed freeway access as a result of the relocation. Thus, it is possible that savings in time costs more than compensate the commuter for the increases in money costs associated with moving further from the job site.

Our investigation looks at a reasonably narrow dimension of speed ; that is, the effect of city size on speed.[7] More specifically, the question that we explore is, what happens to speed as city size increases ? Do we have economies of scale with respect to speed or diseconomies of scale ? These questions will be addressed in the empirical analysis which follows.

EMPIRICAL ANALYSIS

Data sources

The main source of information for this study is the Annual Housing Survey for the years 1975, 1976, and 1977.[8] For each of these years, the Bureau of the Census collected detailed data for twenty different SMSAs through household interviews.[9] Among other variables, the Annual Housing Surveys present aggregate (SMSA-wide) data for heads of households on median travel time, median travel distance, and means of transportation as well as distributions for the travel time and travel distance variables. These distributions are used in the analysis to calculate a weighted average travel time and a weighted average travel distance. It is the natural log of these two variables which we use as the principal dependent variables in the analysis.

The sample size is treated in the empirical analysis as a cross section which implicitly ignores structural changes occurring during the three year period over which the data were collected. Such an assumption is justified by the high degree of aggregation (SMSA level) and by the observation that significant locational changes would be slow to occur such that possible changes in the structure of the urban economy are unlikely to create significant empirical biases. Finally, to the extent that bias due to the temporal inequality of the sample might be a problem, regression results are presented both with and without dummy variables to hold the year of the observation constant when appropriate (i.e., D76, D77 in regression tables. D75 is the omitted category).

Empirical results

Travel distance and travel time

One hypothesis implied by the monocentric city model is that city size should have a strong and positive effect on travel distance (except where $E_L=0$) and an even stronger effect on travel time (due to the increased congestion which follows an increase in population). A simple log-linear regression analysis of the weighted means[10] of travel distance and travel time for the total population of the SMSA (POP, our city size measure) produced the following results (standard errors in parentheses) :

$$(1) \quad LTD=1.64+\underset{(.017)}{.092}\ LPOP \qquad \bar{R}^2=.32\ (n=61)$$

$$(2) \quad LTT=2.03+\underset{(.016)}{.142}\ LPOP \qquad \bar{R}^2=.55\ (n=61)$$

where :

LTD=natural log of the weighted mean of trave distance for the SMSA

LTT=natural log of the weighted mean of travel time for the SMSA

$LPOP$=natural log of the total population of the SMSA

$\bar{R}^2$=adjusted coefficient of variation

n=number of observations.

As indicated by these results, the coefficient on our city size measure (LPOP) is positive and significant in both regressions.

Moreover, the rate of change of travel time with respect to a change in city size is significantly greater than the corresponding measure for travel distance. Alternatively stated, the elasticity of travel time with respect to changes in city size (.142) is 55 per cent greater than the elasticity of travel distance (.092). This result supports our basic hypothesis that, not only do travel time and travel distance increase with population but that travel distance increases more rapidly (due to increased congestion and thus reduced speed). Consequently, the distance parameter which is the central focus of the Alonso-Muth models is likely to be an incomplete characterization of household locational choice since the implicit one to one correspondence between travel distance and travel time does not hold for cities of different sizes. Further, these results are somewhat consistent with the result found by Voorhees *et al.*[14] even though their sample size was much smaller (23 vs. our 61) and his unit of observation is the central city instead of the SMSA as in our study.[11]

Even though these city size coefficients are found to be positive and statistically significant as hypothesized, their magnitudes are relatively small. According to these estimates, a 10 per cent increase in the population of the SMSA would produce a slightly less than 1 per cent increase in the average travel distance and a nearly 1.5 per cent increase in the average travel time.

These basic results raise two further questions which make it necessary to extend the analysis. First, would these results be consistent over different city sizes ? Second, how stable are these simple results when other relevant variables such as income, education, age of the housing stock, and density (as well as other descriptive variables) are added to the analysis ?

With respect to the first question, consistency over city size, our theoretical discussion suggests that the positive relationship between travel distance (or travel time) and population should hold but that this relationship should be weaker as city size increases, especially the relationship between travel distance and city size. This is the predicted effect of the development of subcentres within the SMSA. That is, the larger city, the greater the likelihood that a subcentre or multiple subcentres will be spawned.[12] We would therefore expect that the coefficients on the population variable in our regression analyses would be smaller for a subsample of large SMSAs when compared with a medium or small

SMSA group (especially for travel distance).

To address this first question, we divided our sample into three groups based upon SMSA population differences.[13] Group I contains all SMSAs with a population less than or equal to 625,000. Group II contains all SMSAs with a population greater than 625,000 but less than or equal to 1,600,000. Group III includes SMSAs with populations greater than 1,600,000. The results for these groups are presented in Table 9.2.

TABLE 9.2 : **(Log-linear) Regression results for travel distance (*LTD*) and travel time (*LTT*) on population (*LPOP*) by city size**

	Group I Small SMSAs POP⩽625,000		Group II Medium SMSAs 625,000<POP ⩽1,600,000		Group III Large SMSAs POP>1,600,000	
	LTD	*LTT*	*LTD*	*LTT*	*LTD*	*LTT*
	1	2	3	4	5	6
Constant	1.41	2.90	1.46	2.59	1.98	1.97
LPOP	.129	—.0006	.119	.059	.050	.153
(S.E.)	(.139)	(.1142)	(.064)	(.061)	(.050)	(.050)
R^2	—.01	0	.10	—.01	—.01	.32
n	16	16	26	26	19	19

As can be seen from Table 9.2 there are obvious differences between the three groups in spite of their weak statistical quality. Figures 9.2 and 9.3 illustrate these differences.

In Figure 9.2, the positive (though often statistically insignificant) trend of travel distance with respect to increases in population becomes weaker as we move from Group I (S) to Group III (L). In contrast, the travel time results show the opposite trend. The interpretation of these results is that relatively small SMSAs accommodate an increase in population by spreading the area of the city to the relatively close, inexpensive land at the periphery. Thus travel distance may increase (as shown by the positive coefficient of the population variable in column 1 of Table 9.2) but travel time remains roughly the same (or perhaps even falls slightly) since the increase in congestion may be minimal given the opportunity to develop road systems of

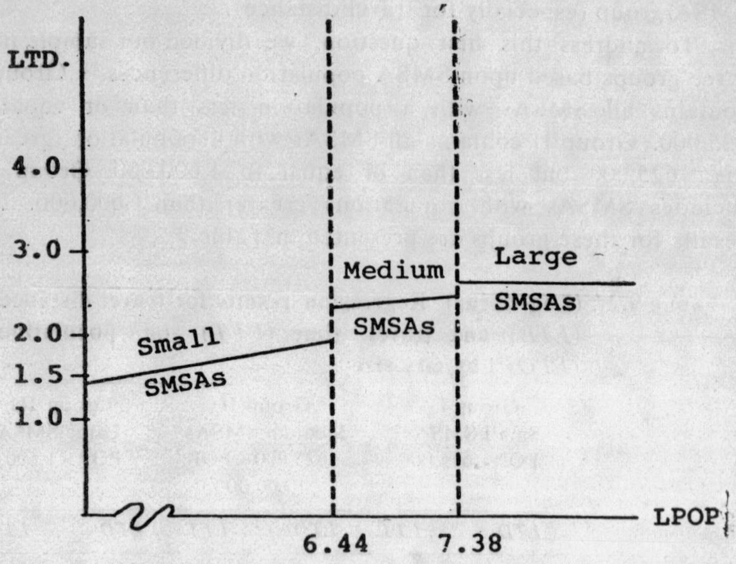

FIG. 9.2 : *Travel distence and city size*

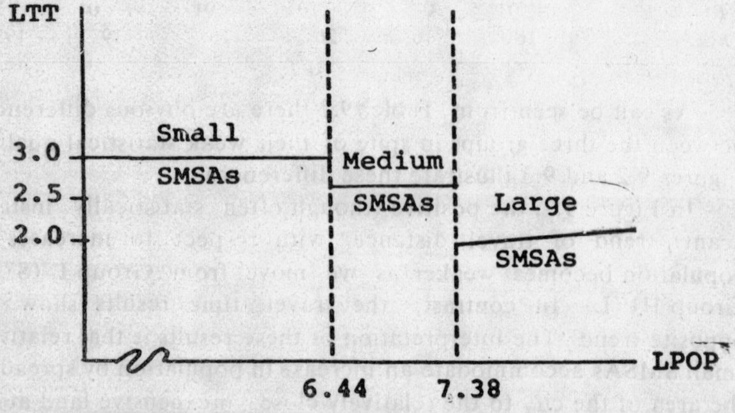

FIG. 9.3 : *Travel time and city size*

minimum efficient scale to handle the increase in traffic, or perhaps a population threshold is reached such that subcentres develop.[14]

This relationship changes with the size of the city. As we move to Groups II and III in Table 9.2, the population coefficient falls for travel distance but becomes positive, increases, and becomes significant for travel time in the largest SMSAs. For Group III, the increase in travel distance for a 1 per cent increase in population is the smallest (with a coefficient equal in size to its standard error) whereas the increase in travel time is greatest for a 1 per cent increase in population (elasticity equal to .153). This result tends to support the hypothesis presented in the theoretical section that large SMSAs are increasingly constrained in the expansion of their land area by supply constraints (river, mountains, etc.) as well as demand constraints (low demand for land at the periphery due to isolation from the economic centre of the city, the CBD). Further, the greater number of subcentres associated with large SMSAs help to accommodate increases in populations. Thus, travel distance is only modestly effected (low coefficient, weak statistical significance as shown in column 5 of Table 9.2). Travel time on the other hand begins to increase more dramatically in the large SMSAs since little new land is available for more subcentres or improved transportation networks and therefore the density of population and development increases to produce slower commutes (i.e., E_L is low for large cities).[15] Further, the increase in population density allows the shift of a greater proportion of the population to mass transit.[16] The higher waiting times implied by that modal choice would contribute to higher travel times overall in large cities. We now move to an examination of the second extension of this basic analysis of the effect of city size on J.T.W. behaviour ; that is, what is the effect of city size on travel time and travel distance in a broader context which includes the influence of other variables ? To address this question, we analyze the multiple regression results listed in Table 9.3.

Columns 1—4 in Table 9.3 present the regression results for travel distance and columns 5—8 report the regression results for travel time. In general, our set of independent variables explains travel time much better than travel distance. The $\bar{R}^2$s in the travel time regressions are always above .70 while the $\bar{R}^2$s for the travel distance equations never exceed .46. As discussed earlier, such a result would be expected since travel distance is only one component of travel time. Further, as has been shown by many researchers, households are more aware of the time dimension of

TABLE 9.3 : **Log-linear regressions equations for travel distance and travel time**

	Travel Distance				Travel Time			
	1	2	3	4	5	6	7	8
LPOP	.090*	—	.093*	.094*	.079	—	.079*	.078*
	(.020)		(.020)	(.019)	(.107)		(.017)	(.016)
DENST	.034*	.050*	.036*	.035*	.026	.035*	.030*	.030*
	(.017)	(.019);	(.019)	(.017)	(.016)	(.016)	(.016)	(.015)
LINC	.288*	.278	.361*	.362*	.303*	.220*	.399	.397*
	(.130)	(.150)	(.146)	(.144)	(.111)	(.119)	(.121)	(.119)
EDUC	—.128*	—.128*	—.132*	—.133*	—(.809)*	—.087*	—.102*	—.100*
	(.057)	(.059)	(.057)	(.056)	(.048)	(.049)	(.048)	(.048)
AGE	—.010*	—.010*	—.010*	—.010*	—.002	—.002	—.002	—.002
	(.003)	(.004)	(.003)	(.003)	(.003)	(.003)	(.002)	(.003)
PPUB	—.490	—.483	—.597	—.596	1.010*	1.010*	.850*	.848*
	(.368)	(.384)	(.382)	(.379)	(.310)	(320)	(.317)	(.314)
TEMP	—.0004	—.001	—.001	—.001	.001	.001	.001	.001
	(.0013)	(.001)	(.001)	(.001)	(.001)	(.001)	(.001)	(.001)
REG	—.598	—.713	—.089	—	—.120	—.179	—.133	—
	(.475)	(.493)	(.644)		(.405)	(.409)	(.534)	

D77	—	—	—.061	—.065	—	—	—0.59	—.053
			(.049)	(.038)			(.041)	(.032)
D76	—	—	—.015	—.016	—	—	—.056*	—.056*
			(.033)	(.033)	—	—	(.028)	(.027)
PD2		.108*				.079*		
	—	(.036)	—	—	—	(.030)	—	—
PD3		.167*				.168*		
	—	(.045)	—	—	—	(.037)	—	—
CON	3.24	3.86	2.82	2.78	2.63	3.30	2.46	2.53
$\bar{R}^2$	.458	.410	.453	.464	.720	.711	.733	.738
S.E.E.	.099	.103	.099	.099	.084	.086	.083	.082
N	61	61	61	61	61	61	61	61

*Significant at the 5 per cent level or better (two-tailed test).

the J.T.W. than distance or the direct money cost *per se*.[17]

The performance and interpretation of most of the explanatory variables are generally similar in each set of regressions in terms of the direction and significance of the coefficients. There are only two variables with opposite signs between the two sets of regressions ; they are, the proportion of the population using public transportation (PPUB) and temperature (TEMP). In the travel distance equations, PPUB is negative but of only weak significance while in the travel time regressions, PPUB is positive and significant. TEMP on the other hand, never achieves statistical significance. (Each of these results is discussed below.) We now analyze the effect of the independent variables on travel distance and travel time.

City size

The variable of primary interest is city size as measured by the SMSA population (in log form, LPOP). The coefficient of LPOP is always positive and significant. The magnitude of the elasticity of travel distance with respect to population is about .09. This means that an increase of 10 per cent in population produces slightly less than a 1 per cent increase in the average length of the work trip. To illustrate by example the size of this response, as we move from an SMSA such as Grand Rapids, Michigan (POP = 570,000) to an SMSA such as Atlanta, Georgia (POP=1,800,000) which is more than three times greater in population, the average length of the work trip would rise by only 19 per cent.[18] Given that the mean travel distance in Grand Rapids is 9.0 miles, the predicted value for Atlanta would be 10.7 miles. (The actual mean travel distance for Atlanta is 11.4 miles.)

With respect to travel time, the estimated elasticity is about .08, indicating that a 10 per cent increase in population leads to a .8 per cent increase in travel time. Again, using the same two SMSAs for the sake of illustration, the additional travel time in Atlanta due to the higher population when compared to Grand Rapids is 2.8 minutes or only a 17.2 per cent increase.[19]

It is important to note that the coefficients of the LPOP variable in the travel distance regressions in Table 9.3 are the same as the coefficient of LPOP reported in equation 1 (in which LPOP is the only explanatory variable). Thus, the introduction of other variables does not effect the estimated relationship between travel distance and city size. In contrast, the estimated effect of population on travel time reported in Table 9.3 is significantly different from the relationship estimated when LPOP was the only independent variable (equation 2 reported at the beginning of this section). The elasticity drops from .142 to the .08 range with the introduction of other explanatory variables.[20] This indicates that the population variable is picking up the added influence of other excluded variables in the travel time regressions but not in the travel distance regressions. As we discuss below, many of these omitted covariates with travel time influence the speed of the commute. Since speed effects travel time but not travel distance (the two definitionally determine travel time), the addition of variables such as DENST, AGE, and PPUB would be expected to impact travel time relationship more than travel distance (to the extent that these variables are covariate with LPOP). Thus, once we include congestion/speed measures, the one-to-one relationship between travel distance and travel time implicitly assumed by Alonso and Muth is restored. The le.son is, of course, that a simple distance parameter can only be applied empirically as the sole measure of household location if the speed of the commute is held constant, either directly or indirectly.

In columns 2 and 6 of Table 9.3, we use a different measure of the city size variable. PD1, PD2, and PD3 are population dummy variables used to categorize the SMSAs in the sample by size. PD1 equals 1 if the city's population is less than or equal to 625,000 (zero otherwise) ; PD2 equals 1 if the city's population is between 625,000 and 1,600,000 (zero otherwise) ; and PD3 equals 1 if the city's population is greater than 1,600,000 (zero otherwise).[21] The excluded category in columns 2 and 6 is PD1, the small SMSA dummy variable.

As can be seen in columns 2 and 6 of Table 9.3, the population dummy variables (PD2, PD3) are always positive and significant. Note that the magnitude the coefficient of the PD3 variable is significantly greater than that of PD2. Further, the rate of increase in travel time is larger than for travel distance as we move from PD2 to PD3.[22] Thus, not only is the predicted positive relationship between city size and travel time/travel distance again borne out but we have a further indication that travel time is more effected by city size than is travel distance.

Density

The density variable (DENST) is defined as total population per square mile for the SMSA. While DENST might be expected to be highly correlated with city size,[23] no significant colinearity problem is evidenced by the results presented in Table 9.3 since DENST clearly adds independent information in explaining our J.T.W. measures. As predicted, the coefficient of DENST is positive and significant in all eight regressions, although modest instability with respect to the size of the coefficient is manifested when we introduce the dummy variable measure of population as opposed to entering LPOP. (Thus, some of the above mentioned colinearity is present.) For travel distance, the positive result indicates that people find the disadvantages of "crowding up" (i.e., higher crime rates ; more noise, dirt, congestion, etc.) to outweigh the advantages (economies of scale in construction, shorter travel distances) and therefore move outward. Given that E_L is greater than zero, this means that the new population causes the city to "spill out" towards its periphery as the monocentric model would predict.

For the travel time results, the positive coefficient reflects two basic forces. First, since higher densities encourage households to live further away from their place of work, the added distance *per se* raises travel time. Second, the positive association between density and congestion might lead to a reduction in the speed of travel. Thus, the travel time could rise because of worsening traffic. Alternatively, if locating further from the job site allows the worker to travel on better roads or forces him/her to drive instead of using the more time intensive alternative of mass transit, travel speed might even increase in spite of the increase in congestion due to higher densities. In such a case, travel time would not increase by more than an amount implied by the greater travel distance. The elasticities of travel distance and travel time with respect to changes in density implied by our results are about .29 and .24 respectively. (No statistically significant difference is manifested.) Thus, the changes in travel time seem to substantially reflect changes in travel distance.

Income

The income variable (in its log form, LINC) is defined as median household income for the SMSA. Economic theory suggests that the effect of income on travel time and distance is likely to be a complicated relationship. Since what a worker can earn as income reflects the opportunity cost of that worker's time, it is expected that the worker would try to cut the time spent commuting as his/her income increased.[24] At the same time, however, a rise in income encourages most households to increase their consumption of housing in general and "space" or land in particular. Thus, households with rising incomes may tend to buy bigger houses at locations more distant from the job site (as land is cheaper outside the CBD). The net effect of a change in income on both time and distance is difficult to predict as these two effects suggest opposite responses. The higher opportunity cost of commuting time suggests closer, "quicker" locations while the increased demand for housing and space suggest more distant locations with higher travel times.

The empirical analysis shows that, for the average household, the second effect (larger houses, more land) dominates the incentive to minimize travel time. The coefficient of LINC is always positive and significant for all Table 9.3 regressions. Further, the elasticities are generally comparable indicating that changes in travel time attributable to changes in income are proportionate and generally seem to reflect the changes in travel distance which follow changes in income.

Education

The education variable, EDUC, measures the mean number of years of formal education for the SMSA population. As a standardizing variable, education is expected to reflect two general attributes of the population. First, the more educated the population, the more efficient will be the exchange of and response to information. For instance, with the dramatic rise in fuel prices that followed the 1973 oil crisis, we would expect households to adjust, perhaps by buying new fuel efficient cars or relocating closer to the job site. Thus, the more educated the population, the quicker the response to changes in the urban environment are expected to be. The education variable indicates that EDUC has a negative and significant effect on both travel time and travel distance, thus confirming our hypothesis. Since the oil crisis, the more informed have apparently acted to save on their transportation cost by reducing travel time and travel distance.

The second characteristic of the population which may be reflected through the EDUC variable is the occupational mix of the city's population. To the extent that more educated populations contain relatively larger numbers of professional workers, employers may be relatively more flexible with respect to employment location. Thus, besides being more informed shoppers when buying or renting housing, the job sites of relatively more educated populations may be more convenient. The negative coefficient for EDUC may in part reflect this accommodation by employers toward white-collar workers.

Age

The weighted average age of the housing stock of the SMSA (AGE) was calculated from an age distribution of housing stock presented in the Annual Housing Survey(s) (U.S. Bureau of the Census).[10] The AGE measure is intended to capture differences in urban structure, particularly the "inertia" or history of the SMSA. Older cities have relatively greater transactions costs associated with adjusting to changing economic conditions than do newer cities which have an infrastructure better designed to accommodate the automobile. Thus, the increased congestion resulting from population growth may be more severe in older SMSAs since these "established" cities adjust to newer transportation technologies more slowly or less efficiently. (One need only drive the contorted expressways of the older northeastern SMSAs to understand the difficulty with which modern transportation was introduced into these cities.) Further, the age of the housing stock should reflect the higher degree of centralization (decentralization) found as an accident of history in older (younger) cities.

The AGE variable enters negatively in all regressions. However, an acceptable level of statistical significance is reached only for the travel distance results. AGE is not significant in the travel time regressions. While the travel distance estimates are strongly reflecting the hypothesized centralization and inertia of older cities, the weakness of the travel time results is probably due to the higher congestion and consequent slower speeds that are associated with the crowded, inefficient highway systems of these cities. Thus, the time saving effect of shorter average travel distances is countered by lower speeds.

Public transportation

The per cent of the population which uses public transportation, PPUB, enters the travel distance regressions negatively but insignificantly, although columns 3 and 4 indicate a nearly acceptable level of significance (t=1.52 and 1.57, respectively). This probably reflects the fact that public transportation is most efficient and most available in densely populated areas. The failure of PPUB to achieve an acceptable level of significance is in part due to the (appropriate) inclusion of the DENST and AGE variables, which may already account for this effect.

The results are quite different in the travel time regressions. Here, PPUB enters positively and significantly. This result reflects the relatively slower speeds of public transportation.[25]

Temperature and the price of gasoline

These two variables are related only in their failure to show any significant effect on either travel time or travel distance. For temperature (TEMP) it was expected that a bad climate (which we define here as low mean temperature during the month of January) would encourage centralization, as people prefer to drive shorter distances, but increase travel time, as driving speed in wintery conditions would be lower. However, neither result is manifested in Table 9.3. (In fact the signs are the opposite of our expectation.)

The price of gasoline (REG) enters most regressions as negative but insignificant. The estimates become especially weak with the introduction of the year dummies, D76 and D77, to hold the year of the observation constant. One would expect that REG would enter both sets of regressions negatively since higher gasoline prices imply higher transportation costs. Our locational models predict a greater centralization as households try to save money by moving closer to the jobsite. The shorter commutes should then imply reduced travel times (with at least a partial offset in time savings caused by increased congestion and/or a switch by households to (slower) mass transit). These effects should be particularly relevant during the period of the analysis, 1975-1977, since the price of gasoline had only recently increased dramatically as a result of the oil embargo of 1973-1974. However, these hypotheses are not confirmed by the results in Table 9.3.

One problem which arises in the measurement of the REG variable is that there are no local deflators available for all (or even most) of the SMSAs in our sample. Consequently, REG is not a measure of *real* gasoline prices. A further problem is that a true centralization process which might follow such a dramatic increase in transportation costs would likely take many years. Thus, the 1975-1977 observations in our sample are too close to the supply shock to which households are expected to adjust. This is especially true when we consider that the immediate effect of the 1973 oil embargo was to throw the economies of the world into a deep recession which significantly reduces both the confidence of consumers and their ability to adapt to a changing economic environment.

(*D75*), *D76*, *D77*. In order to hold constant the year of the observation, year dummy variables were entered into both the travel distance and travel time regressions. D75, the dummy variable with a value of 1 if the observation was from 1975 (zero otherwise), is the excluded category in Table 9.3 regressions (columns 3, 4 and 7, 8). The inclusion of these variables should correct for the fact that our sample is a mix of time series and cross section observations. The coefficients of D76 and D77 are always negative. For the travel distance equations D77 shows only a weak statistical significance for a two-tailed test (i.e., $t = 1.24$ and 1.71 in columns 3 and 4 respectively). D76 is insignificant. The increased magnitude and significance of the year dummy coefficients suggests that a trend toward centralization may be slowly occurring in response to higher energy prices. A similar pattern is evidenced in the travel time regressions except that the significant coefficients are the D76 rather than the weakly significant D77 results. The coefficients are also consistently around −.056 suggesting that whatever centralizing trend is occurring, it does now show an increasing effect with respect to travel time.

The means of transportation choice

As shown in Table 9.1 above, public transportation is utilized by a small and apparently decreasing number of commuters. In 1975, an estimated 23.3 per cent of all households used some form of public transportation (either carpooling, 16.7 per cent, or mass transit, 6.6 per cent). By 1977, this proportion had dropped to

20.7 per cent (15.5 per cent carpooling and 5.2 per cent mass transit). The purpose of this section is to briefly examine household choice of transportation mode.

Theory suggests that commuters would assess the relative prices of different transportation options and choose that option which is cheapest in terms of dollars, time and other associated disutilities (such as crowding on a bus or subway or time spent in traffic jams when commuting by car). Further, these relative prices will in part be determined by the relative efficiency of each mode of transport. For example, the large economies of scale associated with rapid rail transit imply that both the average and marginal cost of a given trip will be lower if the ridership is large. (Thus, fares and the relative price of rapid rail will be attractive.) Clearly, this productive efficiency must in turn depend upon the structure of the city. A truly monocentric city would favour the development of an efficient, low cost rapid rail system since both the density of households and the density of job sites allow for easy collection and distribution of workers. In contrast, the monocentric city discourages automobile commuting since travel times would be high in the relatively congested CBD. Also high parking fees due to the relatively high price of land. And, perhaps, relatively high psychic costs associated with traffic jams and the spotty availability of parking would further discourage travel by private automobile.

On the other extreme, an SMSA with many subcentres may produce the opposite relative prices for modal choice. The decentralization of jobs and people makes rapid rail inefficient and therefore costly while the spreading out of the SMSA through its subcentres makes access by automobile convenient and efficient. Thus, urban structure should play a significant role in determining modal choice.

In order to examine these hypotheses empirically, multiple regression analysis was performed using three alternative measures of modal choice as dependent variables. The first dependent variable specification is PPUB, the per cent of the working households in the SMSA using public transportation, which is broadly defined to include carpoolers and mass transit commuters. The second and third specification break PPUB into its components ; that is, we use PCARP, the per cent of SMSA commuters using carpools, and PMASS, the per cent of SMSA commuters using mass transit (bus and/or rail), as dependent variables. Table 9.4 presents the results for all three specifications.

TABLE 9.4 : **Regression equations for means of transportation choice**

	PPUB (1)	PCARP (2)	PMASS (3)
POP	—.000004	—.000006*	.000010*
	(.000006)	(.000000)[a]	(.000000)[a]
SP	—.471*	—.150*	—.319*
	(.097)	(.078)	(.090)
REG	—.057	—.056	**
	(.199)	(.153)	
AGE	.0007	—.0011	.0017
	(.0012)	(.0008)	(.0010)
PI	—.030	—.022	—.008
	(.025)	(.020)	(.022)
INC	.0013	.0047	—.0023
	(.0030)	(.0024)	(.0027)
DENST	.021*	—.0032	.024*
	(.006)	(.0044)	(.005)
EDUC	.026	—.0099	.035*
	(.017)	(.0135)	(.015)
TEMP	.0005	**	.0005
	(.0004)		(.0004)
D77	—.023	—.015	—.008
	(.014)	(.012)	(.010)
D76	**	—.004	.003
		(.008)	(.009)
Constant	.097	.395	—.296
$\bar{R}^2$	.707	.158	.795
S.E.E.	.031	.024	.027
n	61	61	61

* Significant at the 5 per cent level or better (*two*-tailed test. Standard errors are in parentheses.

** Zero effect. Variable was so insignificant that regression package did not load it.

a Standard error is very small and rounds to zero.

The estimates in Table 9.4 indicate that the choice to carpool is poorly explained by the independent variables ($\bar{R}^2 = .158$) while the choice to use mass transit is reasonably well explained by these variables ($\bar{R}^2$=.795). Further, the overall PPUB equation estimated in column 1 seems to most closely reflect the results estimated for PMASS in column 3. A general result then is that the split between private auto and public transportation is not the only modal choice of interest. Once a choice in favour of public transportation has been made, there is still the separate decision as to which form to adopt, carpooling or mass transit. Since Table 9.4 results suggest that these are very different choices, we will focus here on columns 2 and 3 to high-light these differences.

The first important difference relates to city size. As can be seen for the population variable (POP) the decision to carpool is more likely in small cities as opposed to large SMSAs. This is consistent with the hypothesis that economies of scale in mass transit must be exploited to make mass transit cheap and available. Thus, a threshold effect is reflected by the positive sign on POP in column 3. For carpooling, the bigger cities produce more congestion and thus raise the price of carpooling relative to using mass transit.

In all three regressions, travel speed (SP) enters negatively. This is the expected result since a more efficient flow of traffic indicates lower time costs either because of a better road system or shorter travel distances due to subcentre development. In either case, the relative price of commuting by private car is lower and thus commuters shift away for all forms of mass transit with its many attendant inconveniences.

The price of regular gasoline (REG), performs very poorly in all three regressions. Its expected sign is positive since a higher gasoline price raises the relative price of using a private car (or a carpool). However, REG enters negatively and insignificantly (if loaded at all). One possible explanation is that the *real* price of gasoline during this period was unchanged or possibly even decreased slightly. (As explained earlier, local deflators for our SMSAs were not available. Thus, the nominal price of gasoline is used.)

The mean age of the housing stock variable, AGE, produces opposite signs in the PCARP regression and the PMASS regression. While neither is significant at the 5 per cent level for a two tailed test, the positive coefficient on AGE satisfies the 5 per cent level of significance for a one tailed test (which is appropriate when the sign of the coefficient is predicted *a priori*). As expected, the older, more centralized cities are better structured to produce mass transit efficiently and probably discourage commuting by private auto as congestion in the CBDs of these older cities raises the relative price of both private cars and carpools. (Hence, the negative sign in column 2.) Thus, urban structure does effect modal transportation choices.

Amongst the variables which do not perform well is PI, the per cent of the SMSA population in the central city. Similar to density, this variable was expected to help characterize the urban structure, especially potential market for close-in mass transit riders.

Household income (INC) shows the expected sign for mass transit but is not significant. Historically, the slower, more inconvenient mass transit alternative is avoided by those with the income to drive to and park in the CBD. Further, private automobiles lower the door-to-door travel time and, thus, people with relatively higher opportunity costs to their time will opt for private cars. The positive sign of INC in the PCARP regression though insignificant, suggests that carpools represent the middle ground between private autos and mass transit, at least as far as these choices are effected by income level.

Another interesting contrast between the choice to carpool and the mass transit choice is reflected by the estimates of the population density coefficients (DENST). As predicted for PMASS, more densely structured cities will encourage the development of efficient mass transit. This prediction is supported by the empirical analysis. The opposite would be true for carpooling as congestion rises with density. While the estimate is insignificant, a sign reversal on the DENST coefficient lends weak support to this expectation. Once again, urban structure effects the choice of transportation mode.

The education variable (EDUC) provides still another contrasting result. In the PMASS regression, EDUC enters as positive and significant while an insignificant but negative coefficient is estimated for PCARP. The EDUC variable is most likely capturing differences in the occupational mixes between cities. That is, SMSAs with a more educated population probably have a strong CBD and a higher proportion of professional workers whose job site is in the CBD. In contrast, SMSAs with relatively larger blue collar populations may be better characterized by industrial subcentres in the city's ring. If this tendency occurs the more educated SMSA populations will be correlated with an urban structure conducive to efficient mass transit. Hence, the result is a positive and significant sign for the EDUC variable in the PMASS regression but a negative though insignificant sign in the PCARP estimate.

The climate variable, TEMP, never produces a statistically significant result. We can only conclude that this variable is not well enough specified to capture commuter response to variations in weather.

The year dummy variables, D77 and D76, are weak performers and only serve to show the weak trend away from public transit which was already shown in Table 9.1.

Speed regressions

The purpose of this section is to present a brief analysis of speed of travel as it relates to city size.[26] Since we have no independent observations of the average speed of travel for each SMSA, the dependent variable speed (SP) was constructed by dividing our mean travel distance measure (TD) by mean travel time (TT). SP is thus expressed in terms of miles per minute. If we convert to the more familiar miles per hour measure, the mean speed for all 61 SMSAs in our sample is 28.7 miles per hour, with a standard deviation of 3.6. Thus, a significant degree of variation in speed exists among SMSA's.[27]

The regressions below were estimated to assess the effect of city size on speed (standard errors in parentheses).

$$(3)\quad SP = .501 - .000014^{*}POP \qquad \bar{R}^2 = .14$$
$$\qquad\qquad (.000004)$$

$$(4)\quad SP = .500 - .026^{*}DENST \qquad \bar{R}^2 = .19$$
$$\qquad\qquad (.007)$$

$$(5)\quad SP = .504 - .020^{*}DENST - .000005POP \qquad \bar{R}^2 = .19$$
$$\qquad\qquad (.009) \qquad\qquad (.000010)$$

*Coefficient is significant at better than the 1 per cent level.

In general, these results indicate a negative effect of city size on speed (equations 3 and 5). However, once population density (DENST) is introduced into the regression (equation 5), the significance of the city size variable is lost. The reason that big cities are subject to slower commutes than found in smaller cities is not the bigness of the city *per se* but rather that the larger cities typically are more densely populated. The constraint on speedy travel is the congestion and crowding associated with density. As regression equation 4 indicates, DENST as the sole estimator is as good as the estimation which also includes POP (based on $\bar{R}^2$) and is a better estimator than POP alone.

The above results (equation 4) imply that an increase in the population density of the SMSA from 825 persons per square mile (the mean density of our sample) to 1650 persons per square mile would reduce speed by 1.3 miles per hour. Since the mean travel distance for our sample is 9.9 miles, this result implies an addition of one minute to the average work trip (which is about a 5 per cent increase in travel time).

A similar calculation with respect to a change in population indicates that an increase in population from 1.6 million (the mean in our sample) to 2.8 million would slow travel speed by 1 mile per hour. Therefore, it is expected that the average trip would be extended by about .75 minutes.

SUMMARY

The analysis has shown that the mean SMSA travel distance and travel time of urban commuters is positively and significantly influenced by city size. These results are consistent with predictions made by the monocentric model of urban development, especially as modified to recognize the development of subcentres of urban economic activity. While increases in population seem to have a greater influence on travel time than on travel distance when population is the only explanatory variable, this differential impact disappears when other variables are introduced, particularly those variables which relate to traffic congestion and therefore the speed of urban travel (such as population density, age of the housing stock, and the degree of public transit ridership). The lesson for urban economic model builders is that household location models based on a single distance parameter must hold the speed of urban travel constant if the implicit conceptual equality between travel time and travel distance made by these models is to be effected. This is especially important since households seem to regard travel time with greater sensitivity then travel distance when choosing a location.[28] Other variables shown to significantly influence J.T.W. behaviour are population density, income, education, age of housing stock, percentage of the population riding public transit. Finally, a weak trend toward centralization was identified based on the negative and sometimes significant "year" dummy variables in the travel time and travel distance regressions.

The household choice of transportation regressions produced considerably divergent results between the factors influencing mass transit ridership and those affecting the decision to carpool. The picture which emerges (as might be expected) suggest that mass transit is the choice of those in larger, older, and more densely settled urban areas while carpooling is more appropriate to smaller urban areas. These regressions in particular show that the modal choice for commuters is strongly affected by the structure of the SMSA (age, density, and size). Further, a very important factor in the shift to public transit is the speed of urban travel, which, when slow, tends to encourage both carpooling and mass transit ridership. The price of gasoline did not perform well and does not contribute to an explanation of modal choice, probably because of its poor specifications as a variable (i.e., statewide data and no deflator used).

A final result is that the speed of urban travel seems most directly impacted by the population density as opposed to city size *per se*, although either variable tends to capture the effect of the other if used alone. We interpret these results to indicate that urban congestion is a primary determinant of speed and thus household location. The speed regression results are at best preliminary since more data are needed to capture the effect of the "supply of urban speed" variables (i.e., public investments in road systems, traffic control, parking, and rapid rail) before more complete results can be estimated.

The call for future research in this case is quite straight forward. More observation and better data (especially gasoline price, subcentre counts, and the above mentioned speed variables) are needed with respect to a greater sample size to allow for separate regressions on sub categories of cities, and more reliable results. Once additional years of data are made available with more recent observations on the same 60 SMSAs as those in our sample, further analysis of the evolution of urban structure are possible.

FOOTNOTES

1. The importance of travel time variable can be seen from the findings by Gruen, A.C.[3], "The main finding of this study is that travel time elasticity is substantially greater than the price elasticity" (p. 269).
2. One cannot predict with certainty the effect on travel distance since, even without relocation, the new subcentre might now be closer to the household than the former work site in the CBD. Alternatively, the lower congestion which follows the development of the subcentre may increase travel speed sufficiently to encourage more distant household locations. These empirical questions are explored below.
3. Even with a high elasticity of supply of urban land, the possible development of additional subcentres is realistically limited by the economic linkage these subcentres share with the original CBD.
4. Speed is determined by more than just congestion or the number of cars on the road. Public investments in traffic control, highways, and the provision of public transit alternatives might offset some of the decline in speed created by the increase in congestion, thus the *ceteris paribus qualification.*
5. This finding is consistent with previous studies on the subject [see Mills[6] and Neenan[8]].
6. A further stimulus for carpooling as city size increases would be the increased parking fees in the CBD as land prices rise with population growth.
7. This investigation is somewhat a by product of the J.T.W.—city size analysis which composes the heart of this paper. This is because, by definition, speed is equal to travel distance divided by travel time, the two variables of chief concern to our analysis. Further, because speed depends on such public investment variables as road structure, traffic control, and public parking, which are not included in our data set, a comprehensive analysis of the individual's locational decision with respect to differences in speed is not possible.
8. For a complete list of data sources, see Appendix—I.
9. The sample size for the analysis is 61 SMSAs since the Madison, Wisconsin SMSA was surveyed in both 1975 and 1977. This is the only SMSA to be repeated in the sample. The 1978 Annual Housing Survey has not yet been disturbed. Further, earlier Annual Housing Surveys did not collect travel time/travel distance data so our analysis is constrained to a sample size of only 61 SMSAs. This sample provides sufficient degrees of freedom for the overall analysis but precludes our fully analyzing structural differences between

SMSAs of various size categories by running separate regressions for each category. The empirical analysis does, however present a few interesting but sometimes statistically weak results for separate SMSA categories by size.

10. The weighted averages for travel distance *TD* and travel time (*TT*) are based upon the SMSA-wide frequency distribution(s) of the number of head of families whose J.T.W. characteristics fell into a given range of the distribution(s) (e.g., $0 \leqslant TD \leqslant 1$ miles, $1 \leqslant TD \leqslant 4$, etc., or $0 \leqslant ST \leqslant 15$, $15\ TT \leqslant 30$, etc.). The midpoints (*TD* mid or *TT* mid) of a given range (i) were then weighted by the per cent of the total working families falling into that range $\frac{FAMi}{TOTFAMi}$ · Thus the weighted mean of *TD* (*TT*) equals :

$$\overline{TD}(\overline{TT}) = \Sigma \frac{FAMi}{TOTFAMi} \cdot TD_{midi}\ (TT_{midi})$$

11. The elasticity of travel distance is .19 according to Voorhees *et al.* [14].
12. Because we have no objective measure of the number of subcentres in each SMSA in our sample, we assume that the number of subcentres is positively correlated to population (city size) and thus captured through POP in the regression analysis.
13. The somewhat arbitrary divisions were based upon two considerations : First, after ranking the 61 SMSAs by population, the breaks were chosen at those points where the per cent increase in population was largest along the spectrum of city sizes. This choice was subject to a second consideration, that is choosing roughly approximate sample sizes for the three subcategories. Surprisingly, there was little trade off necessary between these considerations. The only large per cent change that was not used would have separated the largest 5 SMSAs from the rest of the sample. Obviously, the resulting sample size would be too small. While the resulting subsample sizes are somewhat uneven and the estimates are statistically weak for the smallest group ($n=16$) in particular, the breakpoints in the larger sample were based on obvious gaps in the population distribution. A perfect evening of the sample sizes would have been too artificial.
14. Obviously, the above interpretations are speculative as neither the Group I travel time nor the travel distance equation shows a statistically significant result for the population coefficient. Thus, in spite of the sign difference, both effects are statistically equal to zero. However, the consistency of the signs and the consistency of a weak positive distance relationship (*t* roughly equal to 1) and a negative, zero travel time relationship for alternative specifications of these equations (not presented here) suggests that a greater sample size for small SMSAs might produce the results described above. Perhaps, the preferred speculative interpretation is that, for small SMSAs, newly developed subcentres allow workers to keep travel time constant via newly developed highway systems, as they move to the

deeper suburbs, thus slightly increasing average travel distance.

15. In moving from Group I to Group III, the creation of new subcentres implied by population growth seems to have much more success in keeping average travel distance from growing as fast as average travel time. This is possibly the result of a diseconomy of scale in the supply of transportation facilities produced by the division of SMSA's into many subcentres instead one centrally located CBD. On average, the increase in the mean travel distance between Group I and Group III SMSAs is 19.2 per cent while the increase in mean travel time is 42.2 per cent.
16. We test this hypothesis later in this section.
17. R.L. Bish and H.O. Nourse [2, p. 361] sum up this aspect in the following way : "Consistent conclusions from attempts to identify cross elasticities of demand among modes with respect to price and travel time are that (1) . . . (2) the effect of changes in travel time is always stronger than effects from changes in price . . . . ."
18. This heroically assumes that the estimated elasticity is constant over this wide interval. While it is well known that an elasticity is appropriately applied only at the mean, we use this estimate for demonstration purposes only.
19. Actually, the differences in travel time between Grand Rapids and Atlanta is much larger than the 2.8 minutes predicted above (16.5 minutes for Grand Rapids and 24.2 minutes for Atlanta) but this is due to other variables besides population the results for which are discussed later.
20. The standard errors of the LPOP coefficients remain the same even though the coefficients fall in the travel time regressions.
21. These breaks in the population distribution of the SMSAs in our sample are the same as those reflected in the Small, Medium, and Large SMSA regressions reported in Table 8.2. See footnote 13.
22. For travel time, the PD3 coefficient is .17 as opposed to the PD2 coefficient of .08. This is a 125 per cent increase. For travel distance, the coefficient of PD3 rises to .17 from a coefficient on PD2 of .11, only a 55 per cent increase. Once again, however, note that (for PD3 in particular), there is nearly a one-to-one correspondence in the effect of city size on both travel time and travel distance once we include (and thus hold constant) various congestion/speed measures.
23. See for instance I. Hoch[5].
24. Shorter travel time need not imply shorter travel distances. Depending upon the mode of transport or road quality and conditions, a longer trip might be made in less time when two household locations are compared. Still, most locations with increased travel distances are likely to produce higher travel times.
25. The reader is reminded that PPUB is the sum of the proportion of the population which uses mass transit (buses and rapid rail), PMASS, and the proportion which commutes via carpools, PCARP. Since all of these conveyances involve greater time costs for

collecting and distributing [see Mills (6)] riders in addition to the time costs of travelling a given distance, travel time overall is likely to be higher (as the results confirm).

26. A full analysis of the determinants of speed is beyond the scope of this paper. This is principally due to a lack of data which might allow us to measure the structure and quality of the road system, public investments in traffic control, and other variables which effect congestion or speed. Our investigation focuses only on the effect of city size on speed.

27. See Appendix—II, column 6.

28. See footnote 17.

REFERENCES

Alonso, W., *Location and Land Use*, Harvard University Press, Cambridge, Massachusetts, 1968.

Bish, R.L., and H.O. Nourse, *Urban Economies and Policy Analysis*, 1975, McGraw-Hill Book Company.

Gruen, A.C., "Travel Time and Transportation Policy", *Journal of Urban Economics*, September, 1980, pp. 264-71.

Henderson, J.V., "The Economics of Staggered Work Hours", *Journal of Urban Economics*, May, 1981, pp. 349-364.

Hoch, I., "Income and City Size", *Urban Studies*, 1972.

Mills, E.S., *Urban Economics*, 2nd Edition, 1980, Scott, Foresman and Company.

Muth, R.F., *Cities and Housing*, The University of Chicago Press, Chicago and London, 1969.

Neenan, B.W., *Urban Public Economics*, Wadsworth Publishing Company, Belmont, California, 1981.

Ogawa and Fujita, "Equilibrium Land Use Patterns in a Nonmonocentric City", *Journal of Regional Science*, November, 1980, pp. 455-475.

U.S. Department of Commerce and Department of Housing and Urban Development, *Annual Housing Survey*, 1975, 1976, 1977.

U.S. Department of Commerce, Bureau of the Census, *Statistical Abstract for the U.S.*, 1975, 1976, 1977, 1978.

U.S. Department of Commerce, Bureau of the Census, *County and City Data Book*, 1977, *A Statistical Abstract Supplement*.

U.S. Department of Commerce, Bureau of the Census, *State and Metropolitan Area Data Book*, 1979, *A Statistical Abstract Supplement*.

Voorhees, A.M., Factors in Work Trip Lengths, *Highway Research Record*, 141, 1966, pp. 24-39.

Waymire and Waymire, "Effect of Rising Energy Prices on Urban Space", *Regional Science and Urban Economics*, August, 1980, pp. 407-422.

APPENDIX—I

LIST OF VARIABLES, DEFINITIONS, AND SOURCES

Variable	Definition	Source
AGE	Weighted mean age of housing stock in SMSA.	Annual Housing Survey, 1975-1977 [10]
DENST	Population Density : Thousands of people per square mile of area of the SMSA.	State and Metropolitan Area Book, 1979 [12]
D75, D76, D77	Year dummy variables : Value of 1 if observation is from the respective year, zero otherwise.	—
EDUC	Median completed years of schooling of the population in SMSA.	Annual Housing Survey, 1975-77 [10]
INC, (LINC)	Median family income. (LINC is the natural log of this variable.)	*Ibid.*
PCARP	Per cent of heads of households which carpool to work.	*Ibid.*
PD1	Population dummy variable for small SMSAs (POP⩽625,000).	—
PD2	Population dummy variable for medium SMSA (625,000<POP⩽1,600,000).	—
PD3	Population dummy variable for large SMSA (POP>1,600,000).	—
PI	Per cent of the SMSA population living in the central city.	*Ibid.*
PMASS	Per cent of heads of households which use mass transit (rail, bus) to commute to work.	*Ibid.*
POP, (LPOP)	Population (total) of the SMSA. (LPOP is the natural log of this variable.)	County and City Data Book, 1977 [12]
PPUB	Per cent of heads of household using public transportation (=PMASS +PCARP).	—
RFG	Price of regular gasoline ; usually the State average for May of the year during which the respective SMSA was surveyed.	AAA [By correspondence]
SP	Speed of travel, calculated as TD divided by TT (see below).	—
TD (LTD)	Weighted means travel distance for SMSA. (LTD is natural log of this variable.)	Annual Housing Survey, 1975-77 [10]

Variable	Definition	Source
TEMP	Mean SMSA temperature for the month of January.	County and City Data Book, 1977[12]
TT (LTT)	Weighted mean travel time for the SMSA. (LTT is the natural log of this variable.)	Annual Housing Survey, 1975-77 [10]

APPENDIX—II

DISTRIBUTION OF MEAN VALUES OF TRAVEL TIME, TRAVEL DISTANCE, DENSITY, AND SPEED RANKED BY POPULATION*

SMSA Name	Population (thousands)	Travel Time (minutes)	Travel Distance (miles)	Population** Density (thousands)	Speed (4)/(3)
(1)	(2)	(3)	(4)	(5)	(6)
1. New York, NY	9509.0	34.0	12.1	6.87	0.36
2. Los Angeles-Long Beach, CA	7031.0	22.4	10.9	1.73	0.49
3. Chicago, IL	7015.0	29.5	11.3	1.89	0.38
4. Philadelphia, PA	4807.0	25.6	10.3	1.35	0.40
5. Detroit, MI	4370.0	24.2	11.7	1.12	0.48
6. San Francisco-Oakland, CA	3140.0	24.9	11.3	1.27	0.46
7. Washington, D.C., MD-VA	3033.0	29.6	11.2	1.08	0.38
8. Boston, MA	2862.0	24.1	9.4	2.39	0.39
9. Dallas, TX	2673.3	20.9	10.9	0.32	0.52
10. Houston, TX	2423.0	24.2	12.0	0.36	0.50
11. St. Louis, MO-IL	2384.0	22.7	11.4	0.48	0.50
12. Pittsburgh, PA	2294.0	22.4	8.5	0.75	0.38
13. Baltimore, MD	2144.0	26.3	11.8	0.95	0.45
14. Minneapolis-St. Paul, MN	2037.0	19.5	9.7	0.44	0.50
15. Newport News, Hampton, VA	1999.0	21.5	9.7	3.05	0.45
16. Newark, NJ	1969.0	24.4	9.3	1.95	0.38
17. Cleveland, OH	1967.0	23.6	10.3	1.29	0.44
18. Anaheim-Santa Ana-Garden Grove, CA	1801.0	23.2	13.0	2.30	0.56
19. Atlanta, GA	1790.0	24.2	11.4	0.28	0.47
20. San Diego, CA	1585.0	19.1	11.3	0.37	0.59
21. Miami, FL	1440.0	22.8	9.9	0.71	0.43
22. Denver, CO	1438.0	19.5	9.9	0.31	0.51
23. Seattle-Everett, WA	1419.0	21.4	11.3	0.34	0.53
24. Milwaukee,WI	1409.0	19.9	8.8	0.97	0.44

APPENDIX—II : (*Contd.*)

(1)	(2)	(3)	(4)	(5)	(6)
25. Cincinnati, OH-KY-IN	1381.0	22.7	10.9	0.64	0.48
26. Buffalo, NY	1328.0	19.5	9.1	0.84	0.47
27. Kansas City, MO	1290.0	21.1	10.2	0.39	0.48
28. Phoenix, AZ	1254.0	19.1	9.8	0.14	0.51
29. San Bernardino, Riverside, Ontario, CA	1226.0	17.9	11.2	0.04	0.63
30. Indianapolis, IN	1141.0	21.3	10.5	0.37	0.49
31. New Orleans, LA	1094.0	22.8	8.7	0.56	0.38
32. Portland, OR-WA	1083.0	19.7	9.5	0.30	0.48
33. Columbus, OH	1069.0	19.1	9.2	0.43	0.48
34. San Antonio, TX	982.0	20.3	9.3	0.39	0.46
35. Rochester, NY	972.0	21.4	10.3	0.33	0.48
36. Sacramento, CA	908.0	17.2	9.6	0.26	0.56
37. Louisville, KY-IN	887.0	20.6	10.5	0.64	0.51
38. Memphis, TN-AR	886.0	20.1	9.1	0.39	0.45
39. Providence-Pawtucket-Warwick, RI-MA	855.0	19.0	10.2	1.15	0.54
40. Salt Lake City, UT	822.0	19.0	9.9	0.10	0.52
41. Birmingham, AL	800.0	20.6	10.5	0.24	0.51
42. Albany, Schenectady, Tory, NY	794.0	19.0	9.0	0.30	0.47
43. Oklahoma City, OK	762.0	17.4	8.8	0.22	0.51
44. Hartford, CT	732.0	20.3	9.7	0.72	0.48
45. Honolulu, HI	715.0	22.6	9.1	1.20	0.40
46. Allentown-Bethlehem-Easton, PA-NJ	624.0	16.8	8.9	0.42	0.53
47. Orlando, FL	593.0	17.6	10.4	0.23	0.59
48. Omaha, NB-IA	581.0	16.5	7.5	0.38	0.46
49. Grand Rapids, MI	569.0	16.5	9.0	0.40	0.55
50. Springfield, Chicopee, Holyoke, MA-CT	549.0	18.4	8.6	0.94	0.47
51. Raleigh, NC	478.0	17.9	9.6	0.31	0.54
52. Paterson, Clifton, Passaic, NJ	452.0	27.2	11.2	2.35	0.41
53. Tacoma, WA	423.0	20.7	11.5	0.25	0.55
54. Wichita, KA	395.0	17.6	7.8	0.16	0.45
55. Fort Worth, TX	365.0	20.7	11.6	1.60	0.56
56. Las Vegas, NV	346.0	16.7	9.5	0.04	0.57
57. Madison, WI	313.0	16.5	6.7	0.26	0.41
58. Spokane, WA	310.0	16.1	7.7	0.18	0.48
59. Madison, WI	302.0	17.2	7.2	0.25	0.42

APPENDIX—II : (*Contd.*)

(1)	(2)	(3)	(4)	(5)	(6)
60. Colorado Springs, CO	287.0	18.8	8.8	0.11	0.47
61. Saginaw, MI	227.0	18.2	8.9	0.28	0.49

*Sources of data are : Annual Housing Survey for the years 1975, 1976, 1977, Statistical Abstract for the U.S. for the years 1975-1978, Country and City Data Book 1977, and State and Metropolitan Area Data Book 1979.

**Density is measured here in thousands of people per square mile.

TEN

D.C. PANDEY, P.C. TIWARI AND
J.S. RAWAT

CENTRAL PLACE INTERACTIONS
A Comparative Analysis in Hills and Plains

INTRODUCTION

CENTRAL place interactions are referred to as the principal element leading to the organization of space around a focal point (i.e., central place). Various urban geographers and other social scientists have studied the 'interaction areas' either with the help of quantitative techniques or by quantitative or theoretical models and different terms have been used for this purpose. Reilly (Reilly 1931), Dickinson (Dickinson 1934), Smails (Smails 1944), Converse (Converse 1949), Huff (Huff 1963) and Berry (Berry 1967) etc., are eminent scholars who have done an appreciable work in this direction. It has been observed by the researchers that the centripetal and centrifugal forces provide the actual parameters to demarcate the zone of central place interactions and spatial organizations. Two types of complementary areas of a central place can be delineated—zone of an individual function and zones according to the general functional hierarchy.

A chain of continuous spatial interaction is generated between the centres of different orders and their dependent settlements. Lower level central places possess lower order functions and command smaller tributary areas and population and *vice versa*. The main question drawing the attention of researchers in central place studies and planners associated is the areal extent over which a particular central place exerts its influence in a hierarchical order.

STUDY AREA

The present study area includes two development blocks of distinct nature of district Nainital situated in the U.P. Himalaya, viz., Baitalghat and Bazpur. The former is situated in the hills (north), while the latter is in the Tarai tract (i.e., plains—in south). The factors affecting the spatial interaction patterns of central place hierarchies have a different significance for hills as well as for plains. There are marked diversities and complexities in physio-climatic conditions of the above mentioned blocks of the district, which influence the socio-economic and cultural activities of the inhabitants. Out of the total 158 and 192 settlements 8 and 12 were identified as central places in hills and plains respectively.

Methodology

The main theme of this paper is to identify the central place interactions in three-tier functional hierarchy with the help of the quantitative as well as qualitative techniques. The areas of interaction of first, second and third order central places of hills (i.e., Baitalghat development block) and first and second level central places of plains (i.e., Bazpur development block) have been delineated through sociogram technique, while spatial interactions of the lowest level central places of plains have been demarcated through 'Gravity Model' (Pandey & Rawat 1982). The Breaking point concept (Converse 1949) has also been tested.

It has been observed during the field investigation that the spatial interaction patterns of central places were governed by different factors characterizing the two different ecological regions of the district, such as direction, surface slope, transport connectivity and accessibility, etc. Selection of interaction areas as basic planning units or clusters is helpful as a base for making a coherent and integrated area development planning. This clusterization approach has been suggested to solve the problems of location allocation of facilities, which obviously must be fully accessible with respect to interaction areas (Singh & Pandey 1982)

FACTORS AFFECTING SPATIAL INTERACTION PATTERN IN HILLS AND PLAINS

It is generally obvious that the physical as well as cultural phenomena of a region govern and affect the spatial organization and spatial interaction patterns. In reference to the study region, especially in hills, the spatial interaction systems are governed more by physical phenomena and least by cultural environs but it is *vice versa* in respect of plains. Ascending from south to north, i.e., from plains to hills, presence of inaccessible mountain ranges is an acute problem. Therefore, in hills, the movement of men and material, to and from the region is mostly unidirectional towards south. The entire Kumaun hills is almost dependent on the market centres situated to its south in Bhabar and Tarai (which is collectively called here as plains) for all practical purposes especially for foodgrains and other essential commodities. The entire commodity flow to the hills is totally controlled and regulated by the three base towns, viz., Ramnagar, Haldwani and Tanakpur. These towns are sometimes called as 'gate towns' and 'mandi towns' and serve as a mediator of trade and transport between the plains and hills. The freight rates are relatively very high in hills as compared to plains. The costs of goods considerably vary from south to north and this variability acts as a powerful factor and has got direct bearing on consumers perference to the space. The result is that if other things are remaining constant, the consumer would travel a greater distance towards south than towards north to avail a facility or specially to buy goods. The mean ratio difference in travel distances towards north and south was observed respectively as 1.00 : 1.50 km. for the study area, which is a result of spatially varying costs.

Besides the direction, slope is another significant factor and responsible to contract and expand the spatial interaction patterns of a centre. In the mountainous rugged topography, established routes are the only channels of movement, which are never straight lines in hills as they are in plains. Consequently, the straight line distances which are used in application of the gravity model and also in the breaking point concept in delineation of the complementary areas of central places become inoperative in a hilly region.

In regard to distance friction, it was observed that when two equal size centres were at identical distances from a settlement, a consumer will always prefer to the centre which entails lesser gradient as the effort required is less. The mean ratio difference in the travel distances caused by slope factor was observed to be

1 : 2, i.e., chances of the consumers for visiting a centre at a distance of one km. with gradient and a distance of two km. without gradient are equal. In reference to the plains, i.e., in Bazpur block, there obviously has not been any marked correlation between the slope factor and size of the complementary areas.

The third important and common factor, i.e., degree of nodality of transport, clearly governs the spatial interaction patterns. This factor is powerful in plains rather than in hills, because in the Bazpur development block, the rail and road transport net which is more specialized in comparison to hills is accessible for contact outside the region. Railway heads and bus terminuses attract maximum consumers with highest range of travel distance as compared to other locations. It has been observed in the case illustration of hills that the ratio difference of a distance travelled by the consumers in expression of their preferences for a centre at the motor head is 1 : 3. This shows that the centripetal force, or pull of a service centre located on a motor road is three times higher than that of a centre located in the interiors.

Besides the abovementioned factors, there are several other phenomena which also determine the consumer's behaviour pattern to some extent. There are no hard and fast rules and laws to measure human behaviour and human habits which are changable from man to man and place to place.

Application of techniques

The existing central place system and their hierarchical organization have been identified through the study of functional structure of the system. With the help of 18 variables (sub-functions), measurement of centrality has been done by applying the most relevant technique of principal component analysis (PCA), (Johnston 1980). As a result, a total of 8 and 12 central places have been identified in hills and plains respectively, in perspective of district Nainital, i.e., keeping in view the centrality quotient of the two higher order growth centres, i.e., Nainital (Composit Index Value 110.81) and Haldwani (Composit Index Value 104.40). Therefore, in order to cater the sectoral needs of the mass and rationalize the location allocation of the facilities, it is not only necessary to arrange the central places in a hierarchical order but also to demarcate the areas of interaction of different level service centres. Consequently, empirical as well as theoretical approaches have been used for the purpose.

Empirical Approach

There are so many approaches of identifying the service areas of a central place by using various criteria such as distance range and population criteria, existing infrastructural facilities and movements of people and goods, etc. Methods based on a single criterian do not give suitable results of demarcation in comparison to the methods based on multiple criteria.

In the present context, the authors have done a sufficient amount of field work in support of the sociogram technique. Hence, the total 18 sub-functions were grouped in a three-tier functional hierarchy. In the Baitalghat development block (i.e., hills) the space preference data for all the three level centres according to three-tier functional hierarchies have been collected through questionnaires and the interaction pattern between the settlements and central places was indicated by arrows. The demarcation of the zone of influence between the centres has been done keeping in view the physiographical features (i.e., contour lines), e.g., in high altitudes of rugged topography, the ridges often indicate the partition between the zones of two centres. In this way, the zone of influence of higher (1), intermediate (2) and lower (8) order central places of the hill block has been delineated. In regard to the plains, i.e., Bazpur development block, the interaction pattern, of higher (1) and intermediate (5) order central places was also delineated by this empirical approach.

Theoretical Model

An attempt has been made to delineate the areas of interaction of the third order central places in the Bazpur block (plains) with the help of a quantitative analysis. Reilly (Reilly 1931) has propounded a model or the law of retail gravitation for finding out a common point between the zones of influence of two cities. He identified two simple rules concerning the flows of retail trade—one is that the larger a centre is, the more service area it commands and the other is that the centre attracts more consumers from nearer locations.

Converse (Converse 1949) has modified the Reilly's model in

the form of 'new laws of retail gravitation' which is also known as the 'breaking point concept', which states about the zones of influence between the two cities/centres *A* and *B* in miles/km. Berry (Berry 1967) has used number of establishments as a measure of attractive power of a centre. Similarly, distance between two settlements has traditionally been measured in a straight line, but this crow-flight distance has hotly been debated among researchers and social scientists.

It is very confusing particularly in hills that the influences of the two centres will be delimited by using their population sizes and distances. For example, *A* and *B* having an identical population must have equal areas of interaction, whereas in practice, it gives misleading results. A centre which is efficient to serve more by its functions has a larger spatial interaction with maximum number of beneficiaries and *vice versa.* Another drawback of the above model is that sometimes the boundary of the zone of complementary areas either divides a village into two or more than two parts between two or more than two service centres. In order to get more appropriate results of demarcation of service areas of the centres, it would be necessary to adjust the boundaries in such cases, so that a full village may be allotted to the complementary areas of that service centre which includes a greater part of inhabited areas or more than 50 per cent households in its influence. In these typical cases, it is better to have identified such settlement(s) by field observation.

Keeping in view the abovementioned inherent weaknesses, the authors have used here the 'new gravity model' (Pandey and Rawat 1982) of the areas of interaction of central place systems, which can be expressed as follows :

$$D_{px} = \frac{\dfrac{d_{xy} \times P_{tx}}{P_{txy}} + \dfrac{d_{xy} \times W_{fx}}{W_{fxy}}}{2} \qquad \text{...(i)}$$

where,

D_{px} is demarcating point between the central places x and y from x, d_{xy} is the straight line distance between the central places x and y (in km.), P_{tx} is population size of a central x, P_{txy} is the total population of the central places x and y, W_{fx} is the weightage of the function s served by the central place x in a functional hierarchy and W_{fxy} is weightage of the function/s served by the central places x and y in the same functional hierarchy.

SERVICE CENTRES AND THEIR AREAS OF INTERACTIONS

As it has already been discussed earlier, the services and facilities were arranged into three-tier functional hierarchy. It was observed that there exists a high degree of positive correlation between the composite index values and tributary population figures of the both ecological regions ($r=0.917$). On the contrary, there exists very weak correlation between the composite index of the centres and their service areas, especially in hills ($r=<0.40$).

The areas and beneficiary population served by the third order central places of hills and plains have been given in Table 10.1a and 10.1b (Figs. 10.1 and 10.2). Garampani with a composite index value of 57.50 served 4830 tributary population with an area of 34.30 sq. km. of the pilot study region (hills), while Baitalghat, the block H.Q. (with composite index values of 33.68) served 4,170 surrounding population with a large area of 60.40 sq. km. Its service area is comparatively larger than that of Garampani, which indicates that the population in Baitalghat cluster (i.e., service region) is sparsely populated and people have to travel maximum range of >6 km. for the lower order functions. During the field investigation, it has been observed that this cluster is no doubt sparsely populated but the rugged

TABLE 10.1a : **Area and population served by third level service centres in hills**

Name of the Centre	Composite Index	Tributary Population	Area Served (in sq. km.)
Garampani	57.50	4830	34.30
Baitalghat	33.68	4170	60.40
Ratighat	10.90	1560	21.10
Simalkha	8.21	2330	44.50
Bardha	7.61	2420	19.90
Daun	7.25	1780	60.50
Seti Belgaon	6.91	2550	45.50
Binkot	6.71	2470	16.40

TABLE 10.1b : **Area and population served by third level service centres in plains**

Name of the Centre	Composite Index	Tributary Population	Area Served (in sq. km.)
Bazpur	34.09	11340	50.30
Gadarpur	22.00	13110	54.40
Dineshpur	17.96	14090	80.50
Kalia Khera	17.90	6380	36.30
Sultanpur	16.40	6250	38.60
Gular Bhoj	7.65	10170	94.00
Beria Daulat	5.43	8170	31.10
Banna Khera	4.98	7010	60.30
Harsan	4.97	13350	58.00
Sakania	4.94	3090	19.00
Mundia Kalan	4.81	9140	21.40
Masit	4.76	3090	16.20

topography, with inaccessible areas on one hand and non-agricultural and barren land on the other, hampered in evolving new central places in this region.

In hills, the range of the distance travelled by the consumers at this level of functional hierarchy varied from 4 to 6 km. Extremely higher values of the travel distance was observed for the bus stops and seeds and fertilizer distribution centres, a fact which was obvious due to poorly developed transport networks and extension services in hills. In plains, the maximum travel distance for this group of function is 3 to 5 km.

It is clear from Table 10.2a and 10.2b (Figs. 10.1 and 10.2) that there are only two second level service centres in the study area of hilly region, viz., Garampani and Baitalghat. Baitalghat which is situated in Gagar valley has its location on the border of the study area. Only half of its service area and population lie within the study region along river Kosi and the rest of its service area lies in Ratighat, Ramgarh and Kainchi. Baitalghat as a second level centre served more population and larger area than Garampani, whereas Garampani as a first and third order centre was found more efficient to fulfil the demands and needs of the beneficiaries. On the other side in plains, the interaction areas of the five service centres, .e., Bazpur, Gadarpur, Dineshpur, Kalia Khera and Sultanpur, have also been identified. Bazpur

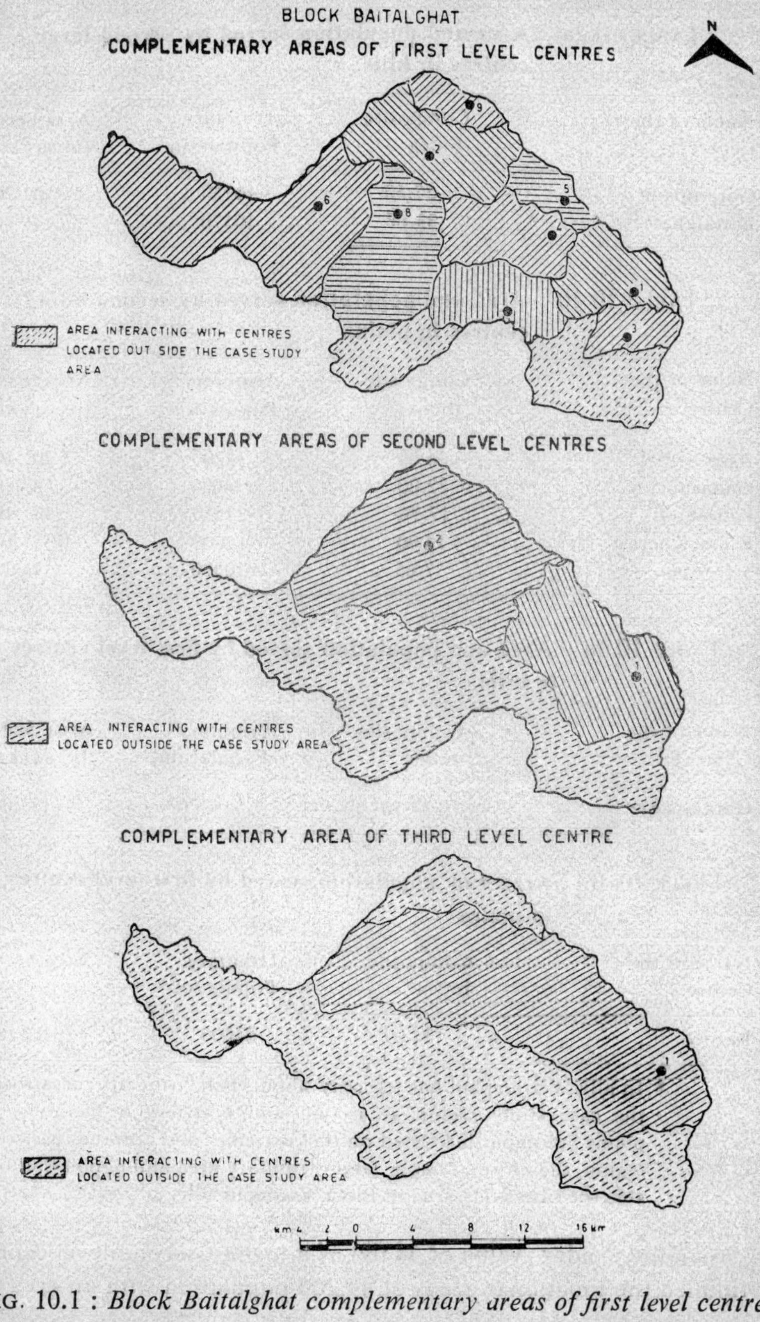

FIG. 10.1 : *Block Baitalghat complementary areas of first level centres*

TABLE 10.2a : **Area and population served by second level centres in hills**

Name of the Centre	Composite Index	Tributary Population	Area Served (in sq. km.)
Garampani*	57.50	10520	102.70
Baitalghat	33.68	10570	148.70

TABLE 10.2b : **Area and population served by second level centres in plains**

Name of the Centre	Composite Index	Tributary Population	Area Served (in sq. km.)
Bazpur	34.09	44200	205.10
Gadarpur	22.00	24030	147.60
Dineshpur	17.96	23550	107.10
Kalia Khera	17.90	12000	57.10
Sultanpur	7.65	10500	43.20

TABLE 10.3a : **Area and population served by first level centres in hills**

Name of the Centre	Composite Index	Tributary Population	Area Served (in sq. km.)
Garampani*	57.50	16270	157.00

TABLE 10.3b : **Area and population served by first level centres in plains**

Name of the Centre	Composite Index	Tributary Population	Area Served (in sq. km.)
Bazpur	34.09	64600	322.60

* In hills, Garampani has its only about half tributary area within the case study region at second and first level of hierarchy. In plains Sultanpur is located on the extreme west of the case study region, therefore, it has a large tributary area and population outside the case study area in Block Kashipur.

(composite index value of 34.09) as a highest second level centre fulfilled the functional needs of 44,200 population with an area of

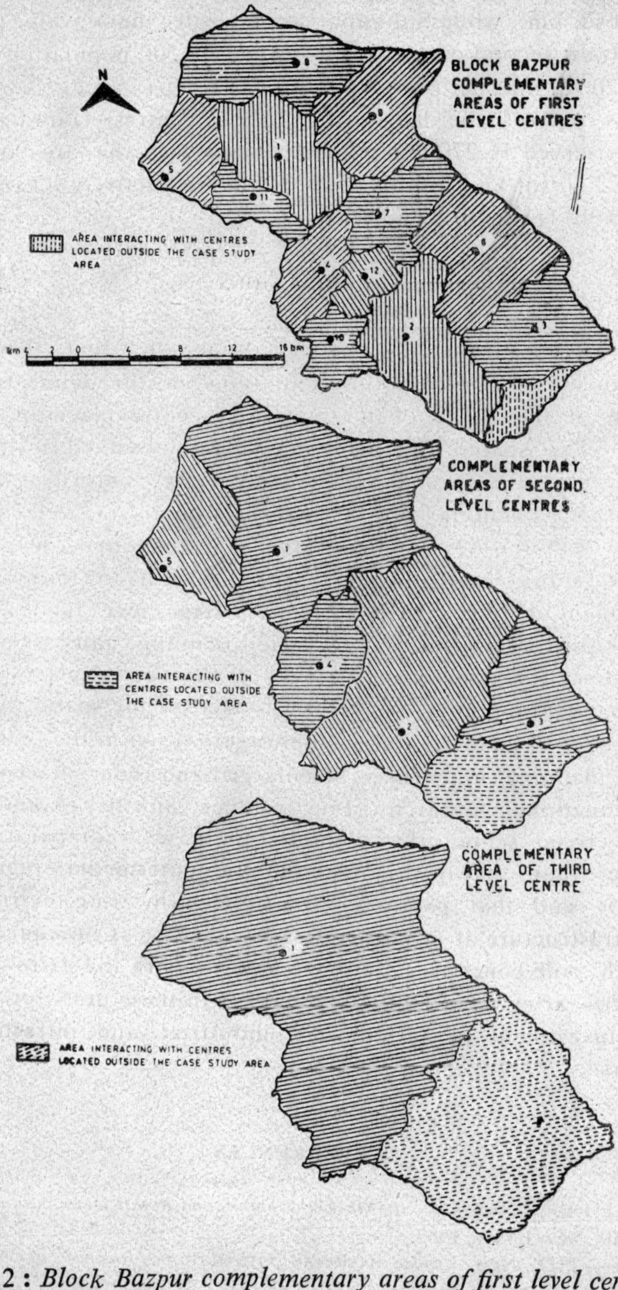

FIG. 10.2 : *Block Bazpur complementary areas of first level centres*

205.10 sq. km., while Sultanpur (composite index value of 7.65) as a lowest second order centre served 10,500 population around its 43.20 sq. km. peripheral areas.

As regards the first order service centres, Garampani and Bazpur served 16,270 and 64,600 persons with the area of 157.00 and 322.60 sq. km. in hills and plains respectively (Table 10.3a and 10.3b) (Figs. 10.1 and 10.2).

CONCLUSIONS

It is obvious from the above discussion that there were fundamental and marked differentiations in the delineation and nature of the areas of interaction of central places of hills and plains. The spatial organization pattern observed in the case study areas has a special significance in the context of location-allocation planning and generalization of a well balanced spatial sectoral development aimed at integrated development of the entire study region. It is difficult to formulate and implement an IAD plan at a single village level and also at a tahsil, district and state as a single planning unit as a whole. Therefore, the interaction areas of the central places taken as basic planning units are helpful to analyse the spatio-functional gaps as well as integrated spatial organization in the region. The basic planning units may be enlarged and reduced according to the functional hierarchy. For instance, in the planning of a junior basic school the planning units will comparatively be smaller than that of the planning of an intermediate college. It can be said that planners often suffer in locating the right type of infrastructure at a right geographical place. Consequently, the growth pole concept is viable enough to mark the extra needs of facilities after identifying settlements in these units for locating new investment in agricultural, industrial and infrastructural sectors.

REFERENCES

Berry, B.J.L., *Geography of Market Centres and Retail Distribution*, Prentice Hall, New Jersey, 1967.

Converse, P.D., New Laws of Retail Gravitation, *Journal of Marketing*, Vol. 14, 1949.

Dickinson, R.E., The Metropolitan Regions of the United States, *Geogl. Rev.*, 24, 1934, pp. 278-291.

Huff, D.L., A Probability Analysis Shopping Centre Trade Areas, *Land Economics*, 39, 1963, p. 81.

Johnston, R.J., *Multivariate Statistical Analysis in Geography*, Longman, London, 1980.

Pandey, D.C. & Rawat, J.S., A New Gravity Model of Interaction Areas of Central Place Systems, in *Prof. Ahmad Felicitation Volume*, 1982, Ranchi (Forthcoming).

Reilly, W.J., *The Law of Retail Gravitation*, New York, 1931.

Singh, O.P. & Pandey, D.C., Spatial Sectoral Planning for Integrated Area Development, Paper presented in the Seminar on *Environment and Development*, NAGI and ISI Sponsored, 11-12 November 1982, New Delhi.

Smails, A.E., The Urban Hierarchy of England and Wales, *Geography*, 29, 1944, pp. 47-51.

ELEVEN

M. M. CHANDNA

LOCATIONAL PATTERN OF SERVICE CENTRES IN THE OUTER HIMALAYAS

A Case Study of District Sirmaur, Himachal Pradesh, India

EVERY inhabited part of the world is characterised by a variety of settlements of human occupance.[1] These settlements may be grouped into two categories from the viewpoint of spatial organisation. The first category comprises of those settlements that primarily serve other settlements and the second category includes others which are served. The places falling in the first category are called service centres.

Service centres exist to provide services to their surrounding areas. They vary in type, quantity and quality of functions and hence differ in their functional status. They interact among themselves in the fashion of a nested hierarchy.

The nature of service centres varies from area to area depending upon the level of socio-economic development and institutional framework operating in a given physical set-up. Service centres in simple agrarian societies differ from those in complex industrial societies. Such variations in the nature of service centres present a fascinating field for geographical research.

The study of service centres is now receiving an increasing attention by Indian scholars.[2] Part of this interest has flown from the potential application of such efforts to developmental planning.[3] Most of these studies are confined to areas located either in the Northern plain or Deccan Peninsula of India.

There is virtually no work on service centres in the Himalayas or its parts, with the exception of a study by Tirtha and Lall.[4]

Also while most of them deal with their functional hierarchy, only a few have looked into their locational aspects. This paper intends to identify all the service centres in the Sirmaur District of Himachal Pradesh and to render a detailed analysis to their locational pattern.

District Sirmaur

A brief description

Situated in the outer Himalayas, Sirmaur is one of the 12 districts of Himachal Pradesh Fig. 11.1). Its present territorial limits have remained unchanged since 1833 (one of the reasons for selection of the study area) when the British in India accorded

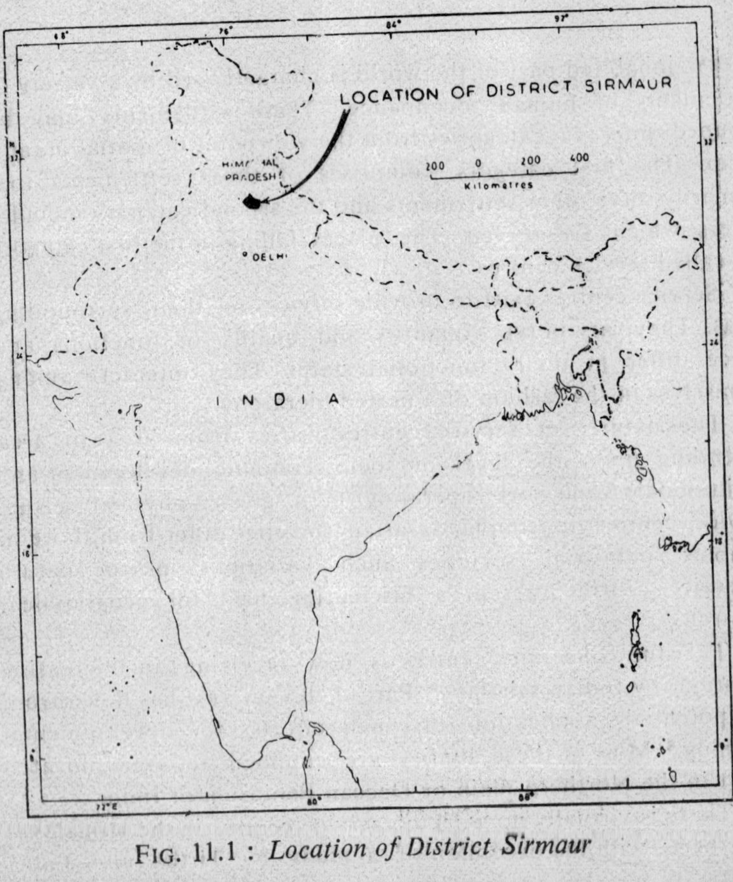

FIG. 11.1 : *Location of District Sirmaur*

recognition to the rule of a local prince over this area. After independence in 1947, the state became one of the districts of Himachal Pradesh. Its area is 2,825 sq. km. and population about 300,000. Barring the 40 km. long and 10 to 20 km. wide valley of Kayarda or Paonta dun in the south and some lowland area of Markanda basin in the southwest, the entire district is hilly and mountainous ranging in elevation from less than 400 to more than 3,500 metres. Over nine-tenths of the population lives in 965 villages each of which is generally fragmented into a number of hamlets. These are confined largely to valleys or hill slopes where some cultivable land and requisite water supply are available. Nahan, Paonta Sahib and Sarahan are the only three urban places. On the whole, the economy is underdeveloped, technology primitive and mobility sluggish in this mountainous region with a legacy of indifferent princely rule for centuries. The consumption pattern of the people is close to subsistence level, their needs few and elementary and purchasing power low.

Methodology

The analysis is based on data collected from all the 965 villages and 3 towns in the district. To accomplish the task of gathering data from nearly one thousand settlements in a mountainous region, the help of malaria and smallpox field workers was sought. Through them a questionnaire was sent to every village. The questionnaire asked for the names of the places from where each village was obtaining services of (i) retail store, (ii) ration depot, (iii) higher order goods centre, (iv) agricultural market, (v) temple, (vi) middle school, (vii) high/higher secondary school, (viii) post office, (ix) veterinary dispensary, dispensary, civil hospital, (x) place providing personal services of a barber, tailor, goldsmith, etc., (xi) bus stand, (xii) panchayat headquarters and (xiii) tahsil/subtahsil headquarters. To verify these data, nearly 10 per cent of villages were personally visited. Moreover, the lists of government instituted services of ration depots, schools, post offices, dispensaries and veterinary centres were obtained from the various offices at the district headquarters of Nahan and comparisons were made with data already collected through questionnaires.

Any place providing one or more of these services to its surrounding area was adopted as a service centre. Presence of a service in itself did not qualify a settlement as a service centre;

it had to serve its surrounding areas as well. A place could for example have a retail store, but if it served only the local population it did not qualify as a service centre. The processing and mapping of data revealed that there were 243 service centres in the district (Table 11.1). A sixfold hierarchy among them could also be identified.[5]

TABLE 11.1 : **Functional hierarchy, median population and mean distance of service centres**

Order of service centre	Number of service centres	Median population	Mean straightline distance in km.	Estimated actual distance in km. (by applying calculated detour index of 1.4)
Highest	1	—	—	—
Second	3	1,475	26.0	35.4
Third	7	885	15.1	21.7
Fourth	20	546	11.4	16.0
Fifth	49	527	8.4	11.8
Lowest	163	231	4.5	6.3

Locational pattern

Service centres occupy specific positions in order to perform functions for their surrounding areas. These positions, ultimately manifest in the locational pattern, are associated with matters like physiographic conditions, transport network and distribution of population. The relative position of service centres in relation to each other is also one of the dimensions of their distribution. Accordingly this paper examines the locational pattern of service centres in relation to (1) physiography, (2) network of transport lines, (3) distribution of population, and (4) mutual dispersion of service centres (Fig. 11.2).

LOCATION BY PHYSIOGRAPHY

By landform regions

The peculiarities of relief, with their direct bearing on accessi-

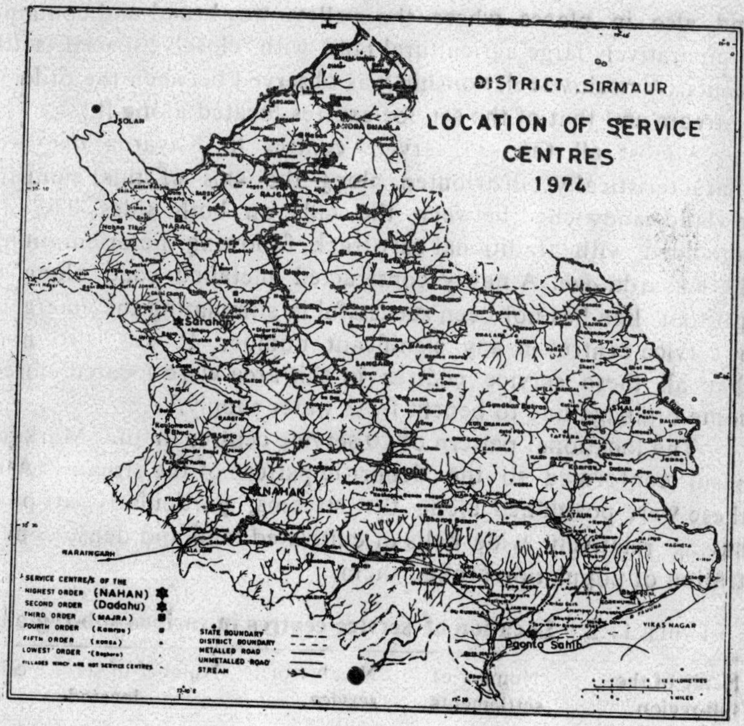

FIG. 11.2 : *District Sirmaur—Location of Service Centres, 1974*

bility, have greatly influenced the locational pattern of service centres in this mountainous region. Among 243 service centres in all, 188 (about 77 per cent) were located in the hilly and mountainous part of the district and the remaining in the low land areas of the Kayarda *dun* and the Markanda basin. This distribution was roughly in proportion to the areas shared by these two broad physical divisions of the district.

Of the 188 service centres in the hilly and mountainous part of the region (including both the trans-Giri and cis-Giri tracts), 146 were sited either on the ridge or near the ridge lines. Such a location enabled a service centre to command the complementary region on both sides of a ridge. The remaining 42 service centres were scattered along the streams or rivulets.[6] These were positioned generally on terraces of the various drainage lines (mostly at points where they were provided with a rope or a *pucca* bridge) and also in places where the valley was broad and contained comparatively large agricultural land with closely spaced settlements. A positive relationship was observed between the order of a stream and that of the service centres located along it.

Almost all the 35 service centres in Kayarda *dun* were characteristically distributed along the axis of this elongated lowland sandwiched between the hills on both sides. The axis coincided with traditional cart track, following the orientation of the Kayarda *dun*. A newly constructed metalled road along the hill-foot line has not been successful in stimulating the emergence of service centres in any significant number. It was also noted that all these service centres in this area were located close to some drainage line to benefit from water supply.[7]

The locational pattern of 20 service centres in the Markanda basin conformed to the dendritic pattern of the streams. All of these were positioned along the streams, particularly at points having relatively wide belts of cultivated land and dense concentration of population around them.

TABLE 11.2 : **Location of service centres in various sub-regions**

Name of the sub-region	Number of settlements	Number of service centres	Number of service centres located	
			On the ridge or near the ridge line	Along the stream
Trans-Giri hills	374	125	95	30
Cis-Giri hills	429	63	51	12
Kayarda *dun*	85	35	—	35
Markanda basin	80	20	—	20
District	968	243	146	97

It follows that the majority of service centres in the region had a ridge or near the ridge line location. It was envisaged that service centres in this region would normally have a valley location. On the contrary, a ridge or near the ridge line location predominated. This location helped them to serve the settlements on both sides of the hill slopes. Drainage lines generally marked the boundaries of complementary regions of service centres.

By altitude groups

In line with their locational pattern vis-a-vis relief conditions, 119 or about a half of the service centres fell in the altitude group of 1,200 to 1,800 metres. Only one-fifth of them (mostly in the Kayarda *dun* and in the lower Markanda basin) were situated below 600 metres. About one-fourth of the service centres belonged to the altitude group of 600 to 1,200 metres. The remaining few, hardly 9 in all, were at an altitude of more than 1,800 metres. There was no service centre above 2,000 metres. The median altitude of service centres was 1,310 metres (Table 11.3).

The altitude pattern of service centres varied in different parts of the region. Almost 80 per cent of the service centres in the trans-Giri hills were situated at an altitude of more than 1,200 metres. All the service centres with an altitude of more than 1,800 metres were also located here. By comparison, the cis-Giri hills recorded about a half of its service centres in the altitude group of 1,200 to 1,800 metres and the remaining half in 600 to 1,200 metres group. In Kayarda *dun* and Markanda basin, more than 90 per cent of the service centres were situated below 600 metres. The remaining few were also lower than 1,200 metres in altitude.

TABLE 11.3 : **Altitude of service centres in various sub-regions**

Number of the sub-region	Number of service centres in the altitude group (in metres) of				Median altitude (in metres)
	below 600	600-1200	1201-1800	above 1800	
Trans-Giri hills	1	28	87	9	1450
Cis-Giri hills	—	31	32	—	1228
Kayarda *dun*	34	1	—	—	425
Markanda basin	14	6	—	—	450
District	49	66	119	9	1310

The preponderance of service centres in the altitude group of 1,200 to 1,800 metres was associated with their position on the ridge or near the ridge line in most of the cases. Beyond an altitude of 1,800 metres, habitations were a few and service centres fewer. The higher regions were too cold and steep to support good agriculture or large population.

LOCATION IN RELATION TO TRANSPORT LINES

Being essentially nodal in character, all the service centres were linked either by roads or mule tracks or cart tracks or footpaths with their complementary regions as well as with one another. Most of them were located at a site where more than one road or track converged.

Of the 243 service centres, 148 (about 60 per cent) were along the mule tracks and the rest were situated along the motorable roads, many of which were earlier mule tracks. A majority of the service centres in the cis-Giri and trans-Giri hills were on the mule tracks. By comparison, most of the service centres in the Kayarda *dun* and Markanda basin were on motorable roads. These differences were related to the level of transport development and functional vitality of service centres in different parts of the district.

Among the first 31 high order service centres, all but five of them were located on motorable roads. They had developed at the junction of roads or mule tracks confirming the role of nodality in emergence of service centres. They were connected not only with one another but also with towns in the neighbouring area outside the district. Evidently their high position in functional hierarchy was associated with the comparatively better transport facility they enjoyed.

LOCATION IN RELATION TO POPULATION DISTRIBUTION

Since service centres evolve primarily to serve their surrounding areas, a close association is expected between the locational pattern of service centres and the distributional pattern of population. A positive relationship was found between frequency of service centres and degree of population concentration.

Service centres were frequent and closely spaced in tracts where agricultural land existed in large patches. This was particularly true of the eastern part of the Kayarda *dun* and the drainage basins of the Pervi-*ka-khala*, Mauth-*ka-khala*, Palor-*ka-khala*, Bhangal *nadi* and Nera *nadi*. These were the pockets of relatively dense concentration of population.

By contrast, there were hardly any service centres on the thickly forested southern slopes of Dharti *dhar* along the Bata *nadi* and in the high altitude tract of Chaur *dhar* in the north. These areas were practically devoid of human habitation. The highly dissected and thinly populated Siwalik hills along the southern margins of the district also had only a few service centres.

Most of the service centres were small in population size in line with small size of settlements in general. About 67 per cent of the service centres had a population of less than 500 each. About a quarter of them belonged to 500 to 999 population size category. Among the remaining service centres, 19 were in the population size category of 1,000 to 2,000 persons. Only 5 service centres, namely Nahan, Paonta Sahib, Majra, Shalai and Bhengani had a population of more than 2,000 each.

Regional variations in population size of service centres were also observed. A quarter of the service centres in the trans-Giri hills and more than a half of the service centres in the cis-Giri hills had a population size of less than 200 persons each. Only a few service centres in the lowland areas of Kayarda *dun* and Markanda basin fell in this category. Some service centres in the eastern half of the trans-Giri hills as well as in the low land areas mentioned above had a population of 200 to 499.

Relatively large service centres, with population ranging from 500 to 999, were more typical of the eastern half of the trans-Giri hills, the Kayarda *dun* and the Markanda basin. A small number of service centres in the trans-Giri hills as well as in Kayarda *dun* had a population of 1,000 persons and above (Table 11.4). The population size of service centres in any part of the region was invariably related to size of settlements in general. The size of settlements was associated, among other things, with the amount of cultivated land available in a locality.

A positive relationship between the population size and spacing of service centres was observed. Relatively large service centres were spaced at greater distance from each other than the small ones. The functional status and population size of service centres were also positively related notwithstanding a great difference in population of service centres belonging to a particular order of hierarchy.

TABLE 11.4 : **Population size of service centres in various sub-regions**

Name of the sub-region	Number (and percentage) of service centres in the population size category of					Median population of service centres
	below 200	200-499	500-999	1000-2000	above 2000	
Trans-Giri hills	31(24.8)*	46(36.8)	36(28.8)	10(8.0)	2(1.6)	575
Cis-Giri hills	42(66.8)	17(27.0)	1(1.6)	2(3.2)	1(1.6)	170
Kayarda *dun*	3(8.6)	13(37.1)	10(28.6)	7(20.0)	2(5.7)	546
Markanda basin	2(10.0)	11(55.0)	7(35.0)	—	—	335
District	78(31.1)	87(35.9)	54(22.2)	19(7.8)	5(2.0)	355

*Figures in parentheses are the percentages.

DISPERSION OF SERVICE CENTRES

A nearest neighbour analysis revealed that the distributional pattern of relatively high order service centres showed a tendency toward regular arrangement. The distribution became successively more and more random in the case of lower order service centres. This was the opposite of what Dacey found in his analysis of central places in a part of south-western Wisconsin (U.S.A.).[8] The nearest neighbour statistic was 1.41 for the first eleven service centres belonging to the highest, second and third orders and 1.31 for the first thirty-one service centres falling in the first four high orders. The nearest neighbour statistic for all the service centres was around 1.0 representing a random distribution.

Most of the relatively high order service centres had evolved over a long passage of time. The low order service centres were generally of recent origin. They owed their emergence to the opening of a retail store by a shopkeeper or allocation of some facilities in the form of schools, post offices and dispensaries by the government. An overwhelming majority of such service centres had only one or two central functions each.

The distribution of service centres in the trans-Giri hills was more even than in the cis-Giri hills. Large patches of uninhabited forested or highly dissected lands in the latter disturbed the distributional pattern of service centres. Likewise the distribution of service centres was more uneven in the Markanda basin than in the Kayarda *dun*.

To sum up

1. Most of the service centres were located on the ridge or near the ridge line rather than in valleys. Such a location enabled the service centres to command the complementary regions on both sides of a ridge. Service centres made a linear pattern in their distribution. Underlying this pattern was the vital role of linear features like ridge lines, drainage lines and elongated Kayarda *dun*.

2. In conformity with their location, the frequency of service centres was the greatest in the altitude group of 1,200 to 1,800 metres. Only a few service centres existed at an altitude of more than 1,800 metres. The service centres located in the Kayarda *dun* and Markanda basin belonged to an altitude group of less than

600 metres.

3. The role of transportation lines was evident. A majority of service centres was located at points where a number of tracks or roads or both converged. High order service centres were linked generally with other service centres in the study area as also with towns in the neighbouring areas outside the district.

4. An overwhelming majority of service centres were small in terms of their population size. Size and spacing of service centres were positively related. The bigger service centres showed a tendency toward regular distribution. The distributional pattern became more and more random in the case of low order service centres.

FOOTNOTES

1. A.K. Philbrick, "Principles of areal functional organisation in regional human geograpy", *Economic Geography*, 33, 1957, pp. 299-336.
2. G.S. Gosal, "Urban Geography : A trend report" in *A Survey of Research in Geography*, Indian Council of Social Science Research, New Delhi, 1972, pp. 203-225.
3. L.K. Sen and others, *Planning Rural Growth Centres for Integrated Area Development : A Study of Miryalguda Taluka*, National Institute of Community Development, Hyderabad, 1971.
4. R. Tirtha and A. Lall, "Service centres in the Western Himalayas", *Journal of Tropical Geography*, 25, 1967, pp. 58-68.
5. Gopal Krishan and M.M. Chandna, *The System of Service Centres in the Outer Himalayas : A Case Study of District Sirmaur, Himachal Pradesh, India*, Man, Culture, and Settlement, N.G.S.I., Research Publication No. 17, 1977, pp. 277-286. Also see Gopal Krishan and M.M. Chandna, "The system of service centres in the outer Himalayas", *Ekistics*, 42, 1976, pp. 62-66.
6. The number of service centres along various streams or revulets was as follows : (i) Giri=17, (ii) Tons=1, (iii) Nera=5, (iv) Jalal=3, (v) Bhangal=2, (vi) Ghaggar=2, (vii) Kawali=1 and other streams=11. Total=42.
7. The number of service centres situated close to various drainage lines in the Kayarda *dun* was as follows : (i) Bata=18, (ii) Giri=10 and (iii) Yamuna=7. Total=35.
8. Dacey, M.F., "Analysis of central place and point patterns by a nearest neighbour method", *Lund Studies in Geography : Human Geography*, 24, 1962, pp. 55-75.

TWELVE

M. L. SONI

HIERARCHY OF SERVICE-CENTRES IN THE UMLAND OF LUCKNOW

INTRODUCTION

THE concept of hierarchy has attracted the interest of a number of geographers in recent years who have conducted empirical studies in specific areas.* The service-centres extend over a complete range, varying in status from places of local significance (village markets) to those whose influence is regional, e.g., Lucknow, Faizabad, Bahraich, Sitapur, etc. The less important a centre the greater is its dependence upon other more important service-centres. Ranged according to status the centres could be made to form an almost continuous list. But as Ian Carruthers writes, 'It is more convenient to think of them as being organised into the ranks or successive orders of a hierarchy or gradation, though the divisions proposed may not always be clear cut or well defined.[1]

Many criteria have been evolved by different geographers for ranking and analysing the various towns and cities in different parts of the world. Christaller has presented the most comprehensive theoretical system of analysing different service-centres from the smallest market towns to the largest cities in Germany

* R.E. Dickinson, A.E. Smails, F.H.W. Green, J.B. Fleming and H.B. Bracey in England ; Christaller in Germany ; H.J. Keuning in Netherlands and John E. Bracey in U.S.A.

and has categorised seven grades* of service-centres based on centrality indices. To measure the centrality of places in Southern Germany, Christaller took the number of telephones as a basis. About twenty years earlier to Christaller, Galpin[2] studied in New York and Wisconsin, but in sociological way. Dickinson[3] considers the provision of goods of service-centres and services to their tributary areas while Smailes[4] considers the essential functions of the towns and the institutions which discharge the functions. Carter's[5] three grades are based on the assessment of selected data with an emphasis on commercial functions. Kolb,[6] while grading, uses some social, commercial and religious services. In some cases a multi-variate functional analysis has been done to grade the various towns. Singh[7] has attempted a tentative classification of towns in the Umland of Banaras by taking into account both the size and service factors. Brush[8] and Philbrick[9] categorised on the basis of size and economic activities and then the distribution has been examined for particular areas. Garrison and Berry subjected the idea of discreteness of level within both a size and functional hierarchy in Snohomish country, Wisconsin to rigorous statistical proof.[10]

An altogether different method has been adopted in the works of Green,[11] Ullman[12] and Taaffe.[13] These works have devised methods to measure the centrality of places by their capacity as transport centres. Godlund[14] derives a set of hierarchies from a centrality index (based on economic activity) and the method has been adopted by K.N. Singh for eastern U.P.[15]

METHODOLOGY

Economically the Umland of Lucknow is still in the mediaeval stage. Modern means of communication are confined only to the bigger towns. Hence the alternative method is adopted for determining the discreteness of level. Size and economic activity of service-centres are considered in this method. Following Godlund the centrality method is applied for grading various

* The grades in the ascending order of hierarchy are :
(1) Marktort, (2) Amstort, (3) Kriesstadt, (4) Bezirksstadt, (5) Gaustadt, (6) Provinzstadt, and (7) Landstadt.

service-centres of the region. But the central functions taken into consideration in the present work are different from those taken by Godlund and K.N. Singh. The latter has considered only the persons engaged in commerce whereas in this paper all the non-agricultural population have been taken into account for centrality calculations.*

Findings

The centrality values as obtained from the calculations are given in Table 12.1 and are also shown by a suitable cartographic method. A close examination of the map reveals that the service-centers in the Umland of Lucknow vary greatly in importance. The centre having the highest centrality (Lucknow Group—31.077) is nearly 1,295 times more central than the lowest (Sheogarh in Rae Bareli district—0.024). The second in order of importance is Faizabad Group (3.831). Only a few with decreasing centrality are Sitapur Group (2.708), Bahraich (2.487), Gonda Group (1.888), Barabanki Group (1.745), Hardoi Group (1.716), Lakhimpur (1.604), Rae Bareli (1.346) and Balrampur (1.195). The rest of the centres have still lower centrality.

Advantage of the method

The centrality of a centre or the capacity to serve the region depends upon the number of persons engaged in the non-agricultural activities, and thus the formula is easily commensurable and provides satisfactory results. The data used in the present work can be obtained for all the settlements in India, and thus enable us to compare with other parts and bring out the regional patterns in the country. It is also realised that the total population of the size of a centre with less population may be assigned even a high centrality rating.

The population sizes vs. centrality index graph

The population and centrality of all the service-centres on a

* The centrality of service-centres is calculated with the help of the formula $C=\frac{N \times 100}{P}$, where '*C*' is the required centrality, '*N*' the number of persons employed in non-agricultural activities in a centre and '*P*' the total number of persons of the region engaged in non-agricultural activities.

TABLE 12.1 : **The centrality of service-centres in the Umland of Lucknow**

Sl. No.	Name of service-centre	Centrality
1	2	3
1.	Hardoi Group	1.716
2.	Sandila	0.717
3.	Pachhiyaon	0.083
4.	Maurawan	0.174
5.	Purwa	0.261
6.	Nihalgarh	0.062
7.	Musafirkhana	0.101
8.	Maholi	0.074
9.	Machhrehta	0.068
10.	Nimsar-Misrikh	0.215
11.	Sarai Pitthu Group	0.131
12.	Sitapur Group	2.708
13.	Laharpur	0.538
14.	Khairabad	0.511
15.	Biswan	0.586
16.	Sidhauli	0.102
17.	Paintepur	0.150
18.	Mahmudabad	0.300
19.	Malihabad	0.187
20.	Chinhat	0.065
21.	Lucknow Group	31.077
22.	Goshainganj	0.106
23.	Amethi	0.135
24.	Sisendi	0.148
25.	Salehnagar	0.043
26.	Tilokpur	0.097
27.	Saadatganj	0.154
28.	Fatehpur	0.345
29.	Dewa	0.105
30.	Barabanki Group	1.745
31.	Jahangirabad	0.114
32.	Masauli	0.179
33.	Zaidpur	0.465
34.	Rudauli	0.383
35.	Rampur-Bhawanipur Group	0.206
36.	Haidargarh	0.096
37.	Ganeshpur	0.036
38.	Bachhrawan	0.121
39.	Mahrajganj	0.077

1	2	3
40.	Rae Bareli	1.346
41.	Jais	0.285
42.	Sheogarh	0.024
43.	Khamaria Pandit	0.081
44.	Oel	0.167
45.	Lakhimpur	1.604
46.	Kheri	0.334
47.	Maigalganj	0.062
48.	Gola Gokarannath	0.923
49.	Palia Kala	0.207
50.	Balrampur	1.195
51.	Utraula	0.424
52.	Khargupur-Imilia	0.091
53.	Dhaneypur	0.123
54.	Gonda Group	1.888
55.	Colonelganj	0.321
56.	Nawabganj	0.223
57.	Mihipurwa	0.115
58.	Maina Bargaon	0.055
59.	Kewalpur	0.101
60.	Nanpara	0.543
61.	Bamhaura Group	0.077
62.	Bahraich Group	2.487
63.	Chakia	0.065
64.	Kaisarganj	0.033
65.	Gilaula	0.032
66.	Dabha Semar	0.035
67.	Faizabad Group	3.831

single graph. This graph has been prepared to test the two aspects—

(a) whether there is any correlation between the size of a centre and its centrality index ;

(b) whether there are any natural break-points on the graph which could be used as reference points for classifying the various service-centres into certain centrality categories.

The graph reveals that the relationship between size and centrality is not consistent at all levels of size of service-centres. The roughly consistent relationship is, however, available up to 15,000 population. Lower down this scale there appears to be less consistence. The less non-agricultural population of a centre keeps its centrality low. The centres located favourably along the routes have obviously high index. Certain specialised centres, e.g., manufacturing, naturally rank higher in the centrality index, such as Gola Gokarannath. Laharpur with higher population (Pop. 20,205 and Cent. 0.538) has lower centrality than that of Biswan (Pop. 19,336 and Cent. 0.586). Likewise Sandila has higher population but low centrality (Pop. 22,365 and Cent. 0.717) while Gola Gokarannath has lesser population but higher centrality (Pop. 21,677 and Cent. 0.923).

The graph reveals that the centrality of a centre is more directly related to route pattern and the nodality of a centre; while the socio-economic factors have their own bearing. The role of administrative headquarters with its various offices and its concentrating power of other functions also are clearly visible in the map.

Hierarchial grades

The graph does not show any discrete points which may help in determining the grades. But as exhorted by Smailes, although any grading must in some measure be arbitrary, since the urban grade is as continuous as the social scale, yet the reality of stratification cannot be denied. The grading adopted in this paper is, therefore, arbitrary and the eight categories of centrality grades are given Table 12.2.

TABLE 12.2 : **Eight categories of centrality grades**

Hierarchial order	Category	Centrality index	Number of centres in the region
I	Regional Capital	Above 4.000	1
II	Regional Centres	2.001 to 4.000	3
III	Sub-Regional Centres	1.001 to 2.000	6
IV	Large Rurban Centres	0.501 to 1.000	6
V	Medium Rurban Centres	0.251 to 0.500	8
VI	Small Rurban Centres	0.126 to 0.250	13
VII	Rural Market Centres	0.062 to 0.125	23
VIII	Market Villages	Below 0.062	7

The Regional Capital of the Umland of Lucknow* is the Corporation City and State Capital—Lucknow with a population of above 0.8 million. It is distinguished by the, (1) it has the regional offices of both government departments and private organisations operating on national and provincial scale; (2) maximum concentration of wholesale and retail traders; (3) a branch of almost all the banks in India; (4) a daily newspaper; and (5) a university, medical college and large general hospitals etc.

The Regional Centres are only three—Faizabad, Bahraich and Sitapur. All these district headquarters are characterized by a wide range of services but having more limited service areas. They also integrate the services of a number of towns around them. The Sub-Regional Centres are six—Hardoi, Barabanki, Rae Bareli, Lakhimpur, Gonda and Balrampur. All of them are also district headquarters except Balrampur which is a tahsil headquarters. Balrampur has a greater nodality hence a sub-regional centre. All are on the important routes.

The large Rurban Centres are six—Sandila, Laharpur, Khairabad, Biswan, Gola Gokarannath and Nanpara. Except Gola Gokarannath and Khairabad all are tahsil headquarters. The two exceptions are recognised for their manufacturing, trade and transport services. On account of their business all have a few branches of important banks, regional co-operative societies, Intermediate colleges (Gola Gakarannath has a degree college), etc. Eight medium rurban centres—Purwa, Mahmudabad, Fatehpur, Zaidpur, Rudauli, Jais, Kheri, Utraula having a population of about 12,000 each except Rudauli (18,933). With the highest population in the group, Rudauli has the minimum percentage (55.9) of non-agricultural working population. However, some of them are vikaskhand headquarters and have their effective service areas chiefly within the vikaskhand boundary. Certainly some of them are tahsil headquarters but are situated away to the main routes like Fatehpur and Purwa. Generally these centres are good commercial and small scale

* Umland of Lucknow has been separately delimited by the author which includes the districts of Lucknow, Barabanki, Bahraich, Gonda, Faizabad, Sultanpur, Rae Bareli, Unnao, Hardoi, Sitapur and Kheri either wholly or partially.

industrial centres. The small Rurban Centres are small administrative-cum-trade-cum-household industry centres. Nimsar-Misrikh and Malihabad are tahsil headquarters but they lack in many services. Maurawan and Colonelganj are noted commercial centres.

Rural Market Centres, some of them old decayed centres, are merely the trade-cum-household industry centres. Market villages are only seven* in the region. These are the centres with a market, a school and a post office in some cases.

Distribution of service-centres

The Umland of Lucknow is an agricultural area and the service-centres exist mainly because of their function as central places for the exchange of goods and services, each for its local trade area. Everywhere the small centres are closely spaced and more numerous; large centres, offering greater services are more widely spaced and less numerous. A perusal tells that the density considered from the point of view of number is higher in the central districts, viz., Lucknow and Barabanki while lower in the peripherical districts like Hardoi, Kheri, Rae Bareli, Gonda and Bahraich. In other words, there is one service-centre after about 342 sq. kilometres in Lucknow district and after about 1,656 sq. kilometres in Hardoi district.

* Salehnagar, Ganeshpur, Sheogarh, Maina Bargaon, Kaisarganj, Gilaula and Dabha Semar.

FOOTNOTES

1. Carruthers, Ian, A Classification of Service-Centres in England & Wales, *Geographical Journal*, Vol. CXXIII, 1957, pp. 371-386.
2. Quoted after Brush, John E., *Geographical Review*, Vol 43, 1953, pp. 381-402.
3. Dickinson, R.E.. The Distribution and Functions of Smaller Urban Settlements of East Anglia, *Geography*, Vol. 17, 1932, pp. 19-31
4. Smailes, A.E., The Urban Hierarchy in England & Wales, *Geography*, Vol. XXIX, 1944, p 41.
5. Carter, Harold, Urban Grades and Sphere of Influence in South West Wales—A Historical Consideration, *Scottish Geography Magazine*, Vol. 71, 1955, pp. 43-59.
6. Kolb, J.H., Trends of Country Neighbourhood, *Research Bulletin*,

No. 117, 1933, p. 38.

7. Singh, R.L., Urban Hierarchy in the Umland of Banaras, *Journal of Scientific Research*, Banaras Hindu University, Vol. VI (2), 1955-56.
8. Brush, John E., The Hierarchy of Central Places in S.W. Wisconsin, *Geographical Review*, Vol. 43, 1953, pp. 380-404.
9. Philbrick, A.K., Principles of Areal Functional Organisation in Regional Human Geography, *Economic Geography*, Vol. 33, 1957, pp. 306-336.
10. Garrison, W.L. and Berry, B.J.L., The Functional Bases of the Central Place Hierarchy, *Economic Geography*, Vol. 34, 1958.
11. Green, F.H.W., Urban Hinterlands in England & Wales—An Analysis of Bus Service, *Geographical Journal*, Vol. 116, 1950, pp. 64-68.
12. Ullman, L., Trade Centres and Tributary Areas of the Philippines, *Geographical Review*, Vol. 50, 1960, pp. 203-218.
13. Taaffe, E.J., The Urban Hierarchy—An Air Passenger Definition, *Economic Geography*, Vol. 38, 1962.
14. Godlund, Seven, The Functions and Growth of Bus Traffic within the Sphere of Influence, Land Studies in Geography, Series B, *Human Geography*, No. 18, 1956, p. 12.
15. Singh, K.N., A Ph.D. Thesis submitted to B.H.U., 1962.

THIRTEEN

K.B. KANKURE, AND P.T. MALSHE

GROWTH, HIERARCHY AND FUNCTIONAL CLASSIFICATION OF URBAN SETTLEMENTS IN MARATHWADA

INTRODUCTION

THE modern civilization is characterised by faster growth of cities in the economically developed areas of the world. The technological innovations have been responsible for industrialization of certain areas and thus, for the growth of urban centres to an unprecedented scale in the history of human civilization. The rural-urban interaction is, therefore, ever on the increase. The urban places play a crucial role as centres of diffusion of culture and knowledge to a very considerable degree during modern times. They are hubs of industrial and commercial activities in a country. In an ancient land like that of ours, the towns and cities bear marks of history.

The science of settlement geography has naturally assumed tremendous significance for this reason, during contemporary times. The growth of urbanization in Maharashtra reveals features of unbalanced growth.[1] The area under study is a relatively less developed with high potential for industrialization/urbanization, considering its rich agricultural endowments. So far as the growth of urbanization in Marathwada is concerned, it is observed that the growth during the past has been extremely poor and, as a result of it, the region's share in total urban population for the

Since the census data for 1981 is not yet published, therefore, it could not be used in the analysis.

state is too less. Though Marathwada shares 20.97 per cent of the state's total geographical area, its share of urban population in the State is only 7.55 per cent (1971). So far as the internal disparities within the region are concerned, it is observed that the three districts of Aurangabad, Nanded and Parbhani have values above the average for the region, whereas, the two districts of Osmanabad and Beed have returned very poor values, as is evident from Table 13.1.

TABLE 13.1 : **Urbanisation—1971**

	Name of the unit	Urbanization (%)
(I)	Maharashtra State	31.17
(II)	Marathwada Region	14.71
(a)	Aurangabad District	16.71
(b)	Nanded District	16.33
(c)	Parbhani District	16.06
(d)	Osmanabad District	12.49
(e)	Beed District	11.61

Source : Census of India (1971) Series 11, Maharashtra, Part II (A).

Methodology

The analysis is based upon cause and effect model with a process approach. Suitable cartographic and statistical methods have been used for this purpose. The functional classification has been attempted according to Nelson's method.

Data sources

The paper is based on secondary data obtained from relevant census publications. Since the data concerning, 1981 census is not available and is not likely to be available in the near future, the data for 1971 census has been used here for analysis. It is very well known that collection of primary data in the field from numerous centres is physically extremely hazardous, time consuming, as well as, tremendously expensive. The secondary data used here is quite suitable for this purpose and the results arrived at speak of regional realities. Since the first author hails from the Marathwada area and has travelled in it considerably during recent times, therefore, he has been able to keep pace with development in the area.

The study region

The area under study is a part of Maharashtra constituting an administrative division. Marathwada, which is made up of five districts, viz., Aurangabad, Beed, Osmanabad, Parbhani and Nanded, is a historical region. It was under Nizam's rule for a considerable period of time. Not much of change occurred during the British rule. However, some changes in agriculture, as well as, in industry are occurring presently through development efforts under the Five Year Plans. The area under study is characterised by diverse relief, i.e., Ajanta hills to the north-west, Balaghat ranges to the south and Godavari valley in the centre (Refer Fig. 13.1). The region is drained by Godavari river and its tributaries. The tahsils occurring along the Western margin of the region are drought-prone areas. Over the rest of the area the amount of annual rainfall is moderate and supports agricultural activities, predominantly. The mainly forested tract occurs in the extreme eastern part of the region in the Kinwat and Bhokar tahsils.

FIG. 13.1 : *Marathwada—General relief map*

Culturally the region has great importance due to existence of important religious centres such as Tuljapur, Parli, Ambejogai, Paithan, etc. Besides this the region contains internationally well-known Ajanta and Ellora group of caves, that obtain along the ancient Kosambi-Paithan highway. This region has lagged behind in economic progress when compared with Bombay-Pune, and Nagpur regions, probably due to its adverse location in relation to the national highways and the main railway routes. Since it is a relatively backward area of the country a peep into the processes of change and realities will provide a clue to the development of the region in future. Thus, it is a vital study of fundamental importance in the context of regional development.

Changing processes and patterns of urban growth in Marathwada

The region of Marathwada was settled during the ancient times (c. 2000 B.C.), particularly the area around Paithan, in Godavari valley, as it was along the north-south ancient highway originating from Kosambi in the north linking, centres with Karnataka plateau towards South.

Later on, this region was under the rule of Satavahanas, with their capital at Pratisthan, i.e., modern 'Paithan'. Paithan was, therefore, the seat of power and a centre of industrial and technological diffusion for a long period of time. It had external links with Nasik towards west and beyond with the Roman empire, Kosambi in the Ganga valley towards north, and with Kanchipuram and other centres of south. During the period of Mohammedan rule the region was under the sway of the Sultans of Bijapur, the emperors of Delhi and after the death of Aurangzeb it passed into the possession of the Nizam of Hyderabad. Ala-ud-din Khilji conquered Devagiri and made this fort his regional capital, as it was useful for his military campaigns further south. When this region came under the rule of Bijapur Kingdom, Aurangabad assumed importance as a place of Muslim culture and learning. Paithan, Ambejogai, Nanded, Tuljapur and Parli were important centres of Hindu religion and culture. Several new forts were built and the old ones repaired in connection with military campaigns at Naldurg, Dharur, Udgir, Parenda and at Daulatabad. New urban centres arose at these places to serve defensive function. Later, Aurangzeb founded the city of Aurangabad at the site of former village 'Kirkee', and fortified it with a strong wall. The military campaigns during this period diffused the settlements into hilly and forested areas, as well as, into the region, away from old highways due to fear of invading armies.

When the British conquered this territory it was under Nizam's rule. However, the British constructed new roads and railways across this territory and as a result of these developments, new and old centres got boost, such as Aurangabad, Jalna, Nanded, Parbhani, Parli, Hingoli, Ambejogai and Osmanabad, etc. Many of these centres contain industrial and commercial activities of modest size during the contemporary times due to facility of transport and nearness to fertile areas.

Considering the growth of urban population in Marathwada during the present century, it is observed that (a) during the first two decades urban population was almost stagnant (Refer Fig. 13.2). This is mainly because of lack of economic growth and

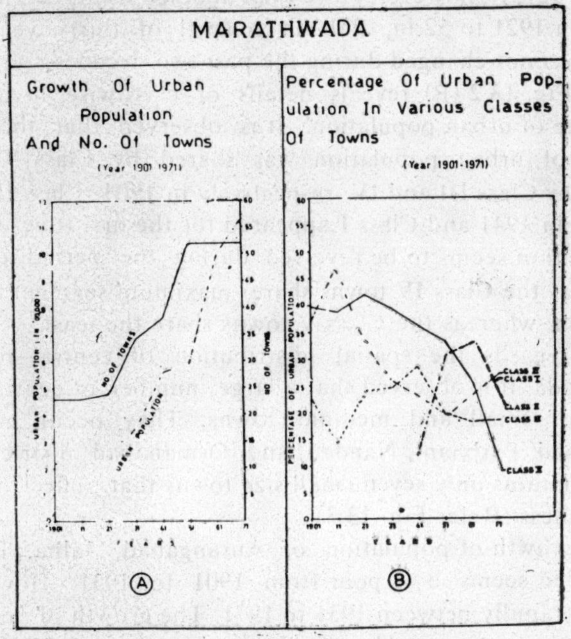

FIG. 13.2 (*A*) : *Marathwada—Growth of Urban population and number of towns*

(*B*) : *Marathwada—Percentage of Urban population in various classes of towns* high mortality rate, due to prevalence of scorges as plague, malaria, and influenza etc., (b) urban population increased two and half times from 1921 to 1951. This growth may be attributed to overall economic development in the Nizam State and thus in Marathwada. (c) The decade of 1941-1951 has registered a growth of 4.33 per cent only. This relatively low value might be explained on the ground that the out-migration of population occurred towards industrially developing areas of Maharashtra and Andhra Pradesh. During census period 1951-1971, a continuous upward trend in the graph is noticed. The urban population doubled itself in this period of two decades. This increase in urban population is due to development of agriculture and industries through various Five Year Plans.

As regards variation in the number of urban centres it is observed from Fig. 13.2(A) that the number rose from 23 in 1901 to 24 by 1921. It, however, more than doubled itself, i.e., increased from 24 in 1921 to 52 in 1951, in a spell of thirty years. This number has not changed during the past two decades.

The Fig. 13.2 (B) reveals details of class-wise break-up of percentage of urban population. It is observed that the largest segment of urban population was shared by Class V centres followed by Class III and IV, respectively in 1901. Class II centres appeared in 1941 and Class I appeared for the first time in 1971. The condition seems to be reversed during the period of seven decades, as the Class IV towns share maximum segment of urban population, whereas the Class V towns share the least.

As regards the spatial distribution of central places in Marathwada, it is observed that a large number of central places consists of small and medium towns. They occur mostly in Aurangabad, Parbhani, Nanded and Osmanabad districts. Bhir district contains only seven small size towns that reflect its utter backwardness (Refer Fig. 13.3).

The growth of population of Aurangabad, Jalna, Parbhani and Nanded seems to be poor from 1901 to 1931. However, it increased rapidly between 1931 to 1971. The growth of population of Latur town seems to be at fairly continuous tempo. The rate of growth of Beed, Ambejogai, Parli and Hingoli, etc., first show a decline of population in 1931 and then increase from 1931 to 1971. The rest of the towns also reveal a poor growth of population due to factors mentioned earlier.

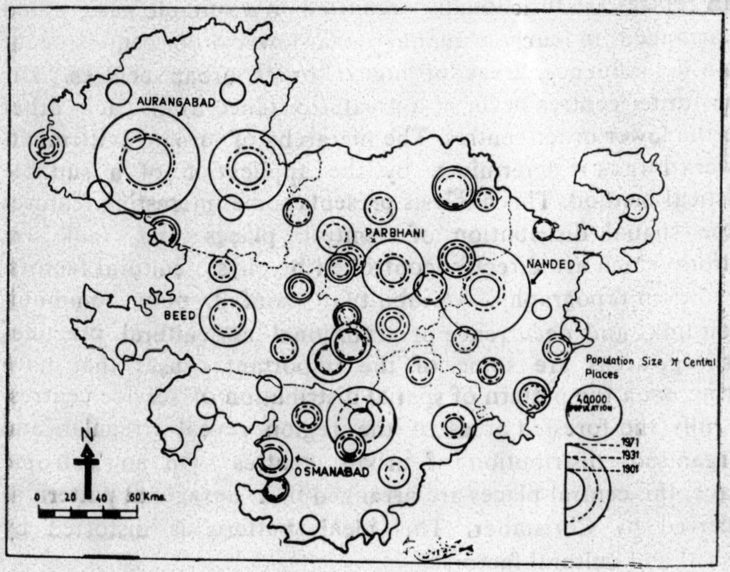

FIG. 13.3 : *Population size of central places in Marathwada (years 1901, 1931, 1971)*

Centrality and hierarchy

A central place connotes a place of manifold activities for the surrounding countryside.[2] A central place can be defined as a permanent human establishment where an exchange of central goods and services for population, other than the local one, exists and which, therefore, commands a tributary region surrounding it. All central places perform certain non-primary functions for the region. The central places vary in size according to their service capacities. The small market centres, the large market centres, sub-regional centres, regional centres, and large regional centres are all central places but they vary in functional characteristics and importance.

Walter Christaller considered the central place as a centre of central functions performed for the surrounding area. Thus, "centrality" is the total amount of functions needed to serve the Umland. "The hierarchy" of urban settlements denotes the ranking of urban centres into successive groups on the basis of population size or some other selected variable. These groups of urban centres are functionally organised in a suitable pattern and are arranged in such a manner that lower order centres occur within the influence areas of higher order urban centres. The higher order centres occur at a greater distance from each other than the lower order centres. The hierarchy of urban settlements in Marathwada is determined by the application of a suitable statistical method. This analysis presents some interesting features in the spatial distribution of central places and rank size relations which are directly controlled by physio-cultural factors. The uneven topography, variability in rainfall, poor communication links and occurrence of traditional agricultural practices over large areas are some of the important causes that have bearing upon the pattern of spatial distribution of service centres. The hilly and forested areas of the region reveal irregular and disorganised distribution of urban centres. On an isotropic surface, the central places are arranged in a hexagonal pattern as conceived by Christaller. This ideal pattern is distorted by physical and cultural factors.

Walter Christaller has made use of number of telephone connections existing at the centres for determining the centrality of service centres in southern Germany.[3] This method is not viable under Indian condition as the rural areas lack this facility. Dickinson in his paper has made use of per capita wholesale business for cities in the United States.[4] Smailes in his study has considered the essential functions and institutions of urban importance such as bank, school, hospital, cinema and newspaper.[5] Green in his paper has made use of bus transport for analysing centrality.[6] Godlund in Sweden has taken retail trade for centrality index.[7]

In this study the centrality has been calculated by adding together all workers engaged in tertiary services by the formula noted below :

$$C=\frac{T\times 100}{P}$$

C=Centrality

T=The number of persons dependent upon tertiary services

P=Total regional tertiary population.

This method is suitable for economically developing countries like India with guided growth and controlled development, which neglects undue advantage of single function such as bus service, telephone, and commerce or others.

Aurangabad is characterised by an assortment of functions, viz., wholesaling, transport, administration and tourism. It is also a place of learning, as well as, publication of regional newspapers in Marathwada. Therefore, it commands the highest centrality value in the hierarchy of settlements. Nanded is a principal trading centre, administrative centre as well as significant for educational and transport services in the south-eastern part of the region. Thus, it commands the second place as indicated in the table in the appendix. Jalna, Latur and Parbhani are important centres for such functions as trading, transport and education. The remaining centres command centrality values less than five. Evidently, these centres are medium and small towns, serving mainly the nearby rural areas (Refer Fig. 13.4).

The concept of hierarchy is based on population size of

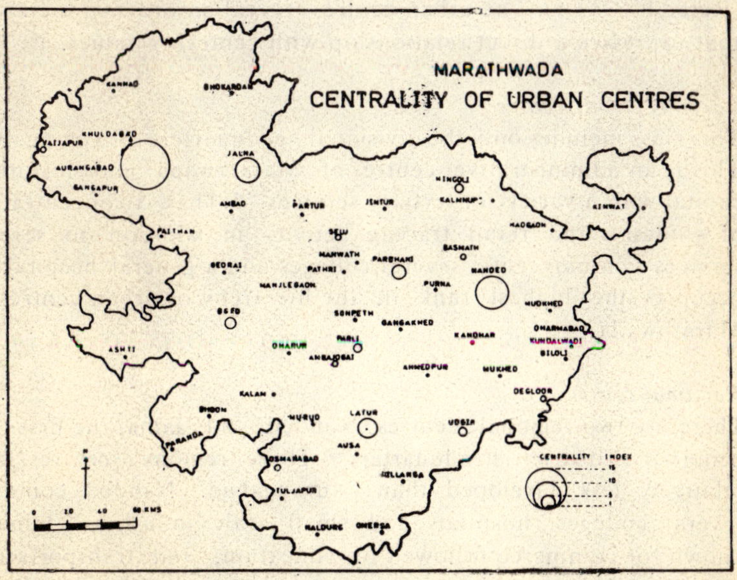

FIG. 13.4 : *Marathwada—Centrality of urban centres*

urban settlements, their functional structure and centrality value. The hierarchy values of central places have been calculated with the help of the following formula :

$$\text{Hierarchy Index} = \sqrt{\frac{C \times TWP \times 100}{WP}}$$

C = Centrality

TWP = The tertiary workers population of a town

WP = Total working population of the town.

The standard deviation has been calculated from the mean of the hierarchy index to find out ranks of the urban centres. One urban centre in this region came up to value of 4 S.D. Further, five categories of central places have been identified based on the standard deviation, viz., (1) Large regional centre, (2) Regional centre, (3) Sub-regional centre, (4) Large market town and (5) Small market town.

Centrally index and Rank of urban centres have been plotted on a graph to get hierarchical grouping of urban centres (Refer Fig. 13.5). The urban centres reveal an order of hierarchy that expresses a direct relationship with centrality values.

Large regional centre

This class includes only the divisional headquarters of Aurangabad. This is an administrative centre of Marathwada and historical capital with a variety of tertiary services. It has a concentration of wholesale and retail trading activity in addition to several services as a university, several colleges and a general hospital. It occupies the highest rank in the hierarchy of urban centres in Marathwada.

Regional centre

There are two regional centres Nanded and Jalna, the first one being the district headquarters. These regional centres are relatively less developed than Aurangabad. Nanded contains several colleges, hospitals and small scale industries Jalna is known for commerce followed by education, and transportation services, etc.

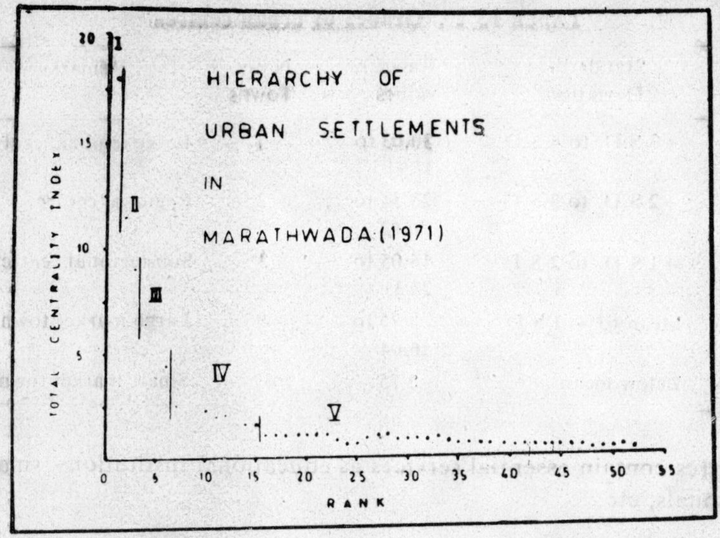

FIG. 13.5 : *Hierarchy of urban settlements in Marathwada (1971)*

Sub-regional centre

Three sub-regional centres viz. Latur, Parbhani and Beed have been identified. They are relatively small in comparison to the regional and large-regional centres discussed above and serve small hinterlands. This group includes two district headquarters (Parbhani and Beed) and one taluka headquarter (Latur). Some small scale industries, colleges and hospitals, etc., occur at these places.

Large market town

Nine urban centres are included in this category. These urban centres include one district headquarter (Osmanabad) and eight taluka headquarters. These centres also have colleges, high schools and centres of entertainment services.

Small market town

There are thirty seven small market centres of class IV and V in Marathwada. They are on the whole widely distributed in the region. All these centres are basically rural service centres. The

TABLE 13.2 : **Grades of urban centres**

Sr. No.	Standard Deviation	Range of values	No of Towns	Remarks
1.	+3 S.D. to 4 S.D.	30.63 to 37.91	1	Large regional centre
2.	+2 S.D. to 3 S.D.	23.34 to 30.62	2	Regional centre
3.	+1 S.D. to 2 S.D.	16.05 to 23.33	3	Sub-regional centre
4.	Mean to + 1 S.D.	8.75 to 16.04	9	Large market town
5.	Below mean	8.75	37	Small market town

centres contain essential services as educational institutions, small hospitals, etc.

Functional classification of towns

In the present study Howard J. Nelson's[8] method of classification has been used. His service classification of American cities is based on "Stated statistical procedure". He calculates the standard deviation from the mean in each of the activity groups and classifies towns and cities according to the degree of variation from the mean. Since this method has been found to be appropriate so far as revelation of regional realities is concerned, therefore, it has been applied with only one modification that the agricultural function has been considered by the authors. This is precisely due to the fact that agriculture is the most dominant economic activity of the region under study and it is significant even in town areas. The total number of urban centres in the region is fifty-two according to 1971 census, and they have been classified according to function, below.

The mean percentages of each activity group to the total workers in each of the fifty-two towns of Marathwada and the mean for each of the activity groups have been calculated. The mean percentage and standard deviation of workers in various activity groups in the towns under study are given in Table 13.3.

Standard deviations from the means have been calculated for each of the eight activity groups of towns to bring out the degree of variation clearly. Standard deviation can be calculated with

TABLE 13.3 : **Mean percentage and standard deviation of workers**

Occupation	Symbol	Percentage	Standard Deviation
Agriculture	A	23.96	16.76
Mining, Forestry, etc.	M	2.90	2.30
Household industry	H	3.38	1.85
Manufacturing other than household industry	MF	11.27	4.83
Construction	C	4.58	3.86
Trade and Commerce	T	19.35	4.63
Transport and Communication	CM	6.55	3.21
Other services	O	27.97	9.36
Diversified	D	—	—

the help of following formula :

$$\text{Standard Deviation}=\sqrt{\frac{\Sigma d^2}{n}}$$

d=difference between each value and the mean

n=number of values.

Using the standard deviation and the means, the towns are grouped according to their appropriate functional categories, e.g., towns with percentages more than one degree of variation from the mean +1 S.D. in agriculture are classed as Agricultural towns, above mean +2 S.D. as Agricultural$_2$ and above mean +3 S.D. are classed as Agricultural$_3$. The same procedure is followed in the case of other occupational groups. Table 13.4 shows mean, standard deviation and three degrees of variation for each of the occupation groups.

Following this method the towns have been classified as given below :

Agricultural towns

Twenty-six towns out of a total of fifty-two urban centres, i.e., exactly half the number of towns are classed as agricultural towns (Refer Fig. 13.6 and Appendix for details). Seventeen of these towns are class four towns and the remaining are class five

TABLE 13.4 : **Average and standard deviation for selected occupation groups**

		Agriculture	Mining	Household industry	Manufac-turing	Construc-tion	Trade & commerce	Trans-port	Other services
1.	Mean	23.96	2.90	3.38	11.27	4.58	19.35	6.55	27.97
2.	Standard deviation	16.76	2.30	1.85	4.83	3.86	4.63	3.21	9.36
3.	Mean +1 S.D.	40.72	5.20	5.23	16.10	8.44	23.98	9.76	37.33
4.	Mean +2 S.D.	57.48	7.50	7.08	29.93	12.30	28.61	12.97	46.69
5.	Mean +3 S.D.	74.24	9.80	8.93	25.76	16.16	33.24	16.18	56.05

FIG. 13.6 : *Marathwada—Hierarchy and functional classification of urban centres (1971)*

towns. Most of these settlements are rural service centres occurring in the agricultural tracts in fertile river valleys. Considerably high value as A_3 is shared by Murud, and A_2 by Bhoom, Naldurg, Pathri and Hadgaon.

Mining and other primary services towns

Only three towns, viz., Osmanabad, Basmath and Naldurg are classed in this category. As these towns occur in the areas of undulating topography and relatively less rainfall, the quarrying followed by livestock and forestry are important economic activities.

Household industry

Nine towns have been classed in this category. Significant amongst them are Jalna, Basmath, Kandhar, Mukhed and Kundalwadi. Most of these towns occur in the fertile agricultural tracts of Nanded and Parbhani districts. Jalna, a leading market-centre, and other centres contain handloom weaving industries as the main household industrial activity. Kandhar shares, the highest value of H_3 due to concentration of this activity ; ten per cent of its workers are employed in household industry.

Manufacturing towns

Only three towns are classified under this head, viz., Nanded, Latur and Purnea. All these centres contain small-scale industrial units, many of them in the M.I.D.C. areas. These centres enjoy railway facilities and road connectivity as well as location in the fertile areas with cotton, as commercial crop.

Construction towns

Aurangabad, Basmath and Paithan occur in this class. Aurangabad has experienced considerable construction activity due to its administrative importance, ever increasing significance as centre of tourism and hotelling industry. Paithan occurs in the Godavari valley and is a place of historical importance.

Trading and commercial towns

Only five towns, viz., Latur, Jalna, Udgir, Pethumbri and Kandhar come in this category. Latur and Jalna are important commercial centres with sizable trade in commercial crops as cotton, groundnuts, other oilseeds and cereal crops. They are well connected by roads and railways. Udgir is a historical place and a regional trading centre.

Transport and communication towns

Jalna, Nanded, Beed and Parli occur in this category. Transportation function is important at these places due to their significance as trading centres, e.g., Jalna and Nanded, and administrative centre, e.g., Beed. Parli contains a big thermal power station for which coal is imported from Andhra Pradesh.

Other service towns

It is a bundle of several services as teachers, doctors, lawyers and others engaged in professional and personal services. Aurangabad, Parbhani and Osmanabad fall in this category. Professional services are important at these centres as they are headquarters of the districts.

Diversified towns

As many as 11 towns come under this category and it is the second largest group of towns. A diversified town is one where the percentage of workers to total workers does not reach above the mean +1S.D. in any of the occupation groups. It is a characteristic feature of Indian towns to have workers engaged in several activities with none attaining a degree of specialisation. Out of these 11 towns, three are in class III, seven in class IV and one in class V.

The analysis of urbanisation, centrality, hierarchy and functional classification of towns occurring in the preceding pages reveals that though the region commands rich agricultural tract, agriculture has not been developed on modern lines and, therefore, several towns still continue as agricultural towns. A developed agricultural activity generates commercial and industrial activities, as found in the irrigated tracts of Ahmednagar, Pune and Kolhapur districts of Maharashtra. This feature is precisely lacking presently in Marathwada. The functional characteristics of the towns might change in future provided development of forestry, tourism, agro-based industries besides agriculture is achieved. The region can grow industrially if the scheme of Bombay-Vishakhapatnam National Highway is executed. It will traverse through Marathwada and will bring the region on the highway system of the country connecting the industrial centres of West coast with those along the East coast.

FOOTNOTES

1. Malshe, P.T., "Settlement System of Maharashtra" in *Settlement System of India*, Ed. by Manzoor Alam & K.N. Gopi, Oxford & IBH Pub. Co., Bombay, 1982, pp. 93-121.
2. Jefferson, M., The distribution of the worlds' city folk, *Geographical Review*, XXI, 1931, p. 453.
3. Christaller, W., Central Places in Southern Germany, translated by Baskin, C.W., Prentice Hall, 1966, p. 143.
4. Dickinson, R.E., The metropolitan Regions of the United States, *Geographical Review*, Vol. 24, 1934, pp. 278-291.
5. Smailes, A.E., The Urban Hierarchy in England and Wales, *Geography*, Vol. XXIX, 1944, part, 2, pp. 41-51.
6. Green, E.H., *Motor Bus centres in S.W. England*, Transactions and

Papers of I.B.G., 1948, Vol. 14, pp. 59-68, RF. p. 59.

7. Godlund, S., The Functions and Growth of Bus traffic within the sphere of urban influence, *Lund studies in Geography*, Sr. B. Human Geography, No. 18, 1956, p. 12.
8. Nelson, H.J., A Service classification of American cities, *Economic Geography*, 1955, Vol. 31, pp. 189-210.

APPENDIX

CENTRALITY, HIERARCHY, RANKING AND FUNCTIONAL CLASSIFICATION OF URBAN CENTRES

Name of the urban centre	Centrality value	Hierarchy value	Remarks	Functional Classification
1	2	3	4	5
1. Aurangabad	17.80	37.43	Large regional centre	C, O
2. Nanded	11.54	27.69	Regional centre	MF_2, CM
3. Jalna	9.28	25.38	Regional centre	T, CM, H
4. Latur	6.73	21.46	Sub-Regional centre	T_2, MF
5. Parbhani	6.10	20.75	,, ,,	O
6. Bhir	4.39	17.08	,, ,,	CM
7. Udgir	2.53	13.03	Large market town	T
8. Hingoli	2.76	12.94	,, ,,	D
9. Parli	2.76	12.64	,, ,,	CM_2
10. Osmanabad	2.35	11.94	,, ,,	M, O
11. Basmath	1.87	10.60	,, ,,	H_2, M, C
12. Ambejogai	1.99	10.30	,, ,,	D
13. Vaijapur	1.57	9.80	,, ,,	D
14. Selu	1.67	9.60	,, ,,	D
15. Deglur	1.67	9.25	,, ,,	D
16. Gangakhed	1.20	8.16	Small market town	H
17. Jintur	1.13	7.89	,, ,,	D
18. Tuljapur	1.00	7.72	,, ,,	D
19. Paithan	1.13	7.61	,, ,,	C_2
20. Purnea	1.16	7.46	,, ,,	MF_2
21. Manwath	1.21	7.30	,, ,,	D
22. Kalamnuri	1.20	7.03	,, ,,	A
23. Kannad	0.86	6.94	,, ,,	D
24. Kallam	0.74	6.42	,, ,,	D
25. Khandar	0.77	6.41	,, ,,	H_3, T
26. Manjalgaon	0.94	6.39	,, ,,	A
27. Partur	1.01	6.37	,, ,,	A
28. Pathri	.92	6.20	,, ,,	A_2, H
29. Kinwat	.82	5.99	,, ,,	A
30. Georai	.73	5.90	,, ,,	A
31. Ahmedpur	.76	5.83	,, ,,	A

1	2	3	4	5
32. Mukhed	.69	5.79	Small Market town	H_2, A
33. Dharmabad	.86	5.46	,, ,,	A
34. Omerga	.64	4.90	,, ,,	A
35. Ambad	.57	4.69	,, ,,	A
36. Nillanga	.63	4.67	,, ,,	A
37. Ausa	.67	4.40	,, ,,	A
38. Khuldabad	.41	4.35	,, ,,	D
39. Bhokardan	.43	4.26	,, ,,	A
40. Ashti	.39	4.21	,, ,,	A
41. Hadgaon	.48	4.13	,, ,,	A_2
42. Biloli	.41	4.00	,, ,,	A
43. Mukhed	.45	4.00	,, ,,	H_2, A
44. Gangapur	.47	3.99	,, ,,	A
45. Paranda	.45	3.93	,, ,,	A, H
46. Sonpeth	.38	3.55	,, ,,	A
47. Kundalwadi	.45	3.39	,, ,,	A_2, H_2
48. Pethumbri	.27	3.37	,, ,,	T_2, H
49. Bhoom	.38	3.34	,, ,,	A_2
50. Naldurg	.35	3.32	,, ,,	A_2, M
51. Dharur	.53	2.43	,, ,,	A
52. Murud	.33	2.33	,, ,,	A_3

FOURTEEN

PRABHA SHASTRI

THE EMERGENCE OF NAGPUR AS A "MILLION PLUS" CITY AND CHANGES IN THE URBAN SIZE HIERARCHY OF VIDARBHA

THIS paper attempts to study the growth of population in Nagpur City which has emerged as a "Million Plus" city for the first time in 1981 census. The paper also analyses how far the urban size hierarchy and primacy indices in Vidarbha have changed during the decade 1971-81 as a consequence of the emergence of a "Million Plus" city. The extent to which the urban size hierarchy deviates from "Rank-size rule" in both the years is also measured.

NAGPUR ON THE NATIONAL URBAN SCENE

During the decade 1971-81 the number of "Million Plus" cities of India increased from 9 to 12 with the addition of Nagpur, Lucknow and Jaipur. Located in the heart of the country, Nagpur is the major city in the eastern part of Maharashtra State (known as Vidarbha). With 1,215,425 Urban inhabitants, Nagpur's population has crossed the "million" mark in the latest 1981 census. Nagpur's population constitutes 2.89 per cent of the population of all "million plus" cities of India. Nagpur's share in the urban population of India is 0.77 per cent in 1981. "Million plus" cities of India are conspicuous not by their growth rate, but by their population size. Though the urban population of the country increased by 46 per cent during the decade 1971-81, it is observed that Class I cities (with more than 100,000 population) record a much higher growth rate—56.8 per cent. On this background the growth rate of "million plus" cities is rather low. Eight out of 12 million plus cities, including Nagpur, record growth rate less than the national urban average. Only 4 cities—Delhi, Bangalore, Pune and Jaipur record substantially higher growth rate than the national average. Though Nagpur ranks 10th in population size among the "million plus" cities, it ranks 7th when the cities are arranged in descending order of growth rates.

GROWTH OF POPULATION IN NAGPUR CITY

Table 14.1 shows the population of Nagpur city at each census since 1901 and the variations therein at decade interval. Population growth during each decade is expressed in terms of percentage over the previous population count. The two curves of absolute population and the rate of growth (Fig. 14.1) reveal that though the population has continued to increase in every decade, (with the exception of 1911 census), the growth has not been uniform throughout. The population increased at a very slow rate at the beginning of this century because of the natural checks operating in this period. The diseases and epidemics like cholera malaria and plague were frequently taking heavy toll of lives resulting in higher mortality. Due to unhygienic conditions and lack of civic amenities, Nagpur was a constant prey to them. The original settlement of Nagpur was over a low-lying area of sluggish drainage towards the east. The drainage system constructed under the Bhosala Government was not maintained

TABLE 14.1 : Nagpur city—Variations in population growth

Year	Population	Increase/Decrease over the previous census	P.C. decade variation
1901	127,734	+ 10,720	+ 9.16
1911	101,415	— 26,319	— 20.60
1921	145,193	+ 43,778	+ 43.16
1931	215,165	+ 69,972	+ 48.19
1941	301,957	+ 86,792	+ 40.33
1951	449,099	+ 147,142	+ 48.72
1961	643,659	+ 194,560	+ 43.32
1971	866,076	+ 222,417	+ 34.55
1981	1,215,425	+ 349,349	+ 40.33

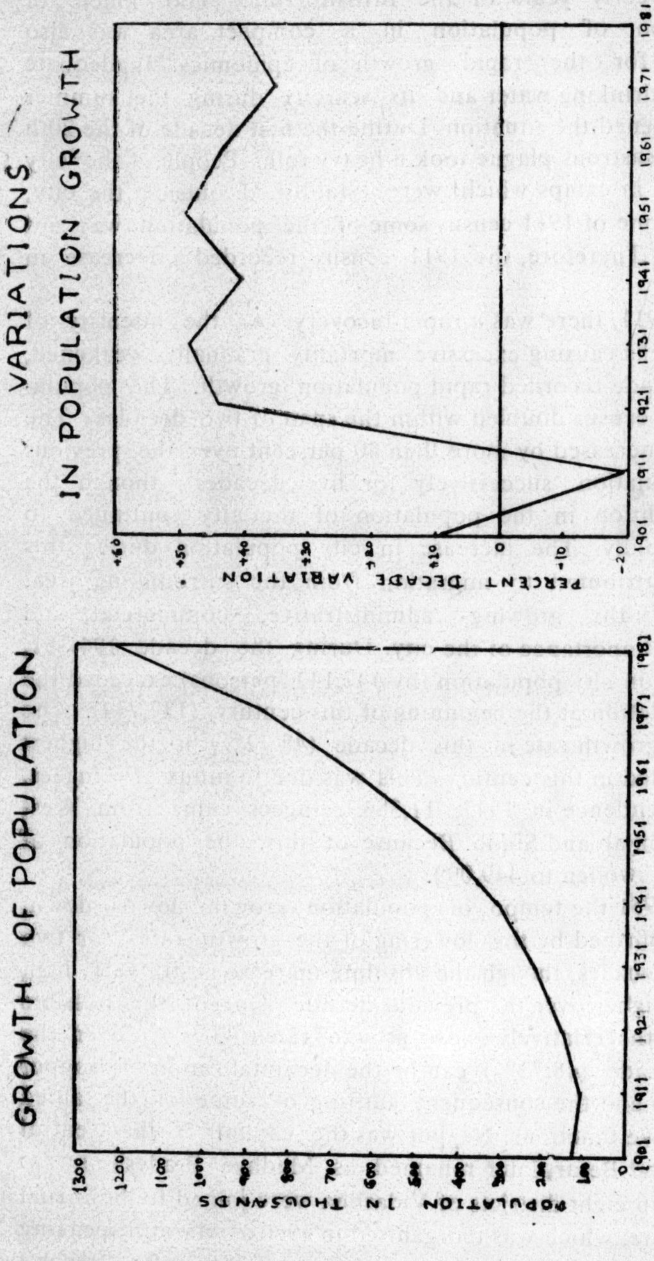

FIG. 14.1 : *Growth of population and variations in population growth*

during the early years of the British rule. Too much of concentration of population in a compact area was also favourable for the rapid growth of epidemics. Inadequate facilities of drinking water and its scarcity during the summer further worsened the situation. During the first decade of the 20th century a disastrous plague took a heavy toll. People of the city came to live in camps which were established outside the city, and at the time of 1911 census some of the population was not enumerated. Therefore, the 1911 census recorded a decrease in population.

After 1911, there was a rapid recovery. As the intensity of natural checks causing excessive mortality gradually weakened, the next decade recorded rapid population growth. The population of 1911 census doubled within the span of two decades. The population increased by more than 40 per cent over the previous census population successively for five decades ; though the absolute addition in the population of the city continued to increase rapidly. The increase in city population during this period is attributed to migration from the surrounding area, because of the growing administrative, commercial and educational importance of the city. During the decade 1941-51, the addition in city population (by 147,142 persons) exceeded the actual population at the beginning of this century (127,734). The percentage growth rate in this decade (48.72%) is the highest value recorded in this century. This was due to influx of refugees. After independence in 1947, 11,383 refugees came from West Pakistan, Punjab and Sindh. Because of this, the population of the city was swollen to 449,099.

Since 1951 the tempo of population growth slowed down, which is confirmed by the lowering of the growth rates for two successive decades, though the absolute increase is still very high and much higher over the previous decade. One of the possible reasons for the relatively slow growth rate (43.32%) over the previous decade (48.72%) can be the decapitalization of Nagpur City in 1956 and the consequent shifting of some of the allied administrative functions. Nagpur was the capital of the Central Provinces and Berar, later renamed as Madhya Pradesh up to 1956. In 1956 eight districts of Vidarbha were joined to bi-lingual Bombay State, which was reorganised in 1960 as Marathi speaking Maharashtra State and Nagpur was given the status of a "second or sub-capital" of the state.

The relatively slow tempo of population growth in Nagpur city may also be regarded as a part of the overall slow rate of urbanization observed throughout India during 1951-61. This slow rate of urbanization can be attributed to "slowing down of the tempo of rural-urban migration on account of a large increase in urban labour force as a result of rapid rate of natural increase in population in urban areas and the existence of a large backlog of unemployed and under-employed persons in these areas, which tend to block the streams of rural-urban migration" (Ashis Bose, p. 23). The industries established after 1947, were located outside the municipal boundaries in Kanhan, Kamptee industrial area to the north-east of the city. The two government sponsored industrial estates within the city boundaries in the north-eastern and western part near the periphery sustained small industries and failed to attract population to a great extent from outside because of the availability of labour force from the city itself. Hence Nagpur's population increased at a relatively slower rate (by 34.55%) during 1961-71.

The decade 1971 to 1981 records the largest addition of population (349,349 persons) in the demographic history of Nagpur city. Because of this huge population addition, and higher growth (by 40.33%) Nagpur could emerge as a "million plus" city on the map of India. The total population of Vidarbha increased by 22 per cent and urban population increased by 34 per cent during this decade. The much higher growth rate of Nagpur city (40.33%) suggests that this excessive increase is the result of migration. Due to Nagpur's central location, it is a major junction of railways, highways and internal air services. Nagpur's easy accessibility to all means of transport and linkages to all parts of India continue to attract people from all directions. Its growing educational and commercial importance is also responsible for migration from the surrounding region. The consequences of this migration are observed in the stagnation of very slow growth of population in the neighbouring small towns and rural areas.

NAGPUR—THE PRIMATE CITY

A primate city represents an important share of the region's population and an even greater share of its urban population. Nagpur, the largest city in population size in Vidarbha, can be termed as "primary city" of the region. The population of Nagpur city constitutes 32.5 per cent of the urban population and 8.48 per cent of the total population of Vidarbha. In 1971 Nagpur's share in the urban population of Vidarbha was 31 per cent and it was 7.4 per cent of the total population. An index of primacy shows how far primate city is disproportionate in population size in relation to the population of other cities within the region. Nagpur's primacy can be established with two primacy indices—two-city index (ratio of the first city to that of the second city) and (2) Four-city index (ratio to 3 other cities next in population size). Two-city index comes to 4.64 and four-city index 2.02. Nagpur is more than four times larger in population size than the second largest city Amravati (1981 population—261,387). In 1971, Two-city index was 4.1 and four-city index was 1.96. The changes in indices can be attributed to concentration of population increase in Nagpur city. 36.73 per cent of the actual addition in the urban population of Vidarbha during 1971-81 is concentrated in Nagpur city alone.

URBAN SIZE HIERARCHY IN VIDARBHA

When towns of a region are arranged in order of size, it is postulated that there is an empirical relationship between the rank of a town and its population size. This empirical relationship is termed as the 'rank-size rule'. The rule depicts a harmonic progression of cities within the urban hierarchy such that if the population of the largest city is known, the population of all other cities can be derived from the rank of their size.

The urban hierarchy in Vidarbha by rank-size rule is presented in Fig. 14.2. In 1981 census, the size of population of Vidarbha's 75 towns ranges from 1,215,425 (Nagpur) to 1,722 (Devalameti). The curve prepared from the actual population of towns and the straight line of expected population of towns derived from detailed calculations, do not exactly correspond with each other. Size of the "primary" city is greater than expected, while 21 towns up to 34,000 population are smaller in size than expected from rank-size rule. 33 towns with 14,000 to 34,000 population are larger in size than expected and 20 towns of less than 14,000 population are again smaller in population than expected from rank-size rule. For primary city Nagpur, the difference in actual and expected population is much higher in 1981 compared to 1971. Difference as p.c. of actual size was 33.3% and difference as p.c. of expected size was 50.1% in 1971. These figures have increased to 37.22% and 59.3% respectively.

CHANGES IN THE URBAN SIZE HIERARCHY

A comparison of the size ranks of towns in 1971 with those in 1981 reveal how much movement has taken place in the urban size hierarchy. A rank-order coefficient of correlation (rho) between the size ranks of towns in 1971 and 1981 provides a summary measure of changes in urban hierarchy. The rho 0.987 suggests that the urban size hierarchies in Vidarbha in 1971 and 1981 closely resemble each other. This does not mean that the ranks of all towns have remained the same at both the censuses. The following (Table 14.2) summaries the changes in the ranks of towns during the decade.

TABLE 14.2 : **Changes in ranks of towns**

Type of change			No. of towns
No change in rank	...	...	14
Change of rank by 1	...	...	18
Change of rank by 2	...	...	18
Change of rank by 3	...	...	7
Change of rank by 4	...	...	5
Change of rank exceeding 4	...	...	7

About one-fifth of towns have retained the same ranks in the urban hierarchy. Number of towns with marginal shifting of ranks (by 1 or 2) is much higher. These 3 categories together constitute over half of total towns in Vidarbha. Table 14.2 provides the type of change, and not the direction of change. When this aspect is studied, it is observed that 29 towns assumed size ranks higher than in 1971 and 26 towns assumed ranks lower than in 1971. If the rates of growth for all towns during the period would have been the same, there would have been no change in their ranks within the hierarchy. The comparison reveals how much movement has taken place and points out that there are variations in growth of towns. Individual towns have increased their population at a rate substantially more or less than other towns.

Deviations from rank-size rule

A glance at Fig. 14.2 reveals that urban size hierarchy in Vidarbha deviates considerably from rank-size rule. An index of deviation is calculated by summing up the differences between the actual and the expected population of towns. The summation is divided by 2 and is expressed as per cent of total urban population. This index represents the percentage of urban residents who would have to move from one town to another to bring about a perfect correspondence between the urban hierarchy and rank-size rule. The greater the index, the less the conformity. For Vidarbha the index comes to 13.88. In 1971 the index was 13.2. Thus the deviation from rank-size rule has increased during the decade. The index is influenced a great deal by Nagpur city, whose size is greater than the expected by 452,477. It alone accounts for 43.57 per cent of the total amount of deviation. In 1971, Nagpur accounted for 38 per cent of the total amount of deviation. Thus primary city Nagpur has an important influence over urban size hierarchy of Vidarbha.

An average discrepancy between the actual and expected size of places independent of their size is found out by calculating a quotient. The difference between the actual and expected size of each town is expressed as a per cent of its actual size. All the percentages are added and divided by the number of towns. The resulting quotient 34.93 per cent shows the average amount that the towns would have to increase or decrease to fit into the rank-size rule. In 1971 this value was 20.1 per cent. Thus the discrepancy between the actual and expected size of towns from rank-size rule has increased substantially during the decade because of the emergence of Nagpur as a "million plus" city.

The per cent error in predicting the population of a town from the rank-size rule is also calculated. The difference between the actual and expected size of each town is expressed as a per cent of the expected population. These percentages are then summed up and divided by the number of towns. The result shows that the expected population of a town in Vidarbha is on

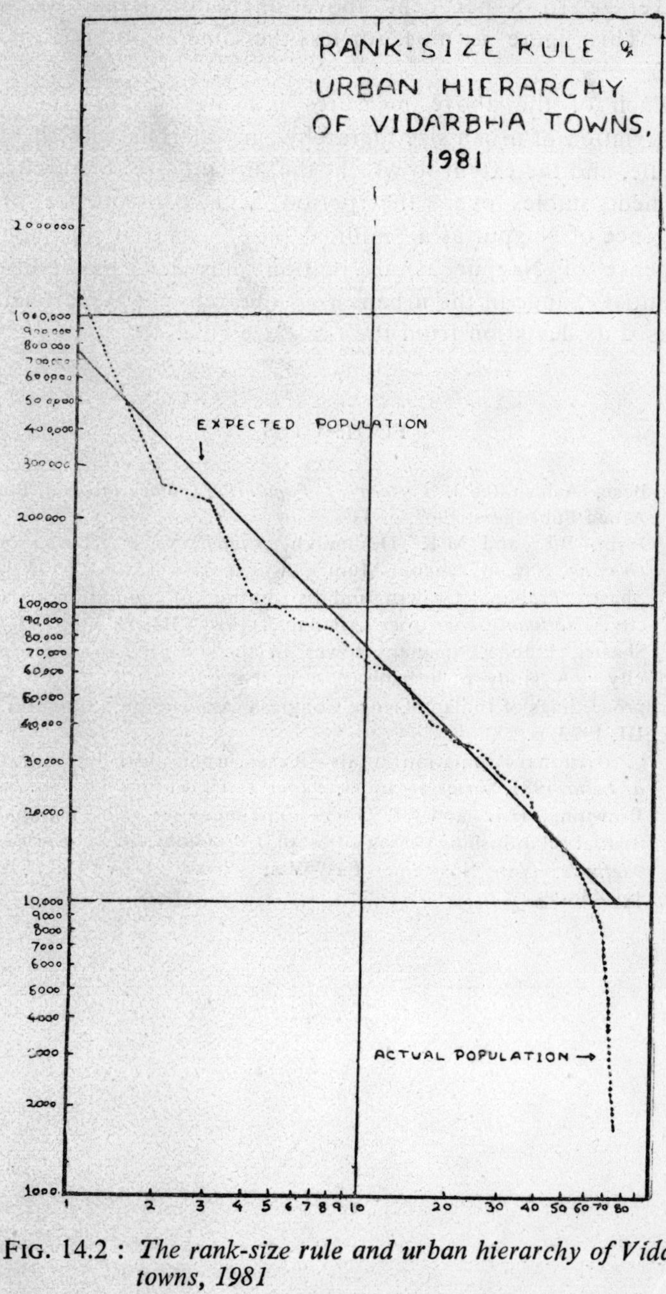

FIG. 14.2 : *The rank-size rule and urban hierarchy of Vidarbha towns, 1981*

an average 16.48 per cent above or below actual size of a town. This figure is more or less the same as observed in 1971 (16.6%).

Each of the above measures indicates the correspondence and deviation of urban size hierarchy in Vidarbha with the rank-size rule, and the extent to which the urban size hierarchy has remained stable over the period as a consequence of the emergence of Nagpur as a "million plus" city. To conclude, the emergence of Nagpur as a "million plus" city has resulted in substantial change in the urban size hierarchy of Vidarbha and increased its deviation from the rank-size rule.

FOOTNOTES

1. Bose, Ashish (ed.), *Pattern of Population Change in India*, Bombay, Allied Publishers, 1967, p. 33.
2. Joshi, P.L. and M.K. Deshmukh, *Nagpur Nagar Sanstha Shatabdi Grantha*, Nagpur, Nagpur Municipal Corporation, 1964, p. 44.
3. Shastri, Prabha, "Growth and distribution of population in Nagpur city." *National Geographer* (Allahabad), Vol VIII, 1973, pp. 63-70.
4. Shastri, Prabha, Stagnant towns in the vicinity of a metropolitan city : A study of urbanization in Nagpur district. Abstracts of proceedings of Indian Science Congress Association, Calcutta. Part III, 1973, p. 272.
5. "Provisional Population totals—Rural urban distribution". *Census of India*, 1981, Series 1—India, Paper-2 of 1981.
6. Browning, H.L. and J.P. Gibbs, some measures of demographic and spatial relationships among cities in J.P. Gibbs (ed.) *Urban Research Methods*, Van Nostrand, East-West Press, New Delhi, 1966, pp. 436-59.

FIFTEEN

MOHAN SINGH

SUB-SYSTEM OF TOWNS WITHIN THE URBAN SYSTEM OF UTTARAKHAND

THE heterogeneity of physical factors presents not only the typical geographical personality but also displays the variable cultural entities. As a cultural artifact the hill towns make a bold appearance in the undulating physical landscape of mountainous region. The functional monotony, the less frequency of alternative routes, the limited and more traditional means of transportation and the pilgrim base of the evolution have resulted the peculiar space relations and interaction in the hill towns.

A considerable number of researches dealing with the cities/towns as system have been conducted by the western scholars. In this connection the central place system of Christaller, the rank-size rule of Zipt and the negative exponential density distance relationship by Craft are the pioneering attempts. Further Berry combined these all techniques and presented his presidential address before the Regional Science Association of U.S.A. in 1933.[1] But most of these attempts are quantified rather than qualified. Hence, the present attempt has made purely on qualified device and takes care of the towns of an under-developed mountainous and hilly region.

The process of urbanisation as envisaged in most of the models of urban growth has not been experienced in hill areas as such. This is why the main purpose of the present paper is to conduct a comprehensive study of systems and sub-systems in the light of the observation, made about of all the towns in the Uttarakhand of Uttar Pradesh located in the central Himalayas.

Its specific objectives are to (i) justify the towns in Uttarakhand as a system, (ii) trace out the sub-systems within the urban system, and (iii) explore the relevance of applying systems approach in the spatial organisation of towns. A brief look in the urbanisation in Uttarakhand may precede the discussion on the points raised above.

URBANISATION IN UTTARAKHAND

Uttarakhand is one of the low urbanised regions of Uttar Pradesh. About 18.2 per cent of its total population was recorded as urban in 1981 against the state figure of 18.1 per cent. The low degree of urbanisation in the region and the state attributed to predominantly subsistent peasant economy, meagre industrial development and the lack of transportation activities resulting the low degree of interaction among various places.[2]

The urban population was scattered in 56 towns mostly small in size. Dehradun the administrative town in Doon was the largest with a population of 2,93,628. Haldwani, a multifunctional foot hill town with a population of 77,581 came next. As much as 38 towns have less than 20,000 population while those having population below 5,000 numbered 25.[3]

The frequency of towns was greater in the Tarai, Bhabar and Doon the most productive parts of the region and also the gateways to the region. As much as 75 per cent urban dwellers of Uttarakhand were residing in these areas.

Services (specially administrative), some market functions, tourism and pilgrimage defined the basic economy of many towns. As much as half of them were either commissionary, district or tahsil headquarters. Industrial and commercial components of population were small and were confined with the towns of tarai and foot hills. Equally feeble was the relationship among various towns. Many of them had stronger links with places outside the region. The mutual interaction among tarai towns was greater due to the physical links.

Towns as systems

A system may be defined as a complex of interacting elements, together with their attributes and relationships. It becomes obvious that the system operates not in a void but in a spatial environment. For any given system, this environment comprises the set of all objects, a change in whose attributes affects the system, and also those objects whose attributes are changed by the behaviour of the system. Thus a system with its environment constitutes the universe of phenomena which is of interest in a given context.[4]

Fig. 15.1 indicates the basic elements in the urban system and environment within which the system operates shows that a system approach to the urban centres is concerned not only with how these are interrelated but with all the implications and ramifications of process. Basically the approach is designed to answer questions, such as what are the forces interacting in various towns of this hilly and mountainous region and what effects have these on the urban landscape.

In the urban system of Uttarakhand the various functions, man as potential mover and physical links are the matter while the push and pull factors and means of transportation are energy. Despite the poor physical links and low connectivity, all the towns of the region are connected with each other by motorable roads. The exception is Kedarnath. This pilgrim centre and seasonal town does not have motorable road. The motor head of this town is Gaurikund about 12 kilometres from the shrine.

The physical links, the commercial links and the administrative links generate the mobility to various towns resulting the movement of goods and human phenomena. The administrative functions of most of the towns link them with each other. The towns of Nainital and Pauri stand on the top of the administrative hierarchy as both of them are the headquarters of Kumaon and Garhwal commissionaries as well as headquarters of Nainital and Garhwal districts.

The next order of administrative hierarchy covers the towns of Chamoli-Gopeshwar, Pithoragarh, Almora, Uttarkashi, Narendra Nagar and Dehradun. These are the headquarters of the respective districts and Tahsils. Further the towns of Dunda, Bhatwari, Chakrata, Devaprayag. Tehri, Kotdwara, Lansdowne, Joshimath, Karnaprayag, Didihat, Dharchula, Champawat, Bageshwar, Ranikhet, Khatima, Kashipur, Kichha and Haldwani-Kathgodam are the tahsil headquarters.

Further, the physical links and links of material supply

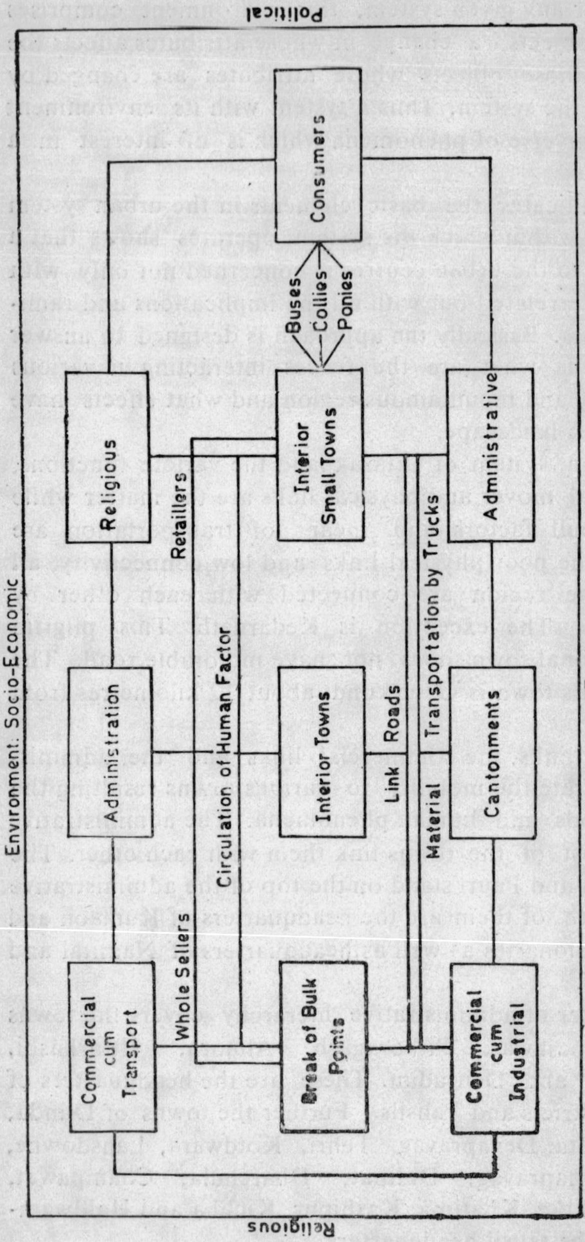

FIG. 15.1 : *A scheme for mountainous urban system*

connect the various towns with each other. The foot hill towns such as Rishikesh, Haldwani, Kathgodam, Ramnagar, Tanakpur and Kotdwara stand on the base point followed by larger and relatively larger inner valley, ridge and spur towns and again further by very small towns and service centres.

Above discussion reveals that people from one town to another migrate due to administrative, ecological and religious factors while materials move due to socio-economic demand and supply. This whole justifies the towns as systems. To understand the system as a whole demands further inquiries about the sub-system in which a system is devided.

The various interacting factors have differences in the association with various towns and various sets of towns. On this basis, the study area comprises of the following six urban sub-system.

Rishikesh-Kotdwara sub-system

The most notable sub-system of towns formulated along the Alaknanda river and its tributaries (Fig. 15.2). Administrative, socio-economic and commercial factors and daily bus services were matter while the push and pull factors and decision of administrators were energy. People from one town to another migrate due to administrative, religious and ecological factors while different goods firstly are unloaded at Rishikesh and Kotdwara, from trains and further transported by trucks to other inner towns such as Srinagar, Pauri, Lansdowne, Karnaparyag, etc. The further distribution of goods carried out by retailers and small whole salers by trucks, buses and ponies and in some cases by collie carriers.

Dehradun-Vikasnagar sub-system

This sub-system has Dehradun in the top of the hierarchical order. The fusion of socio-economic activities have increased the gravity at Dehradun. These gravitational forces exert maximum influence upon the surrounding areas of Dehradun which also influence the relatively farther areas and towns having direct bus links with Dehradun. The sub-system includes Chakrata, Dunda and Bhatwari with Dehradun and its frinze towns.

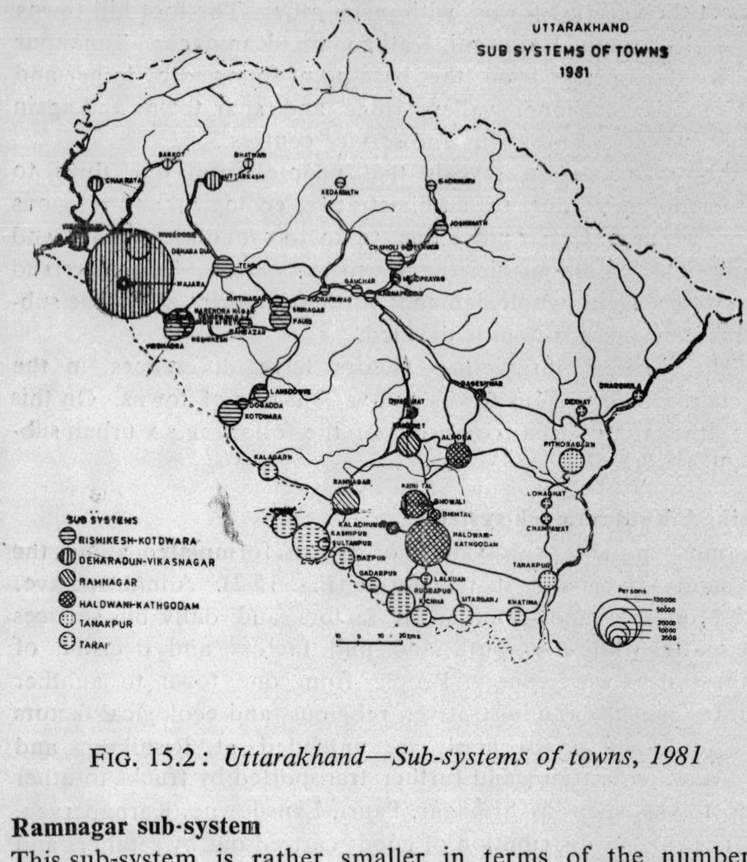

FIG. 15.2 : *Uttarakhand—Sub-systems of towns, 1981*

Ramnagar sub-system

This sub-system is rather smaller in terms of the number of including towns but equally important in terms of area served. This exists along the river Kosi and Ramganga. The main town in this is Ramnagar, which has great influence on the business activities of the surrounding towns Ranikhet, Almora, Dwarahat, Karnaprayag and Nandaprayag.

Haldwani-Kathgodam sub-system

This sub-system operates from Haldwani-Kathgodam and having its reaches up to Ranikhet, Almora, Bageshwar and Pithoragarh. But the bold influence could only be traced in Nainital, Bhowali, Almora, Bhimtal and Kaladhungi. The various towns of this system have commercial and administrative links, resulting the mobility among human factors and material both.

Tanakpur sub-system

River Kali demarcates the border of India and Nepal, in the extreme East. There also, China border attracts the voluminous defence personnels. In the historical past this region has been the link of Indian traders with Tibbet. This is why this was the important sub-system before 1962. But the China war had stopped the trade and pilgrimage to Kailash Mansarovar, hence, the interacting forces have been weak. However, the spread effects of the recent government's developmental programmes have resulted the opening of new towns. This sub-system includes the towns of Champavat, Lohaghat, Pithoragarh, Didihat, Dharchula and Munsiary mostly along the border roads.

Tarai sub-system

The whole tarai belt of Uttarakhand does not match with the physico-cultural personalities of its interior. The plural societies, the fertile and levelled land, the recent colonization and the high nodality paved the way for overall development of tarai, ultimately resulting the concentration of socio-economic activities at the different centres and thus, a chain of towns came up. These all towns not only have the physical links but also equally, links of functions and sentiments.

Above discussion reveals that the towns in Uttarakhand form a system and sub-systems. The sub-systems are emerging along the rivers and roads because of the nodality and fusion of socio-economic activities. The foot hill towns play most important role in the various sub-systems as they not only control the transportation system, but also are the break of bulk points. The tarai towns are typical hence the sub-system, too, is typical as this area does not match with the physico-cultural landscape of mountainous and hilly tracts. Further enquiries and planning may be essential to develop the vast barren areas and town-free tracts so that this backward region may be converted into the state of balanced development.

FOOTNOTE

1. Berry, B.J.L., "Cities as systems within systems of cities" Paper presented at the Annual Meeting of *Regional Science Association,*

Dec., 1963.

2. Singh, M., Towns of Uttarakhand—A Study in Population Geography," Unpublished M. Phil dissertation, Punjab University Chandigarh, 1980.
3. Census of India, *Provisional census totals—Uttar Pradesh,* 1981.
4. Mabogunje, A.L., "Systems Approach to a Theory of Migration", in Emrays Jones (ed.) *Readings in Social Geography,* Oxford University Press, 1975, p. 212.

INDEX